CHANGING PLACES

Published in Canada by
Inanna Publications and Education Inc.
210 Founders College, York University
4700 Keele Street, Toronto, Ontario M3J 1P3
Telephone: (416) 736-5356 Fax (416) 736-5765
Email: inanna.publications@inanna.ca Website: www.inanna.ca

The publisher gratefully acknowledges the support of the Canada Council for the Arts and the Ontario Arts Council for its publishing program. We also acknowlege the financial assistance of the Government of Canada through the Canada Book Fund,

The publisher is also grateful for the kind support received from an Anonymous Fund at The Calgary Foundation.

Note from the publisher: Care has been taken to trace the ownership of copyright material used in this book. The author and the publisher welcome any information enabling them to rectify any references or credits in subsequent editions.

Cover artwork: Catherine McCausland, "Tell Me Again," hand-hooked mat made of reclaimed textiles, Tors Cove, Newfoundland, Canada <www.BallyCatterCrafts.com>.

Library and Archives Canada Cataloguing in Publication

Changing places (2013)
    Changing places : feminist essays in empathy and relocation / edited by Valerie Burton and Jean Guthrie.

Includes bibliographical references.
Issued in print and electronic formats.
ISBN 978-1-77133-084-8 (pbk.). -- ISBN 978-1-77133-085-5 (epub).--
ISBN 978-1-77133-086-2 (mobi). -- ISBN 978-1-77133-087-9 (pdf)

    1. Feminism. 2. Empathy. 3. Change (Psychology).
4. Women -- Social conditions. 5. Women -- Attitudes. 6. Women -- Psychology. I. Burton, Valerie (Historian), writer of introduction, editor of compilation II. Guthrie, Jean (Professor), writer of introduction, editor of compilation III. Title.

HQ1155.C53 2014   305.42   C2013-907351-5
                                         C2013-907352-3

Printed and Bound in Canada.

CHANGING PLACES

Feminist Essays on Empathy and Relocation

EDITED BY **VALERIE BURTON AND JEAN GUTHRIE**

INANNA Publications and Education Inc.
Toronto, Canada

Table of Contents

Acknowledgements

OUR GRATITUDE IS DUE FIRST to the eleven authors of the chapters of *Changing Places: Feminist Essays on Empathy and Relocation*. They stayed with us while a publisher interested in feminist scholarship in the still-emerging area of empathy was found and through the period of revisions suggested by Inanna Publication's anonymous reviewers. We first came to know many of these authors and their research through Memorial University of Newfoundland, mostly during the period when we were responsible for the Master of Women's Studies program and its Speakers' Series. We tapped internal resources, notably the Henrietta Harvey bequest, to bring speakers to the University, and the series also benefited from successive incumbents of Atlantic Canada's Nancy's Chair. But, while this is the place to express our gratitude for institutional finances, we acknowledge those who responded to invitations from a university program to attend the series and become involved. Participation in community networks has contributed importantly to our discoveries and those of the authors, and for this education in empathy a broader spectrum of thanks is due.

The Women's Studies Speakers' Series was an exceptional forum for a program then struggling to achieve full departmental status. It acquired that status in 2007 and the department continues the public series still. Arguably it constituted the most vibrant and challenging continuous inter-disciplinary seminar series that Memorial University has ever hosted. Few who saw its posters could doubt the eclecticism of its subject matter, while those who attended were consistently impressed by the high quality of the presentations. Students as well as more experienced community advocates and scholars presented, and papers were followed by open, supportive discussions: however vigorously points were argued, no voice went unheard. It is fitting that a collection with its roots in this forum argues for empathic, inclusive ways of changing places.

As dedicated teachers, the editors have thought long and hard about the political responsibilities of educators. This volume would not have evolved had the authors not shared our conviction that education can change lives. Accordingly we wanted the introduction to provide undergraduate and graduate students with a clear and detailed overview. We wanted to offer and reflect on paths of discovery to the richness of the chapters; to highlight how far feminist scholars have come in integrating gender and emotion into the ways of knowing that are practiced in universities; and to acknowledge that feminists have learned from resistance to the directions their work is taking. These chapters are studies in gendered reflexivity and because their authors have faced the many quandaries and vulnerabilities of dealing frankly with intellectual and emotional experiences, we renew our thanks to them for trusting to the empathic understanding of their editors when they placed their work in our hands.

Changing Places

An Introduction

VALERIE BURTON AND JEAN GUTHRIE

O N THE COVER OF *Changing Places*, Catherine McCausland's hooked mat shows a woman extending her arm in half-embrace, a gesture which seems to create a space, and to invite her companion to repeat what once passed between them or was already known to them both. Their tender concentration implies a connection between empathy and place: they are on the verge of conversation in an arboreal setting which could be Atlantic Canada, and they seem to be resuming an earlier exchange, less for the sake of recalling it in detail than to re-balance their understandings of each other. The image gives the sense that they will learn on many levels through this intimately framed moment.

I. TELL ME AGAIN

The authors in this volume may be imagined in comparable situations. "Tell me" is the invitation, literal or figurative, they brought to their informants and to documents at the outset of their inquiries. And "tell me again" is not a sign of inattention; rather it suggests, "What have I missed?" and signals a pause for reflecting, modifying a position, or listening to understand, and so staying open to the possibility that exchanging confidences could lead to actions that would change places.[1]

In their discussions, the authors connect social and cultural change with empathic ways of gathering evidence; they consider what empathy as a means of connection can contribute both to the politicization of a feminist, and to sharing in commitments to common causes and interests. These studies indicate how and why women working in the academy or the professions have been trying to do things differently and more empathically in their careers and lives over two generations. While the collection is intended for students of Women's/Gender

Studies, established scholars may also find insights into affect and empathy that invite reassessment of how social life has been modeled in earlier analysis. And we welcome readers from other backgrounds who are perhaps intrigued by the cover to look further. What we offer is a series of studies that reaffirm why it is useful to ask, "Is it really this way?" Empathy is a powerful affect,[2] often undervalued in popular understandings and definitions, not least because of its assumed female associations.

The pedagogical commitment of *Changing Places* leads us to explain empathy as a practical and theoretical proposition.[3] Here we draw out the themes of the eleven chapters with reference to how evolving disciplinary practices overlap with knowing the world empathically, and with understanding the political implications of doing so.[4] Feminism as a critical practice emerged via critiques of objectivity: it has evolved through standpoint theory, and the discussion of experience it encompasses can be philosophical, methodological, ethical, or all of these. Feminists have thus developed a close acquaintance with questions that are increasingly seen as significant by scholars in various fields. As the trend designated "the affective turn" has taken hold in the social sciences and humanities in the last two decades, feminists (among others) have focused on the critical examination of what we do and why we do it. One potential of this reflexive approach is that it can define the relationship between a feminist self-consciousness and empathy.[5]

In Her Shoes

Since the scholarship of affect currently offers greater scope than before for referencing "life itself," we acknowledge the popular image by which empathy is often described: knowing what it is like to be "in another's shoes." It is persuasive, as the curators of Canada's shoe museum testify (Govier). Their project showcases the work of immigrant women who have resumed careers as professional writers. And it has gathered ample evidence for the representational and symbolic scope of shoes. The writers are eloquent in their shoes; does it matter that only one of the forty women writers actually swaps shoes or stands in another's?[6]

"Walking a mile in someone else's shoes" offers the possibility that a privileged person not only imagines the discomforts and discounts experienced by someone less privileged; she takes action to address inequalities. But when a "truth" summed up in an image sends us to a dictionary, we see that accounts of positioning and its epistemic results seem to need more subtle treatment.[7] According to the *Canadian Oxford Dictionary*, empathy consists of "identifying oneself mentally with, and so fully comprehending, a person or object of contemplation." In suggesting that empathy results only when *all* thoughts and feelings of another person are known (or thought to be known), this definition is on shaky grounds, at odds with reconsidered perceptions within feminism (Ahmed, "This Other" 561; Alcoff; Bartky 188-91; Butler 63).

"I Know Just How You Feel"

Over two decades ago, post-modern theorist Donna Haraway linked the repudiation of the "fetishized perfect subject of oppositional history" with greater scope for empathy.[8] She observed that the possibilities for connecting with someone else increase when the person makes the decision to start from notions of herself as fragmented rather than unitary (586; see also Jaggar; Ahmed, "Feminist" 245). Building on Haraway's insight, communications theorist Elspeth Probyn elaborates on the self as generating messages that separate rather than mediate. In the following passage, she explains the contribution of a critical stance informed by empathy:

> [W]e cannot indulge in the fantasy of dialogism wherein "you" can be "me," and "I" can be "you." "I" am not "she" but articulating a working image of the self may allow for a movement of empathy between us. Working within the tensions of a doubled question of "'who is she? and who am I?" forces us to recognize distinction and requires that we work over relations of alterity. (171)

Probyn's contemporary, philosopher Lorraine Code, also recognizes the "space opened to questioning" when the analysis moves beyond normative definitions of empathy (131). Her important essay, "I Know Just How You Feel" (1995), examines the cognitive dimensions of relationships. She is critical of the authority invoked in the claim "I know just how you feel," because it neglects the uneven distribution of speaking positions across the social order. Ostensibly limited by the individual nature of the encounter, the claim to "know just how you feel" has effects that are more widely felt and enacted. The meanings that are made in the ways that subjects are identified and are treated thus enter into the forms and forces that produce human relations, energies, and activities.

Code argues that a notion of empathy that lacks political critique is a "pre-interpretive" mode; she points out that to leave the modality of "speaking for" someone unquestioned reduces women's ability to resist the double-bind of gender entrapment. This happens when women who respond to others' needs with care and help are drawn into the naturalized femaleness of these acts, and they defer bringing political critique to bear on the inequalities from which the need springs. To cite Breda Gray's reference to some of the ethical and political ramifications, this is an example of "the misrecognitions on which the term feminism itself relies" (Gray 226).

More recently, Clare Hemmings describes a subject who realizes that she is positioned differently in the world than she thought, indeed that she is less in command of her life than once she believed, and is conflicted by her politicization: this subject negotiates her existence in the world, but as a feminist she also wants to see the world transformed; and her capacity to feel for others accounts for the changes she would like to see ("Affective Solidarity," 147-48). In her formulation of how empathy and affect are connected in the feminist's sense of her "own" social being, Hemmings has found Probyn's concept of "affective dissonance" useful, and she acknowledges her debt to Probyn's monograph of 1993, *Sexing the Self*, for clarifying how empathy, reflexivity, and affective entanglement are related (149).[9] In doing so, Hemmings is more than scrupulous in acknowledging this inter-generational "conversation." She gives a considered view of what Probyn and her cohort have achieved by dismantling the hierarchical meaning-making that was ingrained in positivism.

Although Hemmings is encouraged by the resurgence of an empirical and theoretical interest in emotions, the extravagant claims of some new affect theorists disconcert her. One of the most thoughtful of current writers on the feminist practice of empathy, Hemmings advances a more detailed discussion than is possible here. We particularly recommend "Affective Solidarity," which, in a few pages, brings conceptual clarity to the issues and practices that arguably separate the proponents of "new" and "old" structures (148-9).

While it is too soon to assess the article's impact, on the eve of this volume going to press the editors welcome Hemmings' intervention on empathy. Beyond partisan issues, her work profiles how feminists have recast the term: from a naturalized capacity to a politicized skill, and from a stance necessitating passivity to one that galvanizes agency, empathy has been central to the shaping of a forty-year project of care and hope.

II. "SOMETHING MUCH MORE GENERAL" (Williams *Resources* 319)

For more than forty years feminist writers have questioned the binary assumptions that colonize and marginalize groups of people by a naturalizing discourse. Feminists have interrogated a gendered world by listening to silences, by finding out how the subaltern speaks (Spivak), and rooting out naively reductionist interpretations of experience (Scott). They have exposed the myth of the dispassionate observer, and variously theorized and moralized investigative and authorial standpoints (Sandra Harding "Introduction"). For a shorter period, feminists have had an institutional presence and practised these strategies as the discipline of WS/GS. And during this time a single phrase, "structures of feeling," has done more than any other formula to maintain the prospect of mainstream academic commitment to questions of ethics, reflexivity, and affect. Often used generically, the phrase "structures of feeling" is more rarely attributed than perhaps it should be (Higgins).

Acknowledging that the phrase was introduced by the cultural critic Raymond Williams does not detract from "unravel[ing] the gendered elements of emotion as a feminist achievement" (Ruberg and Steenbergh 2). Rather it implies that feminists are in some part indebted to Williams' pioneering approach to the complex cultural and historical formations of affect.[10] Our studies would simply not be the same without the significance that Williams placed on each of the following matters: how the emotions embodied or enacted by individuals could be widely shared as the emotional relations of a specific historical location; how they could be simultaneously ephemeral and pervasive (Pribram 21); how they enlarged the concept of experience so that aspects of life beyond the conventionally rational and empirical were recognized without being defined as irrational (Harding and Pribram 871); and, particularly pertinent to the matters under discussion in this section, how hierarchies might be treated when we transcend the cleanly oppositional elements of hegemonic knowledge systems.

Williams was also attuned to the conflation of the emotions with women, and to the historically and contemporaneously restrictive roles of femininity. In the fuller version of the quotation from which the sub-title of this section is taken, he identified "the suppression of tenderness and emotional response, the willingness to admit what is not weakness—one's feelings in and through another. *All this is a repression not only of women's experience but of something much more general*" (319, emphasis added). Williams was prescient about gender in much the way that inspired Haraway, Jaggar, Code, Probyn, and latterly Hemmings, as discussed above, to distinguish between oppressive and progressive articulations of empathy. But Williams did not make a practical proposition out of referencing liminal forms of experience by gender: finding their registers has been largely the achievement of feminists. And this work has benefited from the weakening hold of behavioural models and psychological constructs in humanities disciplines. With this development there has emerged greater scope for both recognizing empathy as an historicized and socialized phenomenon, and elaborating on experiential formations that are gendered, sexed, classed and raced (Jennifer Harding and Pribram 2).

The Impulse to Feminism (Ahmed "Feminist" 238)

If feminists are to establish the strong position for empathy in social theory and empirical research that it deserves, we need work that is expansive, such as that provided by the literary critic and scholar of the classic texts of nation-building and social identity, Ruth Perry. In the first chapter of *Changing Places*, Perry gives attention to the histories of structures of power and of personhood. She recognizes the gendering of the maternal body, and so of womanhood, as a double bind: woman's destiny is seen as motherhood, her body constructed as the site of child-bearing and child-raising; and as a result, she is discounted in orthodox economic and political discourse. Women are thus designated as lacking political substance within a political system that is conceived as exclusively men's business. Perry draws out these characteristics of western society by reading "against the grain" in her interpretation of the symbolic texts of male writers. Rousseau, known as a pioneer of progressive educational methods, she points out, saw education as a field for man's self-realization and constructed women as an ideological abstraction by which to prove the category male. "All women answer his purpose equally well," says Perry (45).

Perry's work helps us interrogate the gendered character of the reason/emotion binary that fosters the denigration of empathy.[11] She treats discourse, but her study emphasizing the significance of motherhood fits with a shift from discourse analysis to examining the substance and significance of matter, materiality, and the body. The result is to bring greater clarity to the structures of feeling that have existed in a range of societies from which our own practices and presumptions derive. While providing an understanding of how the denial of identity and agency to women denies the quality most involved with motherhood, she also shows that this denial underpins men's estrangement from much that humanity might otherwise value in the world. The "permeability" of the body, the capacity to be penetrated, Perry explains, was deployed in the ancient world as an image of unreliability in the political domain. In the slippage from rhetoric to received truth, the maternal or potentially maternal body is designated a political liability.

While she sees the Enlightenment *philosophes* as a major influence in the objectification of women, she also cites twentieth-century authorities, such as Freud, who make the case for accepting the aggressiveness that continues to be regarded as part of masculinity, and thus of the trauma of denial of what male and female bodies might share. The outcomes of processes that use women's bodies are not all biological: women's procreative acts are devalued when they serve patriarchal property lines and reproduce patterns of accumulation. This means that systems of colonial exploitation are indicated in Perry's analysis too. She explicitly calls into question the limits of liberal rights-based discourses of equality, citizenship, identity, the past histories they recall, and the ways they are appropriated by imperialist, nationalist and global capitalist agendas (Gray 215). And when she points to a system of gender with more egalitarian possibilities, it is not modulated on closure, but instead "open to limitless variation" (65).

Working for change means constructing a new model for political life. As to tackling the challenges stemming from sexist and other binaries, Perry highlights alternatives to the subject/object hierarchy that the authors of *Changing Places* seek to realign. The ground is the daily lived experience of people who are different from one another: "The task is to develop a concept of selves as they are constituted dialogically in relation to others and of rights—including rights to bodily integrity—as they emerge from and become the expression of collective aspirations for change" (Petchesky cited by Perry 49). These processes, and the reorientations involved in applying them, make possible a model for political life that does not exclude women, and recognizes the claims of racial or ethnic minorities too.

Philosopher Christine Overall shares Perry's concern that, if we are to make a new future, we should know what we think gender is and what work it does. In chapter 2, she sets out to "trouble" us concerning the uses made of gender analysis. Exercising a philosopher's concern for definition and clarity, she moves between the general and the specific, the abstract and the embodied. She opens up the possibilities of contemplating a world beyond gender. As a university administrator Overall has inhabited classroom and boardroom and her insights are informed by that experience; but for her, "going beyond gender" is not merely an expedient for setting targets that justify withdrawing resources once equity is declared achieved. Her statistics show how few of her counterparts were female; and these statistics perhaps speak to what others had overlooked when they glanced around the university boardroom. Nor does she foresee "beyond gender" as a time in the future when feminist scholars will close their books and happily join others in declaring their work done. Overall's chapter is a place to contemplate the way that gender is articulated collectively and individually. She engages us with the philosopher's practised technique of eliciting "what is meant by?" now applied to presumptions about the future, for if we are going to see society and the lives of its individuals transformed by gender, then we had better be sure what we mean. Overall makes her vision of an empathic university the means of forging connections. And readers should emerge more informed, and more confident in the future, for her insights. With her ironical, provocative, and knowledgeable take on the premise for moving "beyond gender," she gives hope for the future. She reminds her audience this is no simple matter, but offers scope for connection through recognition of human complexity.

Perry and Overall enter as feminists from different ideological positions; but they join in criticizing the de-personalized modes of interaction that have usurped those founded on personal relations. They both wish to see an enlarged space given to collective aspirations for change in the recognition of family, kin, and community. Notably they regret the diminished political authority of women past child bearing. Both envisage a world in which the economics of appropriation has been rejected, women are not conflicted at the expense of their families, nor families set competitively against each other.

But where are these alternative discourses, and even more to our purpose, can we be confident of finding them if a quotidian or "common-sense" conception of "rights" still influences our search? Feminists are persuaded that they must refuse objectification, and must work to reverse the effects of "othering" so that subjectivities denied are recovered. Yet the guidance offered here is still tentative and speculative—an incomplete recommendation of means and ends by the standards of traditional scholarship. Can it be otherwise when the articulation between modernity's fixed place for gender and post-modernity's "beyond gender" (beyond class and race too) are still intangible territory? Thus Overall, who puts the arguments for "beyond gender" most clearly, also warns, "If we try to go on beyond gender, to make gender concepts disappear prematurely, we would simply be ignoring social categories that are still deeply significant in society" (66).

How might we begin to elicit new insights into rights and how they are conceived? What might "rights" look like in texts that are neither symbolically authoritative nor routinely derivative? How does the aspiration to be "beyond gender" in the future affect the formulation of rights here and now?

The Managed Heart

Many feminists, Kathleeen Lahey amongst them, have attempted to understand how women in general and groups of women in particular contribute disproportionately to the world's wealth and well-being but are themselves amongst its poorest and, in terms of their emotional well-being, its most insecure (Benería, Waring). The matter of empathy's naturalization as a specifically female capacity is key; how this is involved in the taken-for-granted components of care; and what the discounting of affective labour has meant for the value taken from women's activities (Straussman, Weeks). Arlie Hochschild's *The Managed Heart*, published in 1983, is possibly the most important study to have treated the making of the under-valued and under-appreciated self. Marxist theory gave focus to Hochschild's interpretation of the loss of the self in self-sacrificial labour, yet her study is better remembered for breaking with the androcentric conventions that left Marxism wanting as a critique of the gendering of capitalist systems of production, consumption and reproduction (Marx, Weeks). Hochschild recognized the need to treat emotional labour outside the household, the usual sphere of Marxist-influenced analysis, and through her concern for "pink-collar" workers, she destabilized the paradigmatic "otherness" of caring as constituted in a binarity with industrial labour, albeit a premise that was not confined to Marxism.

The Managed Heart was a timely response to the merged modes of production and reproduction and the corresponding integration of affective labour articulated by late twentieth century systems of capitalism. Appearing at a time when caring and household labour were being relocated into the market place, the analysis assisted in understanding new forms of feminized, racialised, and globalized wage labour (Hochschild "Emotions"). But the ground has shifted since, notes Kathi Weeks: the old binary divisions of space and gender have broken down and affective labour is not to be identified with a particular gender or specific site (McDowell). Post–Fordist systems of production differ from earlier systems of standardized labour; a vastly greater range of immaterial products has been brought into existence; and most significantly, domestic labour has been re-privatized during recent decades. Women, however, continue to hold primary responsibility for the privatized work of care, and tend still to be "relegated to the gender occupational niches that the domestic division of labour helps to secure" (Weeks 238). In this situation, much that concerns the authors in *Changing Places* may be recognized.

But there is another reason why "The Managed Heart" is the sub-heading for this section and it is connected with another analytical tradition, one that is important to appreciating the basis of Lahey's critique in chapter 3. While true that the labour theory of value is not directly in her sights, she marks the tokenism of neo-liberal policies that make the needs of women and their families into the means of discrimination against them: particularly grating because the proponents of these policies remind women they should first identify with their families. Stunningly inappropriate assumptions about others are at the core of ethical critique in her chapter. Those assumptions come from the liberal progressive imaginary, and Lahey rises to the task of showing how respect for difference has been abrogated as credibility is extended to the onward progress of improvement for all, secured by market forces.

Lahey, like Perry earlier, addresses the nation state. Her analysis transcends the limitations of a constitutional language which discounts the lived experience of gender inequalities. She invokes the discourse of international organizations and conventions to provide the missing perspective: thus an embodied vision of women's economic lives reveals patterns of inequality otherwise disguised. Like the histories of Aboriginal leaders that are recorded by Wadden in a later chapter, this research reminds us that, since the Enlightenment, the body and action have not been dynamically connected with problems of space in the world. Lahey refuses a teleology of progress in Western societies; she rejects the idea that women's enfranchisement has made governments answerable to women, though they are half the electorate. And, like Perry, she questions the abstract notions of women invoked to frame the policies which affect women's lives, as well as the assumption that men can serve as the model for intersubjective relations. "Taking Back the Budget" is her critique of stringency as a cover for deepening financial inequality.

The first part of Lahey's title plays on the familiar chant that resonates in downtown streets each fall as women, children, and male supporters join in the call to reclaim the experience of urban space by transforming the places in which many fear to walk. In this way, it provides an analogue for feminist research in which boldness in taking positions outside conventional intellectual relations has the potential to illuminate new ways of self-imagining and self-construction. All the authors in *Changing Places* are women set upon altering everyday life and culture along with their own destinies. In this first set of chapters, the authors show specifically how their long-term commitment to specialist fields of study is reconciled with a transformative pedagogy. Lahey deploys quantitative analysis to show what might otherwise be lost to the formal language of liberal law-making or neo-classical economics. Her expertise sustains an embodied vision of gender which identifies the gaps in specific economic policies. She uses metaphor to counter the uneasiness many economists feel when metaphor as analytical device enters their purview. What they forget perhaps is that the "invisible hand," coined by Adam Smith in the eighteenth century, has long supplied a rationale for a market which has proved neither fair nor functional in identifying needs or adjudicating the allocation of resources. The metaphor in Lahey's title signals that inequalities arising from gender, race, and class start with policies that are rhetorically justified by the market's hidden "hand."

She questions the limited emotional register of the fiscal experts who advise the Government of Canada: are they unthinking, unsympathetic, lacking in empathy? Lahey's analysis of "Mrs Martin," who is penalized by age and gender, and by her legacy of diminished resources, constitutes a further example of the "misrecognitions on which the term feminism itself relies" (Gray 226). Lahey thus indicates a sad deficiency in the new forms by which bureaucrats cast themselves as empathic. When governments and agencies volunteer with one hand what they then take away, the lives of women are worsened (Berlant 4). As Perry in this volume reminds us, from these disingenuous appropriations follow deepening structural inequality and social institutions that are "empt[ied] of feeling."

In Perry's predominantly historical analysis, "empathy" anticipates a term in a later vocabulary. By the early twentieth century, the term was in use, though as nebulous as any applied to emotions, slippery as they are. Yet when Breda Gray pointedly refers to "modern" empathy, she means to do more than establish its temporality. She is referencing circumstances in which patronizing and appropriative tendencies flow freely in the empathic professions of institutions and individuals in the age of global neo-liberalism (Gray 217; Ahmed 245). The importance of a critic's commitment to empathy defined as involving responsibility, the recognition of difference, and the application of critical reflexivity is clear from Lahey's approach to budget analysis.[12] In the cameo of "Mrs Martin," she has also made apparent that the neo-liberal discourses and assumptions of today fail to grasp the aspirations outlined above for a society that puts a different value on gender, one predicated on a more ethical articulation of economics and politics. As the twenty-first century takes issue with its modernist, Eurocentric past, its progressive critics are challenging the permeability of the female body as definitive, inviting men and women to elide or transgress gender binaries, and deconstructing the rhetoric of "separate spheres." Scholarship must continue to challenge the cultural modalities of difference and sameness that create hierarchies.

Hence the case made here for empathic ways of knowing and their revisionist potential; their emphasis on intersubjectivities and the distinctive part they play in feminist pedagogies; and their attention to the knowledge of the embodied and feeling subject. Gender imbalances in the professions and the academy surely matter: early in this collection Overall provides a balance sheet of the uneven representation of males to females in professional employment; here Lahey documents with recent statistics how short on female expertise Canada is in key areas. One of few women professionally trained in fiscal and legal analysis, Lahey applies multiple specialist skills in a rare combination to argue in effect that every woman should be in a position to see what policy formulations mean when applied to the everyday. Her invitation to women to be involved in the discussion also attaches importance to the interplay of class, race, and age with gender.

While the grouping of the previous three essays suggests the intersection of local, global, and historical processes in women's contemporary experiences of inequality, chapter 4 brings readers to consider more fully rights and equity at discursive and corporeal sites where multiple histories meet. At a time when "difficult dialogues" still characterize media encounters with Canada's Aboriginal people, Marie Wadden, a feminist, and a journalist by profession, practices an empathic mode of crossing the fields of difference (Lewis 9). Mainstream media file their reports under time constraints, but Wadden's journalism emerges from a more consistent and considered presence amongst Aboriginal people. Her early contact with the Innu of Labrador was made in the course of reporting women's protests against military low-level flying exercises, and was sustained after they ceased to make current news. When other journalists returned to report on a crisis of substance abuse by young people, Wadden was there, offering more complex reflections.

Because professional habits are hard to break, journalists commonly adopt the homogenizing references of post-coloniality. They chase breaking news, and their fleeting attention to Aboriginal society reinscribes its marginality, though perhaps unintentionally. Events other than the tragic outcomes of substance abuse call for a media presence. Press conferences, for example, routinely punctuate government attempts at brokering access for business to native lands, and not all of the journalists leaving these events are sanguine about how Aboriginal communities will fare. But critical commentary is truncated in the mainstream media. The meta-narrative of development subsumes critical thinking, and the assumed coherence of neo-liberalism leaves the transparency of its market-oriented logic little questioned in the mainstream press. It is global in reach and Aboriginal leaders can also be persuaded by its explanatory appeal. Empathy can be exercised oppressively or radically, and the recorder—journalist or academic— who intends working in Aboriginal space must see this as a reason to check and recheck her own position.

Health, especially child and adolescent health, has been painfully, if intermittently, foregrounded by the media as a focus for outside concern. Yet international outcry over substance abuse and fetal alcohol syndrome has sometimes been channeled into insinuations that Aboriginal women are to blame for children's deaths by suicide. Wadden's interviews were conducted at a time when the failure of motherhood entered the repertoire of post-colonial subject identification in a dramatic way. The "failed mothers" of the Aboriginal communities where young people were sniffing glue became an object of affective transfer across large parts of the western world.

"The Managed Heart," the subtitle for this section, thus intimates a particularly sombre development for, with affect flowing internationally, the hearts of non-Aboriginal people soon hardened against Aboriginal women for apparent child-neglect. Less had motherhood failed, however, than empathy in its "modern" mode had failed because it was unequal to the circumstances prevailing in Innu settlements. The fragmented and disembodied narratives of mainstream journalism passed over the significance of unfolding negotiations by which outsiders would gain commercial access to land that was being held in trust for future generations of Innu.

Two other contributors to this volume recognize the dense web of emotions and feelings generated by motherhood. And, though Perry (chapter 1) and Jill Allison (chapter 5) concentrate on the non-Aboriginal west, their observations are relevant. Allison's material, gathered in the

Irish state, helps enlarge upon a connection that returns us to health, the concern of several of Wadden's interviewees. Allison's contacts are "failed mothers" too, but identified by involuntary childlessness in a state that sanctifies motherhood. Allison profiles the dualistic coding of motherhood, revealing how it can be held as a sacred trust, and at the same time be an opening to the technocratic management of women's bodies and their lives. The Aboriginal Elders in Labrador, although past child bearing themselves, recognized that their influence in their own communities was weakened by the calumny on women in general. Alternatives to managed health intervention were sought with new political resolve.

Wadden contributes evidence to *Changing Places* from her interviews with ten Aboriginal women: two of those are the basis of our comments here. We draw upon these stories first for the potential of "in-between spaces," for evidence of how the somatic, corporeal, and affective afford new spaces of hope, and also for direction in each story concerning how the moral and affective capacities of media professionals might be changed.

Corporeality emerges from Wadden's essay as key to the different responses of Tshaukuesh (Elizabeth) Penashue and Maggie Hodgson to Aboriginal concerns. In Labrador, a bush walk is an invitation to an altered temporality and spatiality, and to an experience of the different sensibilities that join the Innu of Labrador closely to the land (Mudge). Accompanying the bush-walkers requires an act of imagination greater than any that is given scope in the reduction of land to market value. Penashue has annually issued an open invitation to bush walking, and non-Innu companions accept and join her (Penashue). Women coming together in the in-between space of this landscape represent a use of imaginative capacity which, as Pedwell has argued, is often missing in the neo-liberal "compassion economy (165)."

In talking with Wadden, Maggie Hodgson takes the radical revisioning of space in a different direction, to an institutional and governmental context. Acknowledging Aboriginal diversity and territorial and political autonomy, Hodgson coordinates a pan-Aboriginal apparatus connected with health that is independent of non-Aboriginal development agencies. But *health* is only the most convenient term for indigenous people's widely based commitment to different ways of being in the world. A "public feelings" project might better describe what the organization is working towards. Institutional changes that modify the in-between space of embodied encounters open up the potential for change.

Wadden had no response to her first request for a meeting with Hodgson.

In the fourteen years that then elapsed, Wadden could examine the authority that stems from the performance of her professional identity: where she is known as a journalist she must refuse the immediacy model of news-making and re-think the assumed accessibility of interviewees.[13] As an educated, white, middle class woman she is challenged to rethink the intersubjectivity of their potential encounter as one of unequal affective subjects. If she and Hodgson were to meet in spaces that opened up the potential for changed perspectives, patience was key to arriving at altered understandings of time and space. Wadden's changed position is the lengthy reconciliation of professional and personal ethics during which her passion and politics are engaged and re-engaged. She shares with Perry, Overall, and Lahey a commitment to the forms of consciousness that are not general to society, but which feminists think could make a difference.

The authors of these four chapters do not choose to provide personal accounts, nor do they render an explicit history of feminism, but instead they illuminate its genealogy. They map historical and current forms of neo-liberalism, capitalism and post-colonialism, and they account for the uneven social terrain that they and their subjects inhabit. Readers following their lead will appreciate the importance of what their generation brings to feminist political critique from an anti-hegemonic position. For they are part of a cohort that has sharpened our understanding of social and cultural inequalities and of the knowledge systems involved in naturalizing these inequalities. As scholars and activists, they have worked and continue to work empirically, and their essays reveal some of the ways in which people's well-being depends on this kind of careful analysis. Yet they refuse to sever sentient experiences from the grounds of knowledge and of politics, instead seeing questions of gender as embodied in spaces both metaphorical and lived. Thus they offer a corrective to an empathy that is tokenist, manipulative, or appropriative.

In the next set of essays (chapters 5 to 11) various routes are followed to other economies of knowledge and experience. Material such as cartoons and public art, media representations, and narratives from oral cultures, are treated with a view to disturbing the intellectual practices and social and cultural values of a gender-coded universe. These sources contribute to transformative knowledge and the possibility of action through the affects they produce. Empathy is not self-evident, clichéd, or passive in these studies. It emerges as the vital spark in this work because it is a shifting and unstable basis for engagements with human questions and dilemmas. Self-reflexive modes, flexible analytical strategies, and the eclectic interests of contributors come together in a web of connections via the linkages made in this volume—of empathy and relocation with changing places.

III. EXTENDING THE "GRAIN" OF THE SELF: THE GRAIN OF A POLITICAL PROJECT OF CARE AND OF HOPE (Probyn 173)

In the first paragraph of this introduction a crafted artifact was read for meaning. The mat circulates as its creator planned, as an object with allegiance to place, bearing witness to a specific engagement. Yet, as the artist also intended, it gives meaning to affective intimacy outside of those particular relations and their closeness. Our own structured responses and our emotional and spatial attachments can resemble the textures and surfaces in McCausland's mat (Ahmed "Feminist," 241). She might have found the scraps for her art in our lives and modeled her figures from our gestures, but in the "curve of tenderness" she creates (Sedgwick *Dialogue*, 216), there is room for recognizing difference. Like the feminist project, her art keeps in play the possibility of an affective investment based on seeing the difference in others (Bauer 58-9). Do we perhaps come to inhabit our bodies differently as a result of the intensification of feeling engendered by her image? Could this experience move us to see life articulated along a different grain? If affect increases the register of our senses, do we regard the body simply as belonging to a world of encounters, or might we contemplate the world itself "belonging to a body of encounters" as Gregg and Seigworth propose in *The Affect Theory Reader* (2).

In this way, they suggest, affective moments may be created, imagined, and nurtured "into [the] lived practices of the everyday as perpetually finer-grained postures for collective inhabitation" (2). They envisage experiences as providing for the growth of responsiveness to others by an increased inter-subjectivity of feeling; and they impress upon their readers that these moments do not arise "in order to be deciphered or decoded or delineated"; but they do not take the emotions as self-evident, nor would they say that feeling should prevail over the mind in every case (21; see also Koivunen). They recognize that it is in the nature of affective methods to "shimmer" and shift, and they elaborate on the nurturing which affective moments require: sometimes these moments are to be "smuggled" into the practices-cum-positions of our collective sensibilities, though to produce a more conscious register, Gregg and Seigworth suggest that "direct pressure" may be applied.

Elspeth Probyn's sense for "the grain of the self" extending into the "grain of a political project of care and hope" (173) provides a key reference at this point in the introduction to *Changing Places*. It is useful here as we give closer attention to inter-subjectivities as a source of political insights and consider how they come to create solidarities. The feminist's problem, indeed the problem tackled in *Changing Places* by the authors in general, is finding and explaining a critical stance on experience that attends to thinking *and* feeling. Striking a wrong or false note will cause the project to fail, but it is a condition of success to acknowledge that empathy is precarious; and a researcher who recognizes the political contingency of her position keeps in mind its potential for failure (Gray). In the final section of this introduction to *Changing Places*, we will pay closer attention to how the contributors turn to the task of shaping new patterns and practices of participation. In particular we will consider in what ways they access affective moments bearing on what transforms the "I" into the "we."

Lived Art

Allison's chapter shows how art engages both the intellect and emotions. Noting that art is "at all times lived," Raymond Williams illuminated its significance as a source of the structures of feeling that play in our lives (*Marxism*, 129). Readers who preview the image (chapter 5, figure 3) by Allison's collaborator "Elsa" will find confirmation of this, and the more so when they grasp the circumstances under which the image emerged. It was incorporated into a fund-raising Christmas card and was circulated by an organization that brings an ethical and political challenge to the forms in which motherhood structures feeling in the Irish Catholic state, causing particular discomfort to its involuntarily childless women. With her modification of religious iconography, Elsa complicates the emotional register of affect. We need to view this image more than once: between first and second look, we are already feeling differently. Empathy, but not empathy alone, has produced a circular transformation (Ahmed "Feminist," 249). There is a second strand in Allison's chapter, and it is drawn out in her account of visiting the home of one of her interviewees. Paradoxically while "Elsa's" art helped to open a public platform for issues of infertility, Allison herself found that domestic space allowed her to take only tentative steps in a parallel exploration of the absence of motherhood. Her host's welcome, though warm, is conditional: she determines where and how the lines of connection are drawn. Allison might have preferred to have their conversation unfold differently, but it is not for her to choose its direction. Recognizing the concerns of the person standing in other shoes, she acknowledges that one of those concerns is to resist being the subject of affective identification. Empathy does not fail here, quite the reverse: its precariousness is key to what this study reveals of how the emotions are engaged and disengaged, and how they help us identify the politics of human situations.

When propositions for change turn up in unlikely places and are brought forward with the lightest of hands, they might not be recognized as contending that things should be different. This is the case with Faith Balisch's chapter on the humour of the cartoonist Lynn Johnston. Johnston's comic strip, *For Better or For Worse*, has enjoyed a daily circulation in Canada and the U.S. that would be the envy of many a published feminist. Yet does she belong, even implicitly, in the category? Johnston has rarely, if ever, been identified as feminist, and Balisch is reluctant to apply the term to her work. But then Balisch provides an answer to Overall's question: Johnston helps us to see the difference that gender makes and thus gives a perspective on feminism and its potential to make the future different.

For Better or For Worse has dropped into the mailboxes of North American households for 40 years, its cameo pieces growing into a story of epic proportions. Every day, reader and cartoonist have interacted by means of a hybrid medium that requires fidelity to character and plot, and negotiates familiar territory as problematic. With images and words, Johnston prompts thinking about the reorientations by gender, sex, age, and ability that are needed to reach greater social and economic equality. But unlike many satirists, Johnston avoids giving offence. The barb, the blow, the insult are not in her repertoire, and Balisch defers to this "mistress of the pick you up" (not the "put you down") who refuses the language we have become used to when a male-dominated profession measures comedic effect by blows landed "below the belt."

Balisch's appreciation of Johnston's work helps us see that most of the changes we experience are assimilated longitudinally in family time. This process is not treated as easy or passive, and Johnston avoids any assumptions that the individuals who make up households are all of a piece. While the Pattersons, a middle-class heterosexual couple and their children, are the focus, the emotional challenges of their lives together are real enough, and by way of friends and colleagues, other dilemmas in a world of changing values are introduced. During the time that *For Better or For Worse* has been a syndicated cartoon, its main female character Elly goes from stay-at-home spouse to one who also participates in the formal workforce, and later retires. Paradoxes abound, to be recognized by the cartoon's followers as affording parallels with their own lives. What they see in Johnston's words and images are the ironies of their own or their friends' experiences. If young women with babies in the early 1960s did not think of themselves as trapped, in similar circumstances their daughters have certainly come to do so; and the daughters have accommodated to the new expectation that a family of the Patterson variety will have a second adult wage earner to address any financial stress—not that being working mothers is an entirely seamless experience for these daughters.

Meanwhile the generation who were the mothers in the 1960s and 1970s have adapted to the routine of paid labour via a demographic that often means they have swapped child-care for elder-care. Women who are emotionally conflicted by the contrary pulls of paid and unpaid labour know that something is missing from the dialogue when they are complimented for their talents in multi-tasking. It needs a cartoonist of Johnston's calibre to illuminate how society has devalued caring work and extracted a double burden of labour by perpetuating the gendering of "women's tasks" while calling them by flattering terms. It takes a particular skill as well to explore the conditions of the body's enculturation and socialization in a world which is a "body of [challenging] encounters" for the disabled (chapter 6, figure 5). The subversiveness in Johnston identified by Balisch prevails against a narcissistic, defensive, or redemptive resolution of empathy. Referencing Johnston's professional career, Balisch notes however that critics exemplify a dual standard that has operated to accord her less respect than her male counterparts. And "women's humour" continues to be regarded as a diminished art.

Speaking from the Past

The temporal and spatial scope of *Changing Places* is important and most particularly when the collection comes "home" to NL. Each of the contributors has either lived in or visited NL, though some came here only briefly, and in response to an invitation to speak at Memorial University. Rarely are invitations to the province refused, and some serendipitously enlightening exchanges in the WS/Gender seminar series have been the result. The talks delivered in those series were the genesis of the chapters in this book and with our choice of cover illustration, the editors acknowledge the pull to this place. Often spoken of and written about, the magnetism of NL is experienced daily. Yet people's emotional relations with NL are far from straightforward. When academics have conceptualized these attachments, it is often along the tangled lines of "ties that bind."

The province has a lengthy colonial and capitalist past, and has in recent times seen economic activities involving oil and gas replace those that disappeared with the fish once taken from the cod-rich Grand Banks. Artistic and literary critiques interface with scholarly and popular commentaries on depopulation and repopulation, making this a challenging environment for exploring the cultural dynamics of social and economic relations. And a sociologically, anthropologically, and historically informed feminism has advanced a concern for affect. Amongst Memorial's academics, education professor Ursula Kelly drew from the early literature on gender and affect to provide a thinking and feeling response to loss and recovery in the province. Her work became particularly pertinent when the decline of its fishing communities was accelerated by the introduction of the moratorium. More than a decade later, restrictions on cod-fishing remain in place, and Kelly's work is still shedding light on the different responses to the losses and gains that give the grain to the life of the Newfoundlander ("Learning").

One of the key influences on Kelly is the queer theorist of empathy Eve Sedgwick (*Touching*; see also Harding and Pribram *Emotions*) and it was Kelly who led us to Sedgwick's phrase "curve of tenderness" (*Migration* 144-5). Although we use it here to describe the gesture of empathic identification worked into the mat from Tor's Cove, we acknowledge its original use. In *A Dialogue on Love*, it identifies "the place of a smile, or an intelligence" from which Sedgwick could tell there was a quickening of empathy between her and her students (216). Seeking pedagogically enriched relationships, Sedgwick persistently criticized conventional systems of education. Her sense for the emotional structures of reparation has been an influence on the practice of restorative education in this province as explored by Kelly and others (Kelly *Schooling*). More will be said about teaching and learning practices involving feminist empathic identification for there are chapters in *Changing Places* authored by students who worked with Kelly and her colleagues.

But first another thread in Sedgwick's work: a concern with communication patterns and practices in literate societies that take non-textual forms. In chapters contributed to *Changing Places* by Pauline Greenhill and Willeen Keough, the lively oral tradition of NL, it is argued, reveals the consciousness that exists in the shadow of closed systems of naming and knowing. For Sedgwick, emotions with their free-flowing qualities may disrupt these finished visions of the world, a perception that Raymond Williams in large part shared. Sedgwick, however, considered the emotions as entirely open-ended, while Williams was persuaded to examine a power in circulation differently. "Practical consciousness," the register of the low, the female and the everyday, is understood in his work as socially and materially protean.[14] Nevertheless Williams stressed the social specificity of "thought as feeling and feeling as thought" (*Marxism* 132-3). It had, he observed dominant, indeed hierarchical, characteristics which provided an argument for studying its structural elements with a sense of their history.

In Greenhill's folkloristic treatment of Newfoundland ballads and songs, discoveries are drawn from the vernacular history of seafaring cross-dressing. She gives attention to the real affects of fictive works to reflect on the creative possibilities of sex and gender in these histories where the body is in a dynamic relation to time and space. Her positive view of emotions puts her in step with Sedgwick's sense for the liberatory character of cultural narratives (Ruberg and Steenbergh 14). Using an approach that might indicate what Gregg and Seigworth meant when they referred to the "nurturing" of affective moments, she shows that the embodied experience of affect is capable of linking the individual to others. The world animated as a "body of encounters" is made palpable in this chapter. Keough, however, follows a different course, addressing the heroic accounts of the men who are recognized as the pioneers of NL. Under "direct pressure," different affective truths emerge from these ostensibly plebeian narratives. Having uncovered the spuriousness of their supra-historical temporality, Keough illuminates how the myths have been instrumental in normalizing the displacement of women. But, as she also observes, distinctions divide dominant and subordinate settler groups. Keough's final concern is the cultural currency which English migrants denied to the more egalitarian articulations of gender amongst the Irish. Her findings suggest that the patterns and practices of participation in a predominantly non-literate society are to be considered as no less implicated in the sedimentation of social inequities than are its written texts. Here her insights chime with Williams' sense that we need some historically explicit explanation of a social process that is ultimately inseparable from the re-creation of patterns of capital accumulation, or from their increasingly flexible forms at the present time.

Greenhill concentrates on the idea that the shortening of memory lessens possibilities of a different understanding of gender and sex. And Keough's sense of historicization as a form of cultural production allows her recognition that popular historical accounts should not pass without interrogation if we want a deeper understanding of the work of gender. But both illuminate how the contraction of social memory is connected with the loss of empathic ways of knowing others, and through them knowing the world. These authors stress there is no consistency in the rationalist program for the humanities (since the "gatekeepers" feel no obligation to follow their own rules). Their initiatives in recovering empathic practices displaced from the academy for over a century, open up expanded notions of historical time within which the writers can more fully consider women's lives. Like the Aboriginal women responding to Marie Wadden's invitation to explore their histories and values, Greenhill and Keough appreciate that there are places of learning other than dedicated institutions. Creating the conditions of a new pedagogical exchange, in which empathic sharing is part of professional education, concerns the authors of the last three chapters to be discussed.

Unlearning Lessons

The capacity of the ordinary self to become both learner and teacher is a common thread in chapters by Gloria Montano, Sonya Corbin Dwyer and Danielle Devereaux. The close articulation of these functions in an empathic mode can provide a means for people to resist the foreclosure of the self (Bartky 187; Sedgwick *Touching*). But how and why might a learner become a teacher? And do women who are relatively new to the academy have adequate resources? What is needed in any case if the conventional meaning and modes of learning are to be questioned and the tools of learning and experiment turned over to students (Gore 67-118)? We raise these questions anticipating that some of the readers of *Changing Places* will be undergraduate or graduate students. Yet finding registers of voice, agency, and stance is a formative experience for us all, and this material contributes to the recognition that the roles of empathy in voicing and positioning are complex.

The authors of these three chapters have an institutional connection with Memorial. As students, two (Montano and Devereaux) drew support and inspiration from the scope given to transformative pedagogies in the university, and the third, a faculty member (Corbin Dwyer), reminds us that this commitment is not found everywhere in post-secondary education. Over a decade ago, Megan Boler (xiv) publicized what young women were telling her in personal communications: they had, as one letter-writer confided, "been taught to view emotions as their private problem rather than as a sign that something is wrong with the outside world" (xiv, 270; Probyn

6). Interviews gathered by Corbin Dwyer (chapter 9) document a continuing "chilly climate" for women in educational environments. Her challenge is to present these accounts of emotional journeys in the academy without having them, their speakers, or listeners, characterized as self-absorbed or self-obsessed (Bauer 64-65). An aesthetic structure that incorporates qualities of constructedness and transformability, of repetition and recognition, allows her to rework them as collective and public speech acts: and still they retain their capacity to animate empathic identification (Butler).

Originally Corbin Dwyer's material sustained a quasi-theatrical event in the WS classroom, and it is reproduced here in a form that facilitates re-staging. Women students speak in chorus or, stepping forward, they speak as individuals, but they are articulating what Corbin Dwyer and her collaborator gathered elsewhere. Often their lines concentrate on how women are made to feel uncomfortable about splitting their lives between family and education. At some time, perhaps every member of the audience has been made to feel this way. Empathic identification is thereby encouraged, and it sustains our interest, but there is more subtlety in the interplay of empathy with voice and position than is required simply to hold attention. The speech acts are scripted, and at times they recall the part assigned to a formal female chorus in ancient Greek theatre. These actors, though students, are not to be confused with the informants who first spoke the words. Moreover the listening audience is asked to make other adjustments: as the staged narration unfolds, textual elaboration is provided through PowerPoint projection. This not a piece of realistic theatre, unfolding in a naturalizing grain: rather it is textured so that audience members are caught up in the episodes recounted, and simultaneously positioned to identify and analyze their own responses (Boal 43-45). They see how they have been acted upon. With this careful handling of the potential for empathic identification, the observer is better placed to know and feel what it is to be a young woman in the academy than if the personal testimonies gathered by Corbin Dwyer been more conventionally reported as "research."

Before she was a university student of education, Gloria Montano was a computer engineer, and was much involved in encouraging women into the profession. Wishing to see engineering become more responsive to a range of unmet needs, she joined a prominent equity seeking organization. Through it she hoped to speak to women's unequal access to new technologies. Yet chapter 10 is the account of how her decision to resume formal education was precipitated by her growing unease with what she experienced in that organization. Community-based initiatives were its first approach to exploring women's and girls' ambivalent relationship with technology. But at the next stage, professional reflexes kicked in and her colleagues conceived modular design as the way to multiply their initial successes. Montano was critical as she observed the androcentricism that followed from this development. There had to be other ways of creating new relationships around technology, those that allow for the expression of empathy and joy.

In a chapter that is partly written in first person, Montano acknowledges that becoming estranged from ostensibly like-minded peers is painful. She uses emotional disclosure critically rather than therapeutically however, making her account auto-ethnographical as distinct from confessional. The daughter of a Filipino immigrant family to the United States, she developed determination about career choices early. It now feeds her resolve to change direction mid-career. As she embraces an opportunity for political connectivity with a new community of teachers and learners, it is clear that narcissim has no place in her intellectual or emotional make-up (Ahmed "Feminist," 245; hooks 32). The limits to and capacities for what can be done at any site constitute an important part of what Montano discovers from her lack of fit amongst the women in her profession. Emotional dissonance moves her to find better accounts of affect in a pedagogy that can be applied to technologically mediated experience.

All spaces including the front row were filled in the lecture room at Memorial University when Danielle Devereaux started the video. She had recently returned from a spell as an intern with the Media Education Foundation in the U.S., and now invited an audience to view *Advertizing and the End of the World*. A discussion of its themes would follow, and there were to be other showings and discussions in later weeks. The video began with footage of the popular cultural forms that resonate affectively for consumers, but its momentum would build only if the synthetic popular culture of the advertiser could be displaced by the felt culture of the gathering. While she hoped that the emotional relationships that frame media projections would elicit a critical response, this could not be planned. Devereaux knew only that she needed to avoid manipulative or tokenist interventions that might inhibit the audience. As it turned, out the experience was sufficiently rewarding to inspire her to begin writing about the intersection of critical media, feminism, and pedagogy in the thinking and learning of students, including herself.

Yet none of this had emerged from clearly formulated intentions.

Rather it came from the initial perplexity Devereaux felt about satisfying the unconventional requirements of her post-graduate degree. She was not alone: her fellow students and instructors had asked her how the video screenings could be linked with a program of academic studies; and what in any case was the disciplinary connection, for was she not a student in *Women's* Studies? Devereaux was purposefully under-stated in her response, and educationalist Megan Boler might well have approved of her refusal to conform with others' expectations. Devereaux turned her peers' diminished concept of WS around and from the breadth of what she had gained by embracing her discipline, she drew members of the audience into reflecting on the limitations of their own categories. Far from treating the emotions as a private problem, she animated the possibilities of emotional learning in a public space.

These last three contributors clearly demonstrate that a socialized and pedagogically engaged stance is paramount to extending the grain of the self: Montano by refusing the institutional constraints that were compromising her dialogues; Devereaux by ensuring that a misperception about WS did not stand between her and her audience; and Corbin Dwyer by securing space for an audience to reassess their feelings when the inconsistencies, ironies and outright contradictions of the neo-liberal narrative of women's emancipation achieved were played out before them. The three chapters supply a powerful incitement to break the cycle that can still diminish women's access to graduate education: a fitting conclusion to a group of studies concerned with identifying the places where the North American academy might be reconstructed by attending to more robust models of embodiment and emotion. We return now to one important source of our inspiration for thinking and feeling differently about bold, imaginative applications of empathic scholarly practice.

When Catherine McCausland permitted us to reproduce her hooked mat on the cover of *Changing Places*, we recognized an image that suggests the folds and textures of life itself. And as this image grew on us, we also saw in it a "curve of tenderness," empathic connection, the offer of recognition and acceptance. Could such affective understandings create the conviction that optimism has to be part of the feminist project of care and hope? After all, "Tell me again" can have sharp edges. Its fabrics, old and new, are torn in places.

But to recognize the dissonance as well as the solidarity in the project of empathy is also to open the way to fuller feminist engagement with change and relocation. Our efforts to do both in this introduction to *Changing Places* have been made easier by the work of feminist writers who sense that the dynamics of optimism *and* exclusion shape our existences on the uneven terrains of life. They have considered the shifting, unstable reputation of emotion as a base of investigation or argument, as against established, classic knowledge systems; and they have recognized empathy's contingency with other emotions. In dialogue with their work, we have reflected here on the forms which empathy might take, and its future potential for fostering responsibility, accountability, critical reflexivity, and recognition of difference.

While we have emphasized hermeneutics, or the scholarly application of empathy as a practice, we are also concerned for readers' responses and the ways in which meanings are created in circulation. Empathy is not an "all or nothing occurrence"; and it can never be "a sure fit," the phrase in which Code makes explicit for the reader how "rare and fragile" empathy is (132), not suggesting capitulation to a diminished empathy, but pointing towards the empathic imaginary of the ordinary self doing extraordinary things (see Probyn 170).

[1]Melissa Gregg in Gregg and Seigworth: "I came to notice [in the early 1990s] how affect always points to a future that is not quite in view from the present, a future that scrambles any map in advance of its arrival, if indeed that moment (as a demand on the social) ever fully arrives" (21).

[2]Affect, as defined by Breda Gray "can be understood as an embodied physiological state that emerges in social interaction and relational encounters; it involves an engagement with the world that, although non-reflective, shapes thought.... [A]ffect broadly refers to states of being, rather than their manifestations or interpretation as emotions. In contrast, *emotion* can be understood as the conscious perception of affect. Emotions do things; they are what moves us but also connect us with others" (208-9).

[3]In two further sections of this introduction the chapters are glossed by reference to some of the classic and more recent studies of empathy and affect. "Works Cited" at the end of this chapter acknowledges a long list of sources.

[4]Grouped in two sections, "Something Much More" and "Extending the Grain of the Self" (an abbreviation of the title), the organization of these chapters is a genealogy of how feminists have worked with others across difference to create the conditions for transformation.

[5]We take warning, however, from the editors of "Affecting Feminisms,"

a recent special issue of the journal *Feminist Theory*, who caution against speaking from a superior moral position or over-complicating explanations (Pedwell and Whitehead).

[6]Simten Vural writes of her grandmother's shoes:

Time passed,
She died.
I am in her shoes
She is in me.

[7]While the everyday language of empathy implies the possibility of engaging experientially and affectively with another person, the point here is that a formal definition, especially one cast for brevity, imposes a linearity that does not serve the imagination even in its most practical forms.

[8]The quotation refers to an essentialized and disembodied subject encountered in feminist analysis, but still imbricated with the binary logic of rational knowledge systems. Subjects exist in unhomogeneous social space, and Haraway observes that "there is no way "to be" simultaneously in all or wholly in any of the ... subjugated positions structured by gender, race, nation, and class"(586).

[9]Hemmings also elaborates on the process of moving from affective dissonance to a collective struggle for alternative values. She models this as the recognition among some, if not all, members of a household that something is unjust or wrong. Each is differently positioned and accordingly experiences life in the household differently. The flow of empathy between them is necessary to the reflexive politicization that produces solidarity ("Affective Solidarity" 157).

[10]Williams first identified structures of feeling as a concept with theoretical importance for literary studies in *Culture and Society, 1780-1950* (1958). In *The Long Revolution* (1961) he made the important step of recognizing heterogeneity in social and discursive practices. In "Structures of Feeling," a chapter in *Marxism and Literature* (1977), he considered the interrelationship of public and private processes and historical formations with social structures, and he argued that this interrelationship is active and communicable. In this work too, he elaborated the above concept making it both a practical and theoretical proposition, applied to liminal forms of experience (Williams *Marxism*, 132; Terry Eagleton 28). In its most concise articulation, structures of feeling are "elements of impulse, restraint, and tone; specifically affective elements of consciousness and relationships: not feeling against thought, but thought as felt and feeling as thought: practical consciousness of a present kind, in a living and inter-relating continuity." He further

suggested: "We are then defining these elements as a 'structure': as a set, with specific internal relations, at once interlocking and in tension.... We are also defining a social experience still in process, often indeed not yet recognized as social but taken to be private, idiosyncratic, and even isolating, but which in analysis (though rarely otherwise) has its emergent, connecting, and dominant characteristics, indeed its specific hierarchies" (*Marxism*, 132).

[11]Empathy is observed as a modern word, not existing before the 1920s, but then proving useful to psychologists and cultural critics (Margulies xi). Perhaps "sympathy" provided pre-twentieth century people with a reference to some of what today would be called empathy, though in present-day understandings empathy is more closely linked with compassion and respect than is sympathy.

[12]See also Pedwell's fine critique of the delusions of empathy involved in international development internships.

[13]See also engineer Gloria Montano's similar challenge, treated in chapter 10.

[14]"Practical consciousness is almost always different from official consciousness.... For practical consciousness is what is actually being lived, and not only what is thought is being lived. Yet the actual alternative to the received and produced fixed forms is not silence: not the absence, the unconscious, which bourgeois culture has mythicized. It is a kind of feeling and thinking which is indeed social and material, but each in an embryonic phase before it can become fully articulate and defined exchange" (131).

WORKS CITED

Ahmed, Sara. "Feminist Futures." *A Concise Companion to Feminist Theory*. Ed. Mary Eagleton. Oxford: Blackwell, 2003. 236-56. Print.

Ahmed, Sara. "This Other and Other Others." *Economy and Society* 31.4 (2003): 558-72. Print.

Alcoff, Linda. "The Problem of Speaking for Others." *Cultural Critique* (Winter 1991-2): 5-32. Print.

Bartky, Sandra Lee. "Sympathy and Solidarity: On a Tightrope with Scheler." *Feminists Rethink the Self*. Ed Diana T. Meyers. Boulder: Westview Press, 1997. 177-96. Print.

Bauer, Dale M. "Personal Criticism and the Academic Personality." *Who Can Speak? Authority and Critical Identity*. Ed. Judith Roof and Robyn Wiegman. Urbana: University of Illinois Press, 1995. 56-69. Print.

Benería, Lourdes. "Paid and Unpaid Labour: Meanings and Debates." *Gender, Development, and Globalization: Economics as if All People Mattered.* New York: Routledge, 2003. 54-68. Print.

Berlant, Lauren, ed. "Compassion (and Withholding)." *Compassion: The Culture and Politics of an Emotion.* New York: Routledge, 2004. 1-15. Print.

Boal, Augusto. *Theatre of the Oppressed.* Trans. Charles A. McBride and Maria-Odilia Leal McBride. London: Pluto Press, 1979. Print.

Boler, Megan. *Feeling Power: Emotions and Education.* New York: Routledge, 1999. Print.

Butler, Judith. "Performative Acts and Gender Constitution: An Essay in Phenomenology and Feminist Theory." *Performing Feminisms: Feminist Critical Theory and Theatre.* Ed. Sue-Ellen Case. Baltimore: Johns Hopkins University Press, 1990. 270-82. Print.

Cerwonka, Allaine. "What to Make of Identity and Experience in Twenty-First Century Feminist Research." *Theories and Methodologies in Postgraduate Feminist Research: Researching Differently.* Ed. Rosemarie Buikema, Gabriele Griffin and Nina Lykke. New York: Routledge, 2011. 60-73. Print.

Code, Lorraine. "I Know Just How You Feel." *The Epistemic Authority of Rhetorical Spaces: Essays on Gendered Locations.* New York: Routledge, 1995. 120-43. Print

Code, Lorraine. "Incredulity, Experientialism and the Politics of Knowledge." *Just Methods: An Interdisciplinary Feminist Reader.* Ed. Alison Jaggar. 290-302. Print.

Code, Lorraine. "Taking Subjectivity into Account." *The Feminist Philosophy Reader.* Ed. Alison Bailey and Chris Cuomo. New York: McGraw Hill, 2008. 718-40. Print

Eagleton, Mary, ed. *A Concise Companion to Feminist Theory.* Oxford: Blackwell, 2003. Print.

Eagleton, Terry. "Raymond Williams, Communities, and Universities." *Key Words: A Journal of Cultural Materialism* 1(1998): 28-34. Print.

"Empathy." *The Canadian Oxford Dictionary.* 1998. Print.

Gore, Jennifer M. *The Struggle for Pedagogies: Critical and Feminist Discourses as Regimes of Truth.* New York: Routledge, 1993. Print.

Govier, Katherine, ed. *The Shoe Project.* Web. 13 May 2013.

Gray, Breda. "Empathy, Emotion, and Feminist Solidarities." *Sexed Sentiments: Interdisciplinary Perspectives on Gender and Emotion.* Eds. Willemijn Ruberg and Kristine Steenbergh. Amsterdam: Rodopi, 2010. 207-32. Print.

Gregg, Melissa and Gregory J. Seigworth, eds. "An Inventory of

Shimmers." *The Affect Theory Reader.* Durham, NC: Duke University Press, 2010. 1-25. Print.

Haraway, Donna. "Situated Knowledges: The Science Question in Feminism and the Privilege of Partial Perspective." *Feminist Studies* 14.3 (Fall 1988): 575-99. Print.

Harding, Jennifer, and E. Deirdre Pribram, eds. *Emotions: A Cultural Studies Reader.* London: Routledge, 2009. Print.

Harding, Jennifer and E. Deirdre Pribram. "Losing Our Cool?" *Cultural Studies* 18.6 (2006): 863-83. Print.

Harding, Sandra G., ed. "Standpoint Theory as a Site of Political, Philosophic, and Scientific Debate." *The Feminist Standpoint Theory Reader: Intellectual and Political Controversies.* New York: Routledge, 2004. 1-20. Print.

Harding, Sandra G. *Whose Science? Whose Knowledge? Thinking from Women's Lives.* Ithaca, NY: Cornell University Press, 1991. Print.

Hemmings, Clare. "Affective Solidarity: Feminist Reflexivity and Political Transformation." *Feminist Theory* 13.2 (2012): 147-61. Web. 13 May 2013.

Hemmings, Clare. "Invoking Affect: Cultural Theory and the Ontological Turn." *Cultural Studies* 19.5 (2005): 548-67. Print.

Higgins, John. "'Even the Dead Will Not be Safe': on Dis(re)membering Williams." *About Raymond Williams.* Ed Monika Seidl, Roman Horak and Lawrence Grossberg. Routledge: London, 2010. 117-28. Print.

Hochschild, Arlie Russell. "An Emotions Lens on the World." *Theorizing Emotions: Sociological Explorations and Applications.* Ed. Debra Hopkins, Jochen Kleres, Helena Flam, and Helmut Kuzmics. Frankfurt: Campus Verlag. 2009. 29-35. Print.

Hochschild, Arlie Russell. *The Managed Heart: Commercialization of Human Feeling.* Berkeley: University of California Press, 1983. Print.

hooks, bell. *Talking Back: Thinking Feminist —Thinking Black.* Boston: South End Press, 1989.

Jaggar, Alison M., ed. "Feminist Ethics in Research." *Just Methods: An Interdisciplinary Feminist Reader.* Boulder, CO: Paradigm Publishers, 2008. 457-60. Print.

Jaggar, Alison M. "Love and Knowledge: Emotion in Feminist Epistemology." *Inquiry* 32.2 (1989): 151-176. 1989. Print.

Koivunen, Anu. "An Affective Turn? Reimagining the Subject of Feminist Theory." *Working With Affect in Feminist Readings.* Ed. Marianne Lileström and Susanna Paasonen. London: Routledge, 2010. 8-28. Print.

Kelly, Ursula. "Learning from Loss: Migration, Mourning and Identity." *Despite This Loss: Essays on Culture, Memory, and Identity in Newfoundland and Labrador*. Eds. Ursula Kelly and Elizabeth Yeoman. St. John's: ISER Books, 2010. Print.

Kelly, Ursula. *Migration and Education in a Multicultural World: Culture, Loss, and Identity*. New York: Palgrave Macmillan, 2009. Print.

Kelly, Ursula. *Schooling Desire: Literacy, Cultural Politics, and Pedagogy*. New York: Routledge, 1997. Print.

Lewis, Gail. "Editorial: Difficult Dialogues Once Again." *European Journal of Women's Studies* 16:1 (2009): 5-10.

Margulies, Alfred. *The Empathic Imagination*. New York: W.W. Norton, 1989. Print.

Marx, Karl. "Estranged Labour." *Economic and Philosophical Manuscripts of 1844: First Manuscript* (1844: 2009). Web. 13 May 2013.

Mudge, Andrew. Meshkanu: The Long Walk of Elizabeth Penashue. Black Kettle Films. 2009. Web. 13 May 2013.

McDowell, Linda. "Place and Space." *A Concise Companion. A Concise Companion to Feminist Theory*. Ed. Mary Eagleton. Oxford: Blackwell, 2003. 11-33. Print.

Pedwell, Carolyn. "Affective (Self-)Transformations: Empathy, Neoliberalism and International Development." *Feminist Theory* 13.2 (2012): 163-79. Web. 13 May 2013.

Pedwell, Carolyn, and Anne Whitehead. "Affecting Feminism: Questions of Feeling in Feminist Theory." *Feminist Theory* 13.2 (2012): 115-129. Web. 13 May 2013.

Penashue, Elizabeth. Elizabeth "Tshaukuesh" Penashue Innu Elder and Activist. Blog. Web. 13 May 2013.

Pribram, E. Deidre. "An Individual of Feeling: Emotion, Gender, and Subjectivity in Historical Perspectives on Sensibility." *Sexed Sentiments: Interdisciplinary Perspectives on Gender and Emotion*. Eds. Willemijn Ruberg and Kristine Steenbergh. Amsterdam: Rodopi, 2010. 21-46. Print.

Probyn, Elspeth. *Sexing the Self: Gendered Positions in Cultural Studies*. London: Routledge, 1993. Print.

Ruberg, Willemijn and Kristine Steenbergh, eds. *Sexed Sentiments: Interdisciplinary Perspectives on Gender and Emotion*. Amsterdam: Rodopi, 2010. Print.

Sedgwick, Eve Kosofsky. *Touching Feeling: Affect, Pedagogy, Performativity*. Durham, NC: Duke University Press, 2003. Print.

Sedgwick, Eve Kosofsky. *A Dialogue on Love*. Boston: Beacon Press, 1999. Print.

Spivak, Gayatri Chakravorty. "Can the Subaltern Speak?" *Marxism and the Interpretation of Culture*. Ed. Cary Nelson and Lawrence Grossberg. Basingstoke: Macmillan Education, 1988. 271-313. Print.

Scott, Joan W. "The Evidence of Experience." *Critical Inquiry* 17.4 (1991): 773-97. Print.

Staussman, Diana. "Not a Free Market: The Rhetoric of Disciplinary Authority in Economics." *Beyond Economic Man: Feminist Theory and Economics*. Ed. Marianne Ferber. Chicago: University of Chicago Press, 1993. 54-68. Print.

Vural, Simten. "In Her Shoes." *The Shoe Project*. Web. 13 May 2013.

Waring, Marilyn. *If Women Counted: A New Feminist Economics*. San Francisco: Harper and Row, 1988. Print.

Weeks, Kathy. "Life Within and Against Work: Affective Labour, Feminist Critique, and Post-Fordist Politics." *Ephemera: Theory and Politics in Organization* 7.1 (2007): 233-49. Print.

Williams, Raymond. *Marxism and Literature*. Oxford: Oxford University Press, 1977. Print.

Williams, Raymond. *Resources of Hope: Culture, Democracy, Socialism*. Ed. Robin Gable. London: Verso, 1989. Print.

Woodward, Kathleen. "Calculating Compassion." *Compassion: The Culture and Politics of an Emotion*. Ed. Lauren Berlant. New York: Routledge, 2004. 59-86. Print.

1. The Maternal Body and the State

How Women's Reproductive Capacity Has Undermined Their Share in State Power

RUTH PERRY

THIS CHAPTER TRACES THE LOGIC by which the modern nation state erases the rights of its adult female citizens because of their capacity to become mothers. The murderous opposition to abortion in the United States and lawsuits against pregnant women who smoke or drink—on behalf of the rights of their fetuses—testify that the adult female is not an autonomous individual whose rights the state guarantees, as Julia Epstein discusses. In Canada, too, the state's interest in women's reproductive bodies is apparent in the restriction that comes with the conservative government's aid to developing countries to promote maternal health: the *caveat* that the money cannot be used to fund abortions. Indeed, when one examines historically the symbolic relationship between women's rights and the constellation of ideas about political equality, democracy, liberty, and individual rights—as these ideas surfaced in the Athenian polis, the Italian city states, and most definitively for our culture, in Enlightenment England—it appears that the subordination of women has been integral to the process by which power is democratized among men. What I want to explore here is this doubly contingent move that displaces women. Why has the enfranchising of a broader class of men so often entailed the disempowering of women? What causes this conflation of effects? Or, as Mary Astell asked in 1706: "If *all Men are born free,* how is it that all Women are born Slaves?" (11)

An examination of several models of democratic origin in the western tradition, drawn from different historical periods, shows that conceptually the suppression of the female—and in particular the maternal body—is implicated in the foundation of the "democratic" state. Thus I am arguing that the suppression of maternal power is constitutive of a democratic polity in the same way that Claude Levi-Strauss held that the patterning of incest taboos and the exogamous exchange of women are constitutive of human society. Levi-Strauss posited that social groups define themselves in relation to other social groups by how they draw lines around their women: which ones are "in" or "out" of the family, clan, or tribe, which ones are sexually available, which ones are preferable for marriage, etc. A society's rules about the deployment of its women's sexual and reproductive activities are thus the basis for configurations of kinship.[1] Gayle Rubin, following Levi-Strauss, claims that the incest taboo and the exchange of women are not only the basis of all human society, but are the express substance of the original social contract (192).

This anthropological paradigm describes one way that the suppression of maternal power could be said to be built into the democratic contract among men and the foundation of the nation-state. The connection is overdetermined: it hardly matters whether one believes that the nation-state evolved to suppress the power of families and extended kin communities in which women's role is undeniable, or that the nation-state is built on assumptions about citizenship and equality that exclude women, bodies, and loyalty to families and kin groups. In either case, women's exclusion from the polity because of their reproductive capacity is the subtext that can be traced in most stories of democratic origin. I am not concerned here with particular women in any particular national period; my subject is the cultural symbolism of the western tradition and certain iconic political texts in that tradition. Nor will I be analyzing the power relations among classes of women, ruling class and racialized minority women, colonizer and colonized. I am aware that for eighteenth- and nineteenth-century Anglo-American culture, excellent work by Anna Davin and Felicity Nussbaum has long established that the "cult of domesticity"—the ideology that women are uniquely suited to care for their homes and families—was made possible by the labour of these minorities and colonized women, ironically at the expense of their own homes and families. I am not here concerned with the history of attitudes towards motherhood, but rather with the biological fact of women's reproductive capacity.

Nonetheless, Jessica Benjamin's observations in *The Bonds of Love*, extending the insights of the Frankfurt school, are relevant here. She traces many deformations in our modern society to the devaluing of the mother and maternal labour, and the corollary privileging of the autonomous, self-motivated (male) individual. She describes how the breakdown of intersubjective experience (defined as the tension between self-assertion and recognition of the "other") began with the refusal to recognize the subjectivity of the mother, and leads to relationships of domination and subordination and to a devaluing of intersubjective experience altogether—both at the symbolic level and in everyday life. "Abstract, calculable, and depersonalized modes of interaction," she writes, "replace those founded on personal relationships and traditional authority and beliefs. Instrumental rationality elevates means to the status of ends. Formal procedures (like law) and abstract goals (like profit) replace the traditional values and customs that form a common cultural life and serve to legitimate authority" (185-6).[2] In other words, positing the mother and the maternal functions she performs as irrelevant to the "real" work of the culture erodes one basis for social agreement—our "common cultural life"—and substitutes another in which authority is vested in "formal procedures (like law) and abstract goals (like profit)." Bureaucratic state power thus grows at the expense of the domain of the mother— the personal, intersubjective world of domestic life. What I want to emphasize here, for the sake of my argument, is that the creation of a public sphere governed by formal procedures and abstract goals necessarily entails the suppression of maternal power.[3]

The position of women in democratic theories of the state raises questions about the models that we have taken to be the basis of political power, the possibilities of egalitarian political contracts, and most seriously, about whether states can ever serve the interests of women when those interests are at odds with (male) profit, privilege, or power. In what follows I am not going to look at actual political practices in the Anglo-American tradition such as acts of parliaments, operations of law courts, or even histories of electoral politics— although feminist historians have demonstrated that, long before they had the vote, women participated on the margins of these institutions in Enlightenment England by raising money through their charities for favorite candidates, canvassing and entertaining voters, and formulating political arguments in debating societies established for this purpose (see for example Chalus and Clark). One could also point to the erasure of real women in modern legal practices that recognize a woman's genetic gift but not her reproductive labour in contested cases of "surrogate" motherhood that protect the welfare of a fetus before the rights of an adult woman, and that have attenuated the rights of female citizens to safe medical abortion. But what I want to do here is to analyze a series of symbolic texts in the philosophical tradition of democracy, political fables, and theories that have justified democratic "advances," in order to foreground the pattern of suppression of maternal power (and empathy for mothers) in these stories.

The *locus classicus* of the political double move in which the political power of the state is diverted from women and democratized among men, in the earliest known reference to Athenian democracy, is in *The Eumenides*, the concluding sequence of Aeschylus' *Oresteia* trilogy. In that play, Athena, seeking to end the cycle of blood and retribution set in train by Agamemnon's sacrifice of Iphigenia on the eve of the Trojan war, establishes a tribunal of citizens to judge Orestes' case. She democratizes her power, so to speak, by instructing a group of uninvolved citizens to determine whether or not Orestes should be punished for killing his mother.

The enabling fiction of this court, made up of twelve free male citizens of Athens, is that it is an objective forum, protected from those private feelings which cannot now distort Justice with a capital "J"—newly defined as an interest in the state and in abstract law rather than the family. The choice is structured optimistically, as if it were simply a choice between continuing the cycle of revenge or ending it arbitrarily, substituting the democratic rule of citizens for the blood vengeance of family feuds. But it is also a choice between rule by families or clans— including mothers and sisters—or rule by unrelated adult men. The final verdict—the exoneration of Orestes, the founding move of this new politico-legal system—is understood as a symbolic victory over the inexorable cycle of instinctual, personal revenge: a triumph of culture over nature.

What is excluded from this civilized polis, of course, is the mother, the maternal principle, the starting place and focal point of any family. Froma Zeitlin, in her classic analysis of the repression of "the feminine" in this drama cycle, associates Orestes' story with male puberty rites whose cultural function is to "cure" young men of their dependence on their mothers and to effect their rebirth into a family of men. Thus the first birth from the female is superseded by a second birth, this time from the male. The initiate is born again into the social world of the fathers and is thereby definitively separated from the loving, empathic world of his childhood and his dependence on his mother. The point of these rituals—and, Zeitlin argues, of the carefully symbolic movement of *The Eumenides*—is to effect male bonding at the expense of earlier familial relationships. Loyalty to the new political unit supersedes family loyalty, in fact, the new unit might be said to be established precisely in order to supersede loyalty to the family, and in particular, the mother (Zeitlin 176). Father-right is what matters in Aeschylus' newly fashioned state. Even matricide is permissible when exercised in defence of father-right.

Moving the locus of justice, the site of accountability, from the family to the state appears at first merely to homogenize power among a male citizenry. But in doing so, it creates the public arena from which women are excluded. The public world of civil government, after all, has its meaning only in its differentiation from the family. That is, democratic male power appears to be established and justified at the expense of women, and it is accomplished by separating the polis from the family.[4]

Is this then the mechanism by which women have been denied a voice in affairs of state? Is male individuation so tied to separation from the mother that the subjective differentiation from the mother and from her maternal power must be formally instantiated in the founding of the state? Must the mother—or a symbolic woman—always be implicated in inflecting the difference between the public and the private, as that division has been articulated and rearticulated throughout the history of civil societies?[5] The violence with which the "feminine" is subordinated and denied in political negotiations among men may indicate the urgency of men's need to separate from what is private, familial and maternal—or it may simply reflect the trauma of this separation.

In an article on male prostitution in ancient Greece, David Halperin has shown how, in defining phallic sexual practice as a property of citizenship, the Greeks found another way, grounded in the anatomical features of the body itself, to distribute power among men while simultaneously disenfranchising women. Because the act of sexual penetration was associated with social domination in Greek culture, Halperin argues, a citizen's body was, by definition, "sacrosanct." Violation of its boundaries, whether by physical violence such as torture, or judicial violence such as imprisonment, was illegal. He examines the trial, intended to deprive him of status, of a citizen named Timarchus, said to have been a male prostitute.[6] Given the coding of bodily function as social and political power in that culture, the accusation that Timarchus had voluntarily submitted to penetration is intended to prove his unsuitability for citizenship and to disenfranchise him. This equivalence between the bodily practice of receiving the phallus—of putting oneself at the disposal of another's pleasure—and political untrustworthiness, this equivalence between sexual permeability and political permeability, makes explicit the assumption that the very bodily organization of a woman made her unfit to be a citizen. Halperin also argues that the state-sanctioned system of female prostitution democratized male sexual power while it potentially subordinated all women to all men. Male sexual privilege, then, became the democratic mark of all citizens, leveling unequal degrees of wealth and social standing, and this democratic homogeneity was purchased by privileging a phallocentric sexual practice that sexually subordinated women. In the terms of this volume, one might extend the point that making oneself available for another's pleasure requires a kind of emotional fluidity that is an attribute of empathy.

In analyzing the roles accorded to women in myth and history, feminist scholars have uncovered other ways in which men's political relations are displayed or signaled by reference to women's bodies. Eve Kosofsky Sedgwick's *Between Men: English Literature and Male Homosocial Desire* was the earliest study to identify the pattern in many classic Anglo-American literary texts of male bonding, often across class lines, at the expense of—and often upon the bodies of—women. Nancy Vickers' classic "The Mistress in the Masterpiece" showed the same dynamic in Cellini's bronze bas relief "The Nymph at Fontainebleau," which represents at once Cellini's relationship to his king, his servant, and his mistress, all figured in terms of sexual dominance. Caterina's body, modeled and presented as available to all viewers, becomes the mediating locus through which Cellini confirms his monarch's preeminence, as well as his own superiority to his cuckolded servant, Caterina's husband. Vickers' dramatic example shows how male political power is announced and validated by the appropriation of a woman's body. Indeed, in the last decades we have recognized rape used as a weapon of war, a constitutive act reframing lines of authority among men.[7] With chilling logic, these examples show how frequently women's bodies have been the symbolic sites on which men's arrangements are ratified. Women's bodies, it seems, have functioned throughout the western tradition as the markers of male authority, as interchangeable and mute as Chryseis and Briseis in the famous quarrel between Agamemnon and Achilles.[8]

This might be called the Oedipus complex theory of women's position in political exchange: women as the passive symbolic objects whose fates confirm men's hierarchical positioning of supremacy and control. The classic version is developed by Freud in the last essay of *Totem and Taboo*—his own favourite among his writings—and derives in part from Darwin's attempts to extrapolate pre-history in *The Descent of Man*. In Freud's account of this most primitive of all political challenges, a group of brothers band together to overthrow the father—indeed they devour and thus literally "internalize" him. They take this action because they resent his jealous, monopolistic control of the women of the tribe. Again, women are imagined only as property in Freud's model, the coveted possessions of the father. But once the brothers have done their dirty work, they—and Freud—lose interest in the women, the spoils of the contest, and they drop out of the story of the band of brothers. This, then, is the origin of exogamous incest taboos according to Freud. To keep the peace among themselves after killing the father, in order to avoid fighting among themselves, the "brothers" mutually agree to abstain from sexually possessing these particular women, the ones "in the family" so to speak. Freud concludes this work, surprising even himself with the simplicity of his discovery, that "the beginnings of religion, ethics, society, and art meet in the Oedipus complex."[9]

So it seems that women hardly fare better in a society based on patricide than they do in one based on matricide. In both these stories about the origins of civil government, the formation of the state is grounded in the subordination of women. In the earlier story, the one told by Aeschylus, the polis was predicated on a justification of matricide and women were simply erased from public life. In the Darwinian tale told by Freud, women never had a public presence at all but were rather the occasion for public disputes among men; women were treated as property both before and after the patricide. In this story of democratic triumph, the patriarchal form of government is succeeded by a contractual model in which "the brothers" who challenge the father agree among themselves to an exogamous exchange of women. The seal of democratic practice, the material basis for contractual agreement among men, is agreement about how to dispose of the women.

Anthropologist Christine Gailey, asking why the rise of the nation state in Tonga entailed the reduction of women's traditional power and status, concludes that the loss is contingent upon the separation of productive from reproductive labour. Before contact with Europeans, women's labour in Tonga not only produced goods for subsistence and reproduced children, but also reproduced kin relations, sometimes "concretized in the goods women made and distributed at critical moments in their relatives' lives" (16). In other words, women perpetuated the power of kin-based communities both by physically reproducing the offspring of these communities and by *socially* reproducing these kin-based groups, i.e., by protecting them, validating them, maintaining them, and caring for the members of kin communities. As she describes the process by which the nation-state was established and women increasingly disempowered politically, the devaluation of women is associated with subordination of community and reproduction to state-associated production, and the subordination of kin relations to the production required to generate the surplus needed to support non-producing ruling elites. "In other words," she points out, "where production is for communal use and organized and controlled through reproductive relationships, there is no public/domestic split," and women's labour and participation in decision-making are valued (4). But when productive and reproductive labour are separated, the work that maintains a non-productive ruling class is increasingly privileged, while the work that maintains the kin community is increasingly devalued. Women's power thus founders on the opposition between state power and the power of kin communities, and the distinction between reproductive labour that supports the kin community and the productive labour that supports emerging class relations and the impersonal state. Nation states oppose the self-determination of kinship groups and seek to subordinate them to the imperatives of statehood. "The degree to which women's labour remains highly valued and the degree to which women retain considerable authority depends upon the persistence of [a] kin-based production-for-use sphere," says Gailey (261).

One can see this process operating historically in a global context. Wherever women—usually older women, well past child-bearing—have held sacred or political power in their communities, this power has been denied them by invading colonizers or by "rationalist" forces within their own culture advocating impersonal institutions, as Annette Weiner demonstrates: "Hawaiian priests, Inca rulers, Greek philosophers, Christian clergymen, and Western capitalists, to name only a few, have systematically stripped away women's control over sacred authority and possessions that authenticate rank, thereby denying women's roles in cultural reproduction and restricting them to being wives and reproducing the species" (419).

I have been arguing that the negotiation of the relative powers invested in the family and the state, the economy of public and private, occurs in relation to the body of the mother because that body is the material source of the family and hence a potential symbolic site of family power. How, then, was this exclusion written into the ideological scripts that men take to be the basis of government? By what cultural sleight of hand were women excluded from the benefits of political liberalism in the English enlightenment? Let us bracket all arguments about male psychosexual development, about the exchange of women to mark social groupings and hierarchical status, the state's appropriation of women's reproductive capacity, and the devaluation of the psychological and emotional labour that women do in the traditional sphere of kin communities. Let us turn instead to the founding texts of the liberal democratic tradition—to Hobbes and Locke, Hume and Rousseau—to examine the logic by which they proceed.

John Locke's *Second Treatise on Government*, probably written as early as 1679, was later recast to justify the Glorious Revolution of 1688. Elsewhere I have discussed how this text established the philosophical ground for separating the public life of a citizen from the private areas of his domestic experience ("Mary Astell"). Locke's strategy is to refute the premises of Sir Robert Filmer, who defends monarchical privilege by identifying it with parental power. The *Second Treatise* explains how and why parental power is to be distinguished from magisterial power, how private and public constitute separate spheres of jurisdiction, and how different political imperatives govern decision-making in these two spheres. Of course, the stories of origins resorted to by seventeenth-century political theorists—whether the story of Hobbes' brutes, Filmer's *pater familias* or Locke's rational men living in a state of nature—all fail to take into account women's maternal agency. Thus Locke and Filmer both deny the social and political significance of women's reproductive labour, whether or not they separate the public from the private sphere in discussing the rights of the people *vis à vis* the prerogatives of the king.

It is also worth noting that the Glorious Revolution, for which Locke formulated and circulated his doctrine, reaffirmed male prerogative in its very events and weakened female claims to political power. From the scandalous warming-pan rumours that denied Mary of Modena's maternal (and hence political) agency in producing a Stuart heir (described by Rachel Weil), to the public wifely obedience of the new queen Mary to her husband, William of Orange (including her agreement not to claim the English throne in her own name by right of lineal descent), the Glorious Revolution was another of those democratic "advances" that redistributed power among men while simultaneously leeching away the political privileges of women.

The linchpin of Locke's political theory is his assertion that the primary function of the state—the reason men enter into political contracts with one another—is to protect the unequal distribution of property. In his account, states developed out of pre-existing groups of patriarchal families as the need to protect property arose. Mere paternity offers no justification for political power, he argues, in contradistinction to Filmer. "What Father," he asks, "when he begets a Child, thinks farther than the satisfying of his present Appetite? God in his infinite Wisdom has put strong desires of Copulation into the Constitution of Men, thereby to continue the race of Mankind, which he doth most commonly without the intention, and often against the Consent and Will of the Begetter" (qtd. in Schochet 247). Thus, for Locke, although human society may have begun in clusters of families, these groupings do not provide prudential reasons for constructing a state and entering into a political contract. Those come later, with the unequal distribution of property and the consequent need for its protection.

While he was writing about property and the state, Locke himself was an investor in the major capitalist institutions of his day: the Old and New East India Companies and the Royal Africa Company, which traded in slaves. His relation to the accumulation of property was not merely theoretical, nor was his desire for state protection of unequally distributed wealth, including the property Englishmen held in certain African persons. Although Locke asserted that the most fundamental form of equality among individuals was their equality in property—property in their own persons, in the labour of their bodies and the work of their hands—he never imagined women or Africans as claiming this right. However inalienable the human right of property-in-one's person was for the universal European male, women and Africans apparently never had the right of property in their persons. Locke never assumed that women had property in their bodies, owned their physical or emotional labour, or the work of their hands, for example; he did not even consider that they owned the children that they bore in their bodies and brought forth with their labour, although pregnancy and childbirth would seem to be a pure case of his general theory of how property is created, i.e. by mixing one's labour with the unowned raw materials of the world and producing something new that never existed before.[10] Even now, as Leith Mullings asserts, although female-headed households are increasingly an international phenomenon in both industrialized and developing nations (due to war, genocidal policies, labour migration, unemployment, etc.), such households are considered "pathological" (131).

How could this have happened, one wants to know, this denial of women's procreative power and parental rights? One explanation lies in the emerging segregation of women from the visible production of exchange value in the competitive world of capitalism; these economic developments began to redefine the home as the locus not of production but only of reproduction. The emotional labour of domestic life, needless to say, has never been counted. As with the emergence of the Tongan state, the separation of production from reproduction and the transformation of the conjugal unit to serve a national and even international economy rather than to provide subsistence, resulted in a devaluation of women's labour and women's role in emerging civil society. As C. B. Macpherson pointed out nearly fifty years ago, it was precisely this commercial, consumer, competitive economy, as it was experienced by men, which provided the model for seventeenth-century conceptions of political equality. That is, Hobbes' construct of self-moving, self-directing machines with common vulnerabilities and common appetites must be understood as an ideological abstraction from the existing commercial society of his day, already enormously affected by the conditions of market capitalism. Yet the marketplace hardly describes the reality of most women's lives, engaged by custom and necessity in the physical care of their families. Even when women's unpaid domestic labour is understood as supporting the economic unit of the family in competition with other like units, the meaning of women's activities—and the degree of their alienation—is radically different from that projected by Hobbes.[11] The paradigm of the new individual, in short, was extrapolated from men's lives and not from women's lives, normalizing human relations that lack empathy. It was never intended to describe a woman's relation to her society.

Some feminist theorists such as Gerda Lerner argue that women—because of their valuable reproductive capacity—have always been constructed as belonging to their kin groups, even before the formation of private property or class division.[12] That is, the social ownership of the means of reproduction, necessary to the survival of the species, is guaranteed by the appropriation of women's bodies by their male relatives for the good of the social unit. Even pre-state societies, while they do not idealize women's virginity or chastity and associate it with the honour and integrity of the group as do state societies, nonetheless perceive female sexual power as dangerous and potentially disruptive of the social order and in need of containment by male relatives (as Sherry Ortner discusses). Thus women can never be self-owning in Locke's sense, but are constructed as property themselves, precisely because they are the means of reproducing the family, the tribe, the society. Slave women in the American South and in the Caribbean represent an extreme case of women whose children did not belong to them; they resorted to contraception, abortion, and even infanticide to avoid bringing forth children into slavery. In Aphra Behn's proto-novel *Oroonoko: or, the Royal Slave* (1688), Oroonoko kills his beloved Imoinda because she is carrying their child and they are slaves; he cannot bear that his offspring will be owned by anyone else.[13]

Certainly the legal system of Locke's day constructed women as property. That is, fathers and husbands prosecuted cases of seduction or adultery with lawsuits for the loss of their daughters' or wives' services, as if those female bodies belonged to them and their property rights to those bodies were violated if another man appropriated their sexual services (Susan Staves and Anna Clark separately discuss this). It is not simply fortuitous that there are no women to speak of in Daniel Defoe's *Robinson Crusoe* (1719), that emblematic novel about the quintessentially economic man. The hero, fascinated by his goods and his labours for more goods, isolated from his fellow humans, is necessarily male. How could a woman be depicted as laying up property when she *was* property? Locke never questioned this cultural construction of women as property; and by putting property at the centre of his political theory, effectively disenfranchised women of power in the public sphere.

It seems unlikely that Enlightenment era women considered that they "owned" their bodies. Indeed, it is a modern development in the present day women's movement to raise consciousness on this point. Women in our own day have taken it as a political issue to reclaim their bodies. That is the meaning of the collective, militantly non-expert authorship of *Our Bodies, Ourselves,*[14] the widespread interest in women's weight-lifting and body-building, the insistence on varieties of sexual preference, the passion of the pro-choice campaign: these are signs from our own time of women trying to "own" their bodies.

Yet the term is still not quite right. Possibly because childbearing women share their bodies, first with fetuses and then with nursing infants, "ownership" is not quite the right metaphor. Women do not fit the model of capitalism; mother-child relations do not assimilate to a story about autonomy, competition, and profit. In the west, the bio-social experiences of menstruation, penetration, pregnancy, lactation have rarely been constructed as the means to personal power except in those few class-bound situations in which women have produced politically strategic male heirs. Certainly in the seventeenth and eighteenth centuries, pregnancy was too uncertain, too unpredictable, and too life-threatening to be experienced as a source of power.

If women's relation to their child-bearing bodies does not fit the myth of the autonomous individual creating property, the political theorists of the Enlightenment never confronted this discrepancy. They simply ignored the procreative body as well as women's work in tending the bodily needs of the weak and infirm. Nevertheless, cultural historians of the Enlightenment have observed that attitudes toward the body changed during this era of liberal political theorizing. In the treatment of prisoners, Foucault observes that authorities stopped torturing bodies and began instead to try to recondition the minds of their charges. According to Allon White and Peter Stallybrass, "the suppression and distancing of the physical body became the very sign of rationality, wit and judgment" (105). Norbert Elias in *The History of Manners* constructs a similar argument, that is, that progress and civilization came to be associated with the denial of the body. Political prerogatives that might have been based on claims of the maternal body were similarly suppressed in the founding myths of democracy. The stories told by Hobbes, Locke, Rousseau and other contract theorists about the "state of nature" produced a substitute for the primitive authority of the womb by creating a "body politic" without recourse to women. Carole Pateman makes this point elegantly in *The Sexual Contract*:

> The story of the original contract tells a modern story of masculine political birth. The story is an example of the appropriation by men of the awesome gift that nature has denied them and its transmutation into masculine political creativity. Men give birth to an "artificial" body, the body politic of civil society; they create Hobbes' "Artificial Man, we call a Commonwealth," or Rousseau's "artificial and collective body," or the "one Body" of Locke's "Body Politic." However, the creation of the civil body politic is an act of reason rather than an analogue to a bodily act of procreation. (102)

As Pateman points out in her analysis of Hobbes' *Leviathan*, there is a "connection between the original overthrow of mother-right and the establishment of Leviathan." The conquest of women is a necessary pre-condition for the establishment of the state. "The creation of civil society is an act of masculine political birth; men have no need of a 'helper' in *political* generation" ("'God Hath Ordained'" 68). Joan Landes, too, has argued that "women's (legal and constitutional) exclusion from the public sphere was a constitutive, not a marginal or accidental, feature of the bourgeois public from the start."

Rousseau's account of the birth of society is an exaggeratedly instrumental view of the mother in a state of nature. His *Discourse on the Origins of Inequality* (1755), for example, always assumes the person in the state of nature to be male: "his desires never go beyond his physical wants. The only goods he recognizes in the universe are food, a female, and sleep..." (55). All women answer his purpose equally well. Isolation is his natural state as he wanders through primeval forests.

When Rousseau imagines the origin of speech, he tells two different stories: each illustrates in a different way the absence of women's subjectivity in his projected vision. In his first story of origin, speech is invented anew by every new (male) child in order to tell his mother what he wants. The mother does not herself need to talk, but she learns her child's language so that she can fulfill *his* needs.

> [T]he child, having all his wants to explain, and of course more to say to his mother than the mother could have to him, must have borne the brunt of the task of invention, and the language he used would be of his own device, so that the number of languages would be equal to that of the individuals speaking them, and the variety would be increased by the vagabond and roving life they led, which would not give time for any idiom to become constant. (59)

It is an astonishingly anti-social picture of mankind. Language here arises in aid of instrumental need, not in a social context; as soon as the children can fend for themselves they leave. In time these children and their mother become unrecognizable to each other. No emotional bonds connect them; their relations are merely material. In his discussion of this scenario, Rousseau pointedly disagrees with Etienne Bonnot de Condillac's assumption that a prior society had to exist for language to arise. It was more probable, he asserted, that language "arose in the domestic intercourse between parents and their children," and that it was an individualized, transitory phenomenon.

Rousseau's second account of the origin of language is also remarkable for the extent of its social alienation. Women are entirely suppressed in this account—as are all other forms of society save the solitary company of other competing men. This story begins with a flood or an earthquake, or some other natural disaster, to explain how people might have come to live in proximity to one another in the first place.

> Floods or earthquakes surrounded inhabited districts with precipices or waters: revolutions of the globe tore off portions from the continent, and made them islands. It is readily seen that among men collected and compelled to live together, a common idiom must have arisen much more easily than among those who still wandered through the forests of the continent. (80)

Once "collected and compelled to live together" by geographical accident, people began to form families and live in neighborhoods.

Insensibly the habit grew up among them "to assemble before their huts round a large tree; singing and dancing, the true offspring of love and leisure became the amusement, or rather the occasion of men and women thus assembled together with nothing else to do." This, the invention of language for love and art, is a complementary image to the instrumental picture of a boy inventing language in order to tell his mother what to do for him. Compelled by natural disasters to speak to one another, people come to use their common tongue for expressive and celebratory purposes. But envy and competition are not long in appearing—those high passions that human society always engendered in Rousseau himself. "Each one began to consider the rest, and to wish to be considered in turn; and thus a value came to be attached to public esteem. Whoever sang or danced best, whoever was the handsomest, the strongest, the most dexterous, or the most eloquent, came to be of most consideration; and this was the first step towards inequality, and at the same time towards vice" (81). Rousseau imagines competition rather than simple admiration as the inevitable reaction to others' excellence, in this originary scene of an all-male society cavorting around a large tree.

One final example suffices to demonstrate the profoundly unexamined Enlightenment assumption that the formation of the nation state entailed the subordination of women and their reproductive capacity. In Book III, Part 2, of the *Treatise on Human Nature*, Hume theorizes the relationship between motherhood and the state, explaining how the general interest of society is grounded analogically on the necessity for women's chastity or at least the containment of female sexuality. Hume explains that people agree to keep a nation's laws, keep the peace, and accept its sovereignty, for the same reason that women agree to limit their sexual and reproductive services to one man: to ensure stability of the system. No man would agree to support a child, to "undergo chearfully [sic] all the fatigue and expenses" unless he is sure it is his; and the only guarantee of paternity is a woman's chastity. Men rely on women to stay chaste, to keep peace and order in families, just as the leaders of states rely on the their citizens to be law-abiding if they are to deal with one another on an international level. Thus, he argues, law is based in natural fact; the principle of chastity "is founded on the public interest."

The implication of Hume's odd juxtaposition of these passages about families and international relations is an assumption about property. If the stability of the nation-state depends on the chastity of its women, it is because legitimate paternity and therefore inheritance of property is the cornerstone of the state. "The general interest of society" that guarantees the obedience of (male) individuals to the laws of the nation so that there can be commerce among them apparently also necessitates the chastity of its women. Once again, the best interests of a commercial nation seem to entail the control of women's bodies and reproductive capacity.

Although they arrive at it by different routes, all these scenarios of state formation exclude woman from the newly formed polity on the basis of her reproductive capacity. When a citizen's rights are derived from a division between public and the private, from a distinction between the domestic and the civil order, women are relegated to the private sphere and lose their rights as citizens in the public realm. When rights are guaranteed by the ownership of property—when a citizen is defined as having a material stake in the functioning legal system—the maternal body is a problem because the property it generates (not to mention its manner of generating property) is seen as already owned in some sense by the state or by another citizen. And when rights derive from the social contract entered into freely by individuals living in a "state of nature," females are seen as either already organized by incest taboos, overthrown in their "mother right" by the superior force of males, or, as in Rousseau's narratives, as the merely instrumental means for producing more boy children to grow up in a state of nature.

So where does this leave us? How can we construct a model for political life that does not exclude women—not to mention racial or ethnic minorities—and that is grounded in the daily, lived experience of people who are different from one another? We must recognize varieties of bodily experience and not separate and hierarchize different forms of labour—emotional labour vs. productive labour or the labour of hands vs. the labour of minds—or privilege production for exchange value over production for use value and the production of material goods over the reproduction of children and social networks. We need a political practice based not on abstractions that deny particularity and difference, but one that grows out of the patterns of life as it is lived, based not on the human relations constructed by production for an impersonal market but on human relations conditioned by a combination of subsistence production and reproduction. We must find ways to recognize and reward the emotional labour that is essential to parenting and domestic life, as well as other manifestations of empathy in public life that ground the respect for difference.

The organization of communal work, the celebration of seasons, the ritual marking of stages in human life—these social functions need to be preserved and recognized by communities as essential rather than peripheral. We need a model of democracy that takes into account the needs of human hearts and bodies as well as rational minds, and of the female body as well as the male body. Reproductive labour needs to be recognized and rewarded as a service to society, not appropriated by men or by the state. Attention to the education of the young and care and preservation of the old would be features of a society organized around reproductive labour—which is to say the preservation and perpetuation of kin relations and the passing on of culture from one generation to another. As Rosalind Petchesky writes, "the task is to develop a concept of selves as they are constituted dialogically in relation to others and of rights—including rights to bodily integrity—as they emerge from and become the expressions of collective aspirations for change" (400). It is high time to re-think the legacy of the Enlightenment and those political models that evolved to facilitate market capitalism—as other forms of social organization are swallowed up by its instrumental economic success. Feminist intellectuals in particular should be wary of political models that separate productive from reproductive labour and that marginalize families, kin groups, and communities within an impersonal bureaucratic state. The legalistic corporate ethos that has come to dominate our workplaces and our schools, promoting property rights and short term profitability rather than human welfare, must give way to more sustainable systems of responsibility to one another and to the environment, identifying individual good with the good of the whole society, and prizing the mutual recognition and obligation that lie at the heart of the concept of empathy.

[1] Feminist thinkers as disparate as Gayle Rubin, Luce Irigaray, and Gerda Lerner have incorporated Levi-Strauss's analysis.

[2] In a summary statement Jessica Benjamin writes: "Gender polarity deprives women of their subjectivity and men of an other to recognize them. But the loss of recognition between men and women as equal subjects is only one consequence of gender domination. The ascendancy of male rationality results finally in the loss and distortion of recognition in society as a whole. It not only eliminates the maternal aspects of recognition (nurturance and empathy) from our collective values, actions, and institutions. It also restricts the exercise of assertion, making social authorship and agency a matter of performance, control, impersonality—and thus vitiates subjectivity itself" (218). Carol Gilligan draws a similar conclusion in her meditation upon individualism when

she notes that in western culture individual power is understood to be antithetic to love. "Psychological development is usually traced along a single line of progression from inequality to equality, following the incremental steps of the child's physical growth. Attachment is associated with inequality, and development linked to separation. Thus the story of love becomes assimilated to a story about authority and power" (247).

[3] An important collection of essays by political theorists demonstrating the danger for women of "the public/private dichotomy as a principle of social organization" can be found in Seyla Benhabib's and Drucilla Cornell's *Feminism as Critique: On the Politics of Gender.*

[4] One effect of the separation of public from private—still relevant to our society with its permitted forms of private violence such as wife-battering and incest—is that if political rights are defined within the public sphere while women are relegated to a private sphere, women will not be perceived as having political rights. For a discussion of these implications see MacKinnon. An interesting book by Connelly suggests that women in ancient Greece played significant roles in religious ritual, which gave them a place in the polis that has been hitherto unrecognized.

[5] For discussion of the political implications of the division between public and private, see Elshtain, and for an historical analysis of the separation of men's and women's spheres, see Cott; Davidoff and Hall give a more recent historical account in the English context. Vickery, among others, has debated this division and argued that women in the early modern period operated more in the public, commercial world than this "separate spheres" doctrine would suggest. See her "Golden Age to Separate Spheres?" and *The Gentleman's Daughter.* My skeptical appraisal of this position can be found in the *History Workshop Journal.*

[6] This famous Athenian case is also discussed by K. J. Dover (19-23; 24-31; 34; 36-41; 46-53).

[7] See Jean Franco's "Rape: A Weapon of War." This article speaks particularly of the civil wars in Peru and Guatemala, but rape was used as a weapon in the wars in the former Yugoslavia as well and in more recent African conflicts.

[8] For critics who develop this connection, see Froula, Fineman, and Silver and Higgins.

[9] See also Lynn Hunt's fascinating working out of this model in the context of the French Revolution.

[10] In his section on slavery in the *Second Treatise,* Locke justifies appropriating another's labour with the argument that if a captor has the right of life or death over his captive and delays in acting upon

that right—that is, delays in killing his captive—there is nothing wrong with the captor's making "use of him to his service" in the meantime (Chapter IV, 17-18).

[11]Evelyn Keller, dissecting the concept of individualism as biologists use it in theories of evolution, has pointed out the slippage between the notions of autonomy and competition—a legacy this biological construct owes to its originating economic model.

[12]The relation between property and reproduction in Lerner's formulation is illustrated in Margaret Atwood's modern parable *The Handmaid's Tale*. First the new right-wing government disinherits women *en masse*, dispossessing them of their property overnight by computer and assigning their bank accounts to their male next-of-kin, and then they appropriate the childbearing women as property themselves, as machines of reproduction for the state. If they are to produce citizens efficiently for the brave new world, women themselves, it seems, must be disenfranchised and dispossessed of their property.

[13]The Norton edition of *Oroonoko* contains several excellent essays about gender and slavery.

[14]*Our Bodies, Ourselves* began as a discussion group in Cambridge, MA; its earliest circulation was as stapled newsprint lists of non-sexist doctors and advice. In 1973 the first commercial edition was published; by now it has been translated into many languages and has gone through 12 editions, not to mention the books about teen sex and older women's sexual issues that it has seeded and sponsored. The policy I refer to here was a deliberate decision of the members of the collective never to appear individually on TV or radio but always to have at least two of them visible in any media event so as to emphasize the collective nature of the authorship of the book. This was done, in part, to demonstrate that these women were ordinary, non-expert women who pooled their research and experience to produce the book.

WORKS CITED

Aeschylus. *Aeschylus I: Oresteia*. Trans. Richmond A. Lattimore. Chicago: University of Chicago Press, 1991. Print.

Astell, Mary. "Preface." *Some Reflections Upon Marriage*. 3rd ed. John Nutt: London, 1706. *Inventing Maternity: Politics, Science, and Literature 1650-1865*. Ed. Susan C. Greenfield and Carol Barash. Lexington: University Press of Kentucky, 1999. 111-37. Print.

Atwood, Margaret. *The Handmaid's Tale*. Toronto: McClelland and Stewart, 1985. Print.

Behn, Aphra. *Oroonoko: An Authoritative Text, Historical Backgrounds, Criticism*. Ed. Joanna Lipking. New York: Norton, 1997. Print.

Benhabib, Seyla, and Drucilla Cornell, eds. *Feminism as Critique: On the Politics of Gender*. Minneapolis: University of Minnesota Press, 1987. Print.

Benjamin, Jessica. *The Bonds of Love*. New York: Pantheon, 1988. Print.

Boston Women's Health Book Collective. *Our Bodies, Ourselves: A Book By and For Women*. New York: Simon and Schuster, 1976. Print.

Chalus, Elaine. "'That Epidemical Madness': Women and Electoral Politics in the Late Eighteenth Century." *Gender in Eighteenth-Century England: Roles, Representation and Responsibilities*. Ed. Hannah Barker and Elaine Chalus. London: Longman, 1997. 151-78. Print.

Clark, Anna. *Women's Silence, Men's Violence: Sexual Assault in England, 1770-1845*. London: Pandora Press, 1987. Print.

Clark, Anna. "Women in Eighteenth-Century British Politics." *Women, Gender and Enlightenment*. Ed. Sarah Knott and Barbara Taylor. London: Palgrave, 2005. 570-86. Print.

Condillac, Etienne Bonnot de. *Essay on the Origin of Human Knowledge*. Trans. and ed. Hans Aarsleff. Cambridge Texts in the History of Philosophy. Cambridge: University of Cambridge Press, 2001. Print.

Connelly, Joan Breton. *Portrait of a Priestess: Women and Ritual in Ancient Greece*. Princeton, NJ: Princeton University Press, 2007. Print.

Cott, Nancy. *Bonds of Womanhood*. New Haven: Yale University Press, 1977. Print.

Darwin, Charles. *The Descent of Man*. 2 vols. London: John Murray, 1871. Print.

Davidoff, Leonore, and Catherine Hall. *Family Fortunes*. Chicago: Chicago University Press, 1987. Print.

Davin, Anna. "Imperialism and Motherhood." *History Workshop Journal* 5 (1978): 9-65. Print.

Dover, K. J. *Greek Homosexuality*. New York: Random House, 1980. Print.

Elias, Norbert. *The History of Manners*. 2nd ed. Trans. Johan Goudsblom. New York: Urizen Books, 1978. Print.

Elshtain, Jean Bethke. *Public Man, Private Woman*. Princeton: Princeton

University Press, 1981. Print.

Epstein, Julia. "The Pregnant Imagination, Women's Bodies, and Fetal Rights." *Inventing Maternity: Politics, Science, and Literature 1650-1865.* Ed. Susan C. Greenfield and Carol Barash. Lexington: University Press of Kentucky, 1999. 111-37. Print.

Fineman, Joel. "Shakespeare's *Will*: The Temporality of Rape." *Representations* 20 (Fall 1987): 25-77. Print.

Foucault, Michel. *Discipline and Punish: The Birth of the Prison.* New York: Pantheon, 1978. Print.

Franco, Jean. "Rape: A Weapon of War." *Social Text* 91.25.2 (Summer 2007): 23-37.

Freud, Sigmund. *Totem and Taboo: Some Points of Agreement Between the Mental Lives of Savages and Neurotics.* New York: Norton, 1950. Print.

Froula, Christine. "The Daughter's Seduction: Sexual Violence and Literary History." *Signs* 11.4 (1985-86): 621-44. Print.

Gailey, Christine Ward. *Kinship to Kingship.* Austin: University of Texas Press, 1987. Print.

Gilligan, Carol. "Remapping the Moral Domain." *Reconstructing Individualism: Autonomy, Individualism, and the Self in Western Thought.* Ed. Thomas C. Heller, Morton Sosna, and David E. Wellbery. Stanford: Stanford University Press, 1986. 237-52. Print.

Ginsburg, Faye, and Rayna Rapp, eds. *Conceiving the New World Order: The Global Politics of Reproduction.* Berkeley: University of California Press, 1992. Print.

Halperin, David M. "The Democratic Body: Prostitution and Citizenship in Classical Athens." *One Hundred Years of Homosexuality.* Ed. David Halperin. New York: Routledge, 1990. 88-113. Print.

Hume, David. "Of Chastity and Modesty." *A Treatise of Human Nature.* Ed. T. H. Green and T. H. Grose. 2 vols. 1886. London, Darmstadt: Scientia Verlag Aalen, 1964. Vol. 2.330-33. Print.

Hunt, Lynn. *The Family Romance of the French Revolution.* Berkeley: University of California Press, 1992. Print.

Irigaray, Luce. *This Sex Which is Not One.* Trans. Catherine Porter. Ithaca: Cornell University Press, 1985. Print. Trans. of *Ce sexe qui n'en est pas un.* Paris: Editions de Minuit, 1977.

Keller, Evelyn Fox. "Language and Ideology in Evolutionary Theory, Part I." *Secrets of Life, Secrets of Death: Essays in Language, Gender, and Science.* New York: Routledge, 1992. 115-126. Web. 23 Aug. 2010.

Landes, Joan. "Jurgen Habermas, the Structural Transformation of the

Public Sphere: A Feminist Inquiry." *Praxis International* 12.1 (April 1992): 106-27. Print.

Lerner, Gerda. *The Creation of Patriarchy.* New York: Oxford University Press, 1986. Print.

Levi-Strauss, Claude. *The Elementary Structures of Kinship.* Boston: Beacon Press, 1969. Print.

Locke, John. *The Second Treatise of Government.* Ed. and intro. Thomas B. Pearson. Indianapolis: Bobbs-Merrill, 1952. Print.

MacKinnon, Catharine A. *Feminism Unmodified: Discourses on Life and Law.* Cambridge: Harvard University Press, 1987. Print.

Macpherson, C. B. *The Political Theory of Possessive Individualism: Hobbes to Locke.* Oxford: Clarendon Press, 1962. Print.

Mullings, Leith. "Households Headed by Women: The Politics of Race, Class, and Gender." *Conceiving the New World Order: The Global Politics of Reproduction.* Eds. Faye Ginsburg and Rayna Rapp. Berkeley: University of California Press, 1992. 122-39. Print.

Nussbaum, Felicity. *Torrid Zones: Maternity, Sexuality, and Empire in Eighteenth-Century English Narratives.* Baltimore: Johns Hopkins University Press, 1995. Print.

Ortner, Sherry. "The Virgin and the State." *Feminist Studies* 4.3 (1978): 19-37. Print.

Pateman, Carole. *The Sexual Contract.* Stanford: Stanford University Press, 1988. Print.

Pateman, Carole. "'God Hath Ordained to Man a Helper': Hobbes, Patriarchy and Conjugal Right." *Feminist Interpretations and Political Theory.* Ed. Mary Lyndon Shanley and Carole Pateman. University Park, PA: University of Pennsylvania Press, 1991. 53-73. Print.

Perry, Ruth. "Mary Astell and the Feminist Critique of Possessive Individualism." *Eighteenth-Century Studies* 23.4 (Summer 1990): 444-57. Print.

Perry, Ruth. "Women and Daughters." *History Workshop Journal* 47 (Spring 1999): 292-96. Print.

Petchesky, Rosalind Pollack. "The Body as Property: A Feminist Re-vision." *Conceiving the New World Order: The Global Politics of Reproduction.* Eds. Faye Ginsburg and Rayna Rapp. Berkeley: University of California Press, 1992. 387-406. Print.

Rousseau, Jean-Jacques, and G. D. H. Cole. *The Social Contract and Discourses: Translation and Introd. by G. D. H. Cole.* London: Dent, 1973. Print.

Rubin, Gayle. "The Traffic in Women: Notes Toward a Political

Economy of Sex." *Toward an Anthropology of Women.* Ed. Rayna Reiter. New York: Monthly Review Press, 1975. 157-210. Print.

Schochet, Gordon. *Patriarchalism in Political Thought: The Authoritarian Family and Political Speculation and Attitudes.* New York: Basic Books, 1975. Print.

Sedgwick, Eve Kosofsky. *Between Men: English Literature and Male Homosocial Desire.* New York: Columbia University Press, 1985. Print.

Silver, Brenda, and Lynn Higgins. *Rape and Representation.* New York: Columbia University Press, 1991. Print.

Stallybrass, Peter, and Allon White. *The Politics and Poetics of Transgression.* Ithaca, NY: Cornell University Press, 1986. Print.

Staves, Susan. "Money for Honor: Damages for Criminal Conversation." *Studies in Eighteenth-Century Culture* 11 (1982): 279-97. Print.

Vickers, Nancy. "The Mistress in the Masterpiece." *The Poetics of Gender.* Ed. Nancy K. Miller. New York: Columbia University Press, 1986. 19-41. Print.

Vickery, Amanda. "Golden Age to Separate Spheres? A Review of the Categories and Chronology of English Women's History." *The Historical Journal* 36.2 (1993): 383-414. Print.

Vickery, Amanda. *The Gentleman's Daughter.* New Haven: Yale University Press, 1998. Print.

Weil, Rachel. "The Politics of Legitimacy: Women and the Warming-Pan Scandal." *The Revolution of 1688-89: Changing Perspectives.* Ed. Lois Schwoerer. Cambridge: Cambridge University Press, 1992. 65-82. Print.

Weiner, Annette. "Reassessing Reproduction in Social Theory." *Conceiving the New World Order: The Global Politics of Reproduction.* Eds. Faye Ginsburg and Rayna Rapp. Berkeley: University of California Press, 1992. 407-24. Print.

Zeitlin, Froma I. "The Dynamics of Misogyny in the *Oresteia.*" *Women in the Ancient World:The Arethusa Papers.* Ed. John Peradotto and J. P. Sullivan. Albany: State University of New York Press, 1984. 159-94. Print.

2. Sexism and the Gendering of the University

CHRISTINE OVERALL

Y OU MIGHT SAY THAT AN ACADEMIC is someone who first went to school at the age of four or five, and then never left. I am a (former) university student, a faculty member for more than thirty years, and a (former) university administrator for eight years. In this chapter I offer a framework for thinking about sexism and the gendering of universities. I do not cite a lot of empirical studies or statistics. Instead I mainly draw upon decades of observation of academia. Experience-based philosophy attempts to use empathic insight into both one's own institutional position and the positions of others, noticing our similarities, our connections, and our differences. At the same time, experience-based philosophy reveals the absence of empathy in oppressive relationships and institutions.

I will start by clarifying my key concepts, gender and sexism. Feminists have provided many different definitions of "gender." However, the term can be usefully defined in two general ways.[1] First, as an attribute of *individuals*, gender is *the identification or presentation of self* as being a woman or a man. In this sense, gender potentially includes femininities, masculinities, and all the variations on and resistances to them. I will call this "Gender(I)" (Gender [Individual]). The normative form of Gender(I) requires both heterosexual self-presentation and activity and stereotypical procreative and productive behaviour.

Second, as *a mode of social organization*, gender is a cultural institution, a way of organizing how human beings live (Lorber 1), and in particular, how they do or do not (or ought and ought not) to interact sexually and reproductively. It is racially coded (Markowitz 391) and inflected by class, religion, ethnicity, and age. Gender in this sense is "the social organization of social difference .... Gender is the knowledge that establishes meanings for bodily differences" (Nicholson 290). I will call this sense of gender, "Gender(S)" (Gender[Social]). Gender(S) conventions are prescriptions for policies, organizations, institutions, rituals, and values, prescriptions that, whatever their content might be, are founded upon a conceptualization of humanity as divided into two distinct groups, based upon their sex. Although there is some variation in which traits are taken, in different social environments, to constitute masculinity and femininity, these concepts almost always incorporate the domination and superiority of those beings labelled "masculine" over those labelled "feminine."

Sexism is unjustified discrimination and domination on the basis of a person's sex, mostly but not always directed at women. Sexism is made possible, in part, by the absence of empathy: the inability to recognize the reality and uniqueness of a particular person because of a commitment to defining and understanding her only in terms of her genitalia. Sexism is made possible by the existence and power of Gender(S) as a system, and reinforced through Gender(I). So, sexism is not just a matter of individual injustice; it is founded upon and sustained by a system, a system that pervades our culture. If we want to do away with sexism, we have to ask ourselves how to cope with the gender system on which it is based.

Virtually all past cultures took for granted that one's sex mattered, was always significant, and determined one's status, in almost every domain of human action. People's sex—whether they were female or male—was treated as if it truly determined who they were and what they could and could not, should and should not, be and do within their society. A commitment to the definition of others only in terms of their sex apparently precludes any need to try to understand others' individual needs, capacities, or perspectives.

It is only in the last forty-five years or so that more and more people—feminists, and also their allies, those who are committed to social progress and the end of invidious stereotyping and injustice—have said that in most human activities one's sex is not particularly relevant to what one can do. The fact that I am female should not be relevant to whether or not I can vote, hold political office, drive a car, go out in public unaccompanied, wear jeans rather than a skirt, or attend the religious organization of my choice. The fact that I am female should not be relevant to whether I can play hockey or lacrosse, decide whether and when to have children, study any subject of my choosing, or become an engineer, lawyer, doctor, or university professor.

My sex, the fact that I am female, *ought* not to be relevant to any of these things, although unfortunately in some societies it is. Being female can mean that one has little or no control over one's sexuality and procreative abilities, that one has few or no political or civil rights, that one has no religious freedom, and that one does not have open access to education or to paid work. Societies such as these are intensely gendered, and women are the victims of systemic sexism.

But it would be a mistake to suppose that by contrast, Canadian society is not gendered and that sexism has disappeared. Within the context of universities, it is not hard to think of examples of sexism that are familiar either indirectly or through first-hand experience. These examples reflect the ways in which sexism precludes empathy, making it impossible for the perpetrators to identify with their victims, imagine their perspectives, or even recognize any need to identify with those whom they perceive as totally other:

- the dangers on campus of sexual harassment and assault against women;
- heightened attention to women's sexuality;
- the use of sexist words and remarks;
- so-called "chilly climate" issues of disrespect, disparagement, and plain old inattention, both casual and calculated, for female faculty, staff and students (Jaggar 33);
- treating women as if they were either invisible, or as if they represent all women;
- discouraging women students from studying certain subjects; having different standards, whether higher or lower, for female students and faculty;
- devaluing women's work, whether in the classroom, in publication, or on the lecture circuit;
- the operation of what is often called the "old boys' network"; failure to tenure, promote, or even hire women faculty members; assuming that hiring and tenuring women in large numbers may be incompatible with excellence;
- inequities in salaries and benefits for female faculty and staff;
- the assumption that all women, whether students, staff, or faculty, are alike;
- the requirement that women faculty carry heavier teaching and/or committee responsibilities than men faculty;
- the expectation that women faculty and staff will nurture anyone in need, and will provide domestic services like bringing coffee and running errands;
- the absence or inadequacy of university policies for childcare and eldercare;

•petitions by some male students to be exempted from working with female students;

•the absence or under-representation of women, whether in certain scholarly disciplines or in administration; and

•the unequal availability of resources for women in areas such as athletics, graduate funding, research funding, and mentoring.[2]

Not all of these are present at any given institution. And some, perhaps many, institutions are in the process of improving; it is easier now to be a woman student, staff member, or faculty member than it was forty-five years ago. Still, as one of my women colleagues rather delicately expressed it, "Things are not quite perfect."

I will not discuss all of these lingering manifestations of sexism in this paper. Instead I shall concentrate on only one issue, and that is the fact that there are often strong disparities between what women students and men students focus upon. For example, a recent Canadian report indicates that while women constitute 61.1 percent of all bachelor and first professional degrees,[3] they are only 41.9 percent of all Ph.D. candidates (Robbins and Ollivier). Even more telling, if we compare the disciplines in which women and men enrol at the Ph.D. level, we find that women are 69.8 percent of those in education and 50.4 percent of those in the humanities, but only 27.6 percent of those in mathematics and computer science, and a paltry 19.3 percent of those in engineering and architecture. There are many other interesting disparities between women's and men's participation in university education. For example, in general there are more men in philosophy departments (especially at the graduate level), in physics courses, and on football teams; there are more women in schools of nursing, in fine arts, and on gymnastics teams.

Now the question is, How should we interpret these differences between what female students and male students study and engage in at university? Do they indicate the presence of sexism? Why or why not? And if they do indicate the presence of sexism, what, if anything, might be done about it? These questions force us to think about the *value* of gender, and in particular, the value of gender within education. Can we have a gendered society without having a sexist society? Can we have a gendered university without having a sexist university? Both feminists and non-feminists have, historically, proposed a variety of different perspectives on the value of gender. In what follows, I discuss several of them and apply them to the context of universities.

TRADITIONAL GENDER: A GENDER(S) SYSTEM THAT EMPHASIZES DIFFERENCES IN GENDER(I), AND VALUES MASCULINITY MORE THAN FEMININITY

Consider first a Gender(S) system that emphasizes and reinforces differences in Gender(I), and that values masculinity more than femininity. Such a system is, in fact, a key feature of many cultures in the past and present. The idea is that women and men both *are* and *should be* inherently different, and that the education system must maintain and support the differences between women and men. From this point of view, the gender differences between what male and female students study and participate in at this time, in twenty-first century Canada, would be considered entirely acceptable, and might in fact be criticized for not going far enough.

In education, emphasizing differences in Gender(I) and valuing masculinity more than femininity lead to the segregation of women's and men's education in order to support the establishment and maintenance of different curricula for girls and boys.[4] Men must be educated for leadership and paid labour in the public sphere. Women, on the other hand, must be educated for their role as caregivers for husband, children, and home. And so it was not so long ago that girls and women were not allowed to study medicine, engineering, or law, and were believed to have abilities mainly suited for attracting men, homemaking, and childrearing.[5] Boys and men, on the other hand, were assumed to be good at mathematics and science, and to be interested in both highly theoretical inquiry and also practical world-changing work like politics and engineering. Hence, nursing and so-called domestic science were women's fields, while engineering and philosophy were men's fields. Clearly this approach to the gendering of the university is sexist: It precludes the empathic identification of genuine differences or similarities among people by defining everyone in terms of their sex. There is no good reason for assuming that a man is better suited to be a doctor than a woman. Making educational opportunities available on the basis of sex closes off many educational opportunities for women and also potentially for men; it squanders the unique and individual abilities of members of both sexes. In the not-so-distant past, a woman who wanted to study medicine was thought to be endangering her femininity and even putting her childbearing capacities at risk. At the same time, a man who was interested in stereotypical women's fields was considered to be not a "real" man,[6] and therefore deeply deviant. In both cases, individuals who sought education outside the dominant

Gender(I) norms were regarded as compromising their very identity as a woman or as a man. So, emphasizing Gender(I) differences and valuing masculinity over femininity forecloses on empathy and reinforces sexism in education by its insistence that sex differences must determine the educational opportunities for women and for men.

DIFFERENT BUT EQUAL: A GENDER(S) SYSTEM THAT REVALUES FEMININITY, THAT IS, THE "FEMININE" FORM OF GENDER(I)

In response to the traditional heavy emphasis on the importance and value of males, some feminists have offered a different approach: a Gender(S) system that values women and femininity, the "feminine" form of Gender(I). This kind of gender system says that men and women are indeed different, and sex differences truly are significant and relevant to the running of society. But women and men are nonetheless morally equal, and the transformation of gender and the ending of sexism must take place through a greater appreciation of those traits and behaviours associated with femininity (e.g., Heilbrun xvi; Sommers 815). This Gender(S) system emphasizes differences in Gender(I), but also evinces a kind of empathy by positively valuing femininity at least as much as masculinity is valued. From this point of view, the gender differences in areas of study and activity between female and male students would not necessarily be a problem; they might just be the result of women and men making different choices, both of which should be valued.[7]

An education system that retains Gender(I) dualism but values women and femininity in this way is likely to validate what some feminists have called "women's ways of knowing," as well as girls' and women's strengths in text-based endeavours like English and History, their so-called "intuition," their interest in and understanding of human relationships, and their tendency to focus on the human implications of most disciplines.[8] As a result, some universities and colleges have taken steps to make traditionally male fields like engineering, mathematics, computing, technology, and science, as well as theoretical disciplines such as philosophy, more feminine-friendly.[9] Often there is an emphasis on the applications of these fields, especially applications within what are taken to be women's experience and interests. In addition, some argue that girls and young women do better, scholastically, when they study and learn together without the influence of boys and young men, so some schools set up special science, mathematics, or computer courses that cater to female interests and abilities.[10]

This approach to ending sexism in education represents significant progress beyond the first that I discussed, for it no longer seems to curtail opportunities for females just because they are female. Instead, it attempts to adapt to what are taken to be the unique and valuable characteristics of females. But a Gender(S) system that emphasizes Gender(I) differences and highly values femininity in this way has some pitfalls, and does not necessarily avoid sexism in education. It fails to permit genuinely empathic recognition of individual characteristics. The commitment to Gender(I) differentiation, however positive the perception of genders, still imposes restraints on individual persons based on the biological characteristics with which they are born. It makes the mistake of assuming that all girls and women tend to be similar. But what happens, for example, if a girl wants to be just like the boys? She wants to play football or hockey, not become a synchronized swimmer or a gymnast. What if a young woman wants an education that will train her to compete in the so-called men's world as an aggressive politician or businessperson? She does not want an education that reinforces feminine traits, however much they may be valued; she wants to become as tough and forceful as men are purported to be. For that matter, what if a boy actually prefers to learn in the same way girls supposedly do, and is interested in intuitive, relationship-oriented approaches to intellectual disciplines? Should these people be confined, because of their sex, to forms of education that are thought appropriate for their Gender(I)? A Gender(S) system that values femininity and masculinity, and that educates girls and boys differently as a result, is stultifying for people of either sex who do not conform to Gender(I) norms. Such a system is unlikely to avoid sexism.

ANDROGYNY: A GENDER(S) SYSTEM THAT ADVOCATES COMBINING GENDER(I) DIFFERENCES

So far, the Gender(S) systems I have discussed—both the one that regards men as superior, and the newer one, which hopes to revalue femininity equally with masculinity—require the existence of two distinct Genders(I). In any "different but equal" Gender(S) system, there are problems of reconciling the differential treatment of members of each sex with the moral goal of equal worth and equal treatment. As a result, some feminists, echoing a centuries-old tradition, have argued that the Genders(I), masculinity and femininity, should not be regarded as distinct and separate. Instead, each human being should be encouraged and educated to combine Gender(I) characteristics. As human beings, women and men have much more in common than we have differences, and, moreover, there is a tremendous amount of variation *among* women and *among* men. Women can be masculine; men can be feminine. Both feminine characteristics and masculine characteristics are valuable. So, why should we think of masculine and feminine attitudes and behaviour in stereotyped ways, as if each can only be aligned with the members of one sex? Why not, instead, seek to combine the best of femininity and the best of masculinity within one person? An individual of either sex could be both assertive and nurturing, both strong and gentle. The idea is that people should become "androgynous," a word that signifies the combination of masculine and feminine characteristics. This approach appears to permit a more empathic understanding of individuals, because it encourages a greater mix of characteristics within each one of us.

In some areas of education, the ideal of androgyny is already being applied. These days, for example, most children in kindergarten are encouraged to play with both dolls *and* trucks. In primary school they are able to take both home economics *and* shop (provided these subjects have not been abolished altogether, in the interests of cost cutting!). High school teachers aim to help their students become good at English *and* at mathematics.

When androgyny is the ideal, the aim is no longer to make men masculine and women feminine. The ideal of androgyny, that human beings of both sexes should exemplify the best of femininity and the best of masculinity, raises the expectation that there should, eventually, be approximately equal numbers of women and men in all the different university disciplines and at all the different levels and ranks. From this point of view, it would be a source of worry that there are so few women in science and engineering, and so few men in teacher's colleges. If the promotion of androgyny were successful, then in future, its supporters predict, as many young women as young men would study engineering, mathematics, and computing. As many young men as young women would train as nurses and primary school teachers. Instead of graduate schools containing a large majority of male students, the split would be more like 50:50. There would be equal numbers of men and women among the support staff. And instead of only a minority of full professors and administrators being women, half of all full professors and administrators would be women.

Yet, depending on how it is interpreted, androgyny, too, may present certain problems, both theoretical and practical. First, as an ideal, the concept of androgyny literally retains, in its etymology, a significant dualism, the dualism between femininity and masculinity. It is this dualism that endows individuals' sex with great significance, and hence makes sexism possible.

More importantly, on a practical level, some feminists have argued that androgyny requires too much: Although it may not be sexist, such an approach overrides genuine empathy by demanding that every individual be a kind of renaissance person, combining all the positive traits, attitudes, and capacities formerly parcelled out separately to women and to men. While androgyny appears to allow for individual differences, it might tend to ignore many of them. For although some people find the androgynous ideal comfortable and readily attainable, the fact is that some girls and women just do seem to have so-called feminine interests and abilities, and some boys and men just do seem to have so-called masculine interests and abilities. Perhaps even more significantly, some girls and women seem to have so-called masculine interests and abilities, while some boys and men seem to have so-called feminine interests and abilities. Should we really expect each of these people to focus on developing abilities and expertise for which they may not have much capacity? Such a system does not seem to sufficiently recognize individual differences.

ON BEYOND GENDER: THE DEMISE OF COMPULSORY GENDER(I) AND THE DISMANTLING OF GENDER(S) AS A SYSTEM

All three approaches that I have discussed so far retain as a key concept the very idea of gender, with its dualism of masculinity and femininity and its historically situated tie to biological sex characteristics. Gender's meaning is entirely tied up with femininity and masculinity, female and male. Given that sexism is "unjustified discrimination and domination on the basis of the person's sex, mostly but not always directed at women, a phenomenon made possible by the existence and power of Gender(S) as a system, and reinforced through Gender(I)," then preserving the concept of gender—of masculinity and femininity, manliness and womanliness—runs the risk of preserving, at least implicitly, the invidious conventional values associated with these concepts. Would human society, including our systems of education, be better off without them? Certainly the concept of androgyny points us forward, toward valorizing human abilities and virtues *independent* of their associations with masculinity and femininity. Perhaps, then, the compulsory nature of gender must be challenged, and the idea of gender may have to be rejected.

This argument takes us to a further proposal, which I like to call the project of going "on beyond gender." In the children's book *On Beyond Zebra*, by Dr. Seuss, the narrator proposes that we move beyond the last letter of the alphabet, beyond "zee" and "zebra" into hitherto unexplored conceptual realms. Seuss writes:

In the places I go there are things that I see
That I *never* could spell if I stopped with the z.
I'm telling you this 'cause you're one of my friends.
My alphabet starts where *your* alphabet ends!"
(n.pag., emphasis in original)·

Going on beyond gender is like that: I am talking about the demise of genders as significant categories. Gender(I) distinctions would no longer be compulsory; Gender(S) would be dismantled and deinstitutionalized. But going "on beyond gender" is not a plea for unisex or being neuter. It does not mean the end of sexuality. It does not mean compulsory sameness, but instead the opportunity for and empathic celebration of lots of differences. What we have in common is our humanity. We also have in common the fact that each of us is unique. If we give up a system based on two concepts, it does not follow that we must have a system based only on one. Instead, potentially, we could have a system that is open to limitless variations.

A gender-free culture is easier to describe in terms of what would likely disappear than in terms of what might develop: No more condemnations for walking, running, sitting, talking, or throwing like a girl. No more "M" and "F" boxes on applications for school or university, passports, or licenses to drive or to marry. No more obligatory categorizations by gender of human jobs, knowledge, skills, art forms, leisure and recreation activities, sports, clothes and other adornments, child care, law, ritual, patterns of consumption, housing, food and eating, artefacts, religious/spiritual practices, political activities, friendships, social life, family constitution and practice, struggle and conflict, emotions, or sexualities.

What would going beyond gender mean within education? If we truly moved beyond gender, there would not be schools for girls and schools for boys, subjects for women and subjects for men. Such distinctions would make no more sense than having one set of schools and subjects for people with O-positive blood, and separate schools and subjects for people with A-positive blood. In a culture that no longer engages in compulsory designations of females and males, we would no longer need to be concerned about the numbers of men and numbers of women in the student population or among the faculty. It would not be meaningful to do so. We would no longer need special efforts to recruit women into engineering, whether as students or as faculty; nor would we need campaigns to get men into primary school teaching or nursing. There would simply be a variety of different people in these various fields. The end of the gendering of the university would necessarily mean the end of sexism in post-secondary education.

However, although there are many merits to the idea of going on beyond gender, it also generates some problems. For it is difficult to figure out how to get there from here. Individual empathy is not enough. We certainly could not go directly from our current deeply gendered social system to a system without the concepts of gender. One obstacle arises from what Martha Minow has called the "dilemma of difference": on the one hand, if you emphasize difference you reinforce it, and run the risk of exacerbating the disadvantages that may be associated with that difference. That is the kind of problem in systems that preserve and enhance gender: when gender differences are emphasized, then the framework is in place for sexism. On the other hand, if you attempt to ignore or go beyond difference, you run the risk of ignoring or overlooking something that genuinely matters and makes a difference in people's lives. So if we try to go on beyond gender, to make gender concepts disappear prematurely, we would simply be ignoring social categories that are still deeply significant in society. We cannot ignore the ways in which existing people have been shaped, sometimes benefited, and often harmed by Gender(S) and its individual Genders(I). We cannot make sexism go away by ignoring the system that creates sexism. We cannot pretend that gender does not exist. The idea that "there's no one here but us people" is like pretending that race does not exist.

Ironically, then, even if we take "on beyond gender" as a long-term goal, in the short term we must still pay attention to gender, both as a social system and as individual ways of being. In the culture in which we *now* live, gender is always relevant, because culture makes it relevant. In this world, at this time, no one can be free of Gender(S) (although Gender(S) takes different forms in different world cultures). Gender(I) as self-presentation is potentially subject to individual change, but Gender(S) as social institution cannot be changed by any one individual.

So, it seems, we come full circle, back to an emphasis on gender in both of its main forms. Here, however, the goal is not to reinforce sexism but rather to dismantle it, by working toward making gender categories obsolete or irrelevant in most and perhaps all circumstances. The key success of feminism is that it has taught us to *pay attention* to gender and sexism, with the ultimate goal of *ending oppression* based on gender.

But how can we pay attention to gender without reinforcing sexism? Doing so requires the exercise of empathy at the institutional or policy level. This institutional empathy recognizes individual needs, capacities, and perspectives while also acknowledging the social context that continues to prevent the full expression of individuality. Within universities, we need educational policies that do not pretend that sexism is over, but rather seek to educate people about the gendering of the university and the rest of society, and encourage people to think critically and creatively about it. We need male and female role models and mentors within higher education. We need equity policies that promote and support diversity—in family formation, culture, race, age, ability, and sexuality, as well as gender. We need practices that support respect and prevent harassment, bullying, and disrespect. We need a critical mass of women, from the widest possible variety of class, ethnic, racial, and cultural backgrounds, at all levels of education and in all fields (and a critical mass of men in those fields where they are a minority). We need transparent and fair processes of appointing, renewing, tenuring, and promoting faculty members. We need open and fair expectations about the subjects to be taught, who can teach, and the effort and accomplishment expected and rewarded. We need policies that support maternity leaves, parental leaves, childcare and eldercare, that provide benefits for same-sex relationships, that make the campus fully accessible for people with disabilities, that provide for continuing education for staff, that make the campus financially accessible to people from poor and working class backgrounds, and that do not discriminate against staff, faculty, or students on grounds of their sexual orientation.

We also still need women's studies and gender studies. And we still need feminism. While feminism, women's studies, and the study of sex and gender can to some degree be integrated into the various disciplines, the existence of sexism means that they are still also necessary as separate areas of study. We should be engaged in research and teaching about gender, in order to better understand sexism and the injustices resulting from compulsory gender systems.

In student admissions and staff and faculty hiring, in what is taught and how it is taught, in curricular and extra-curricular activities, in sports and athletics, in the distribution of educational resources, in our private and public interactions, and in our efforts to make the campus safe for all, we still have to be aware of the difference that the institution of Gender(S) makes, and the sexism it allows and reinforces. And so we are left with what may seem to be a paradoxical proposal to end sexism in education: We must *focus* on understanding and evaluating gender in education, in order to move *beyond* the gendering of the university and the sexism that it entails.

For comments on earlier versions of this paper, I am grateful to the audiences at the Philosophy, Politics and Educational Policy Spring Speaker Series at the University of Tennessee, Knoxville, Tennessee, March 14, 2003; the Stapleford Lecture at the University of Regina, Regina, Saskatchewan, March 11, 2004; the Women's Studies Speakers' Series at Memorial University, St. John's, Newfoundland, January 19, 2007; and an anonymous reviewer.

[1]The following definitions of gender, and the perspectives upon gender described later, draw upon my paper, "'Return to Gender, Address Unknown?' Reflections on the Past, Present, and Future of the Concept of Gender in Feminist Theory and Practice" (Overall).

[2]Paula Caplan provides even more examples.

[3]The growing disparity between women and men at the undergraduate level might be thought to represent a problem for men. However, it is not the case that men's participation in undergraduate education is declining; it is simply not growing as fast as women's. Also, in times of relative prosperity, men often go straight into the work force from high school, where they can make more money than women who work full-time after high school. Hence, women have, in effect, more to gain than men from a university degree. Nonetheless, I would not deny that there could be problems in the declining percentage of men as undergraduates. Might it be because university education is declining in prestige, so men are less attracted to it? What I do not accept is the idea that men are so different from women that they must have a different form of teaching in order to prepare them for university. Instead, there should be a wide repertoire of teaching modes, to reach and benefit all students.

[4]This was the education envisioned by Jean-Jacques Rousseau, in his treatise, *Émile* (1762).

[5]Here is an example of this kind of stereotyping. At Wheeling Jesuit

University, women students in two single-sex dormitories had to clean their own bathrooms and buy toilet paper, but the bathrooms in all-male dorms were cleaned by housekeepers, who also stocked the toilet paper. Why? According to Corey A. King, Vice President for Student Affairs, "The impression I got was, the guys were much messier, so they needed the additional help" (Rooney A10).

⁶In general, whenever women are found in large numbers in a particular area of study or work—whatever it may be—it tends to have low prestige, and men avoid it. An obvious example is primary school teaching, which (in contrast with about a hundred and thirty years ago) is dominated by women, offers relatively low wages, and (therefore) is not attractive to men. I also wonder whether the decline in the prestige of the humanities in the last couple of decades might be related to the fact that women are found in greater and greater numbers in literature, languages, and history.

⁷This attitude toward gender is evident through much of contemporary education in the West. Consider, for example, the provision of separate sports for females and males. The idea is that girls and women have different athletic capacities from those of boys and men. But instead of preventing girls and women from playing sports (which was the attitude in Victorian times), most educational institutions now provide physical activities designed to respond to what are taken to be the interests and abilities of females. For example, most young women do not play football, but they do well at synchronized swimming and gymnastics, so universities provide football teams for men and synchronized swimming and gymnastics teams for women. The assumption is that the members of each sex have separate strengths and talents, so each will be catered to.

⁸Other famous examples come from Carol Gilligan's work, which urges us to value the moral thinking most characteristic of women (although it is also found in some men), and from the ethics of care interpreted as a "feminine approach to ethics" (Noddings).

⁹Interestingly, some experts complain that primary schools are now so feminine-friendly that they are not appropriate for boys' needs and interests.

¹⁰One recent Canadian report on this approach says, "Girls are a lot more timid in the presence of boys. They're extremely worried about the boys' opinion. Once they're separated, the girls are more willing to explore ideas. They're a serious part of the discussion, unlike before. And the boys don't need to posture in the classroom any more. As a result, they're more attentive" (Peritz F8).

WORKS CITED

Butler, Judith. *Gender Trouble: Feminism and the Subversion of Identity*. New York: Routledge, 1990. Print.

Caplan, Paula. *Lifting a Ton of Feathers: A Woman's Guide to Surviving in the Academic World*. Toronto: University of Toronto Press, 1993. Print.

Gilligan, Carol. 1982. *In a Different Voice: Psychological Theory and Women's Development*. Cambridge, MA: Harvard University Press, 1982. Print.

Heilbrun, Carolyn G. *Toward a Recognition of Androgyny*. New York: Harper and Rowe, 1973. Print.

Jaggar, Alison M. "Gender, Race, and Difference: Individual Consideration Versus Group-Based Affirmative Action in Admission to Higher Education." *Southern Journal of Philosophy* 35 (1996): 21-51. Print.

Lorber, Judith. *Paradoxes of Gender*. New Haven: Yale University Press, 1994. Print.

Markowitz, Sally. "Pelvic Politics: Sexual Dimorphism and Racial Difference." *Signs* 26.2 (2001): 389-414. Print.

Nicholson, Linda. "Gender." *A Companion to Feminist Philosophy*. Ed. Alison M. Jaggar and Iris Marion Young. Oxford: Blackwell, 1998. 289-97. Print.

Noddings, Nel. *Caring: A Feminine Approach to Ethics and Moral Education*. Berkeley, CA: University of California Press, 1984. Print.

Overall, Christine. "'Return to Gender, Address Unknown?' Reflections on the Past, Present, and Future of the Concept of Gender in Feminist Theory and Practice." *Marginal Groups and Mainstream American Culture*. Ed. Yolanda Estes, Arnold Lorenzo Farr, Patricia Smith, and Clelia Smyth. Lawrence, KS: University of Kansas Press, 2000. 24-50. Print.

Peritz, Ingrid. "Where the Boys Are." *Globe and Mail* 1 Feb. 2006: F8. Print.

Robbins, Wendy, and Michèle Ollivier. "Feminist and Equity Audits: Selected Indicators for Canadian Universities" 2006. Web. Aug. 11, 2012.

Rooney, Megan. "Cleaning Up Their Act." *Chronicle of Higher Education* 6 Dec. 2002: A8+. Print.

Rousseau, Jean-Jacques. *Émile* [1762]. Trans. Barbara Foxley. London: J. M. Dent and Sons, 1974. Print.

Seuss, Dr. *On Beyond Zebra*. New York: Random House, 1955. Print.

Sommers, Christina. "Philosophers Against the Family." *Vice and Virtue in Everyday Life: Introductory Readings in Ethics*. 2nd ed. Ed. Christina Sommers and Fred Sommers. Fort Worth, TX: Harcourt Brace Jovanovich, 1989. 728-754. Print.

Williams, Joan. 1991. "Deconstructing Gender." *Feminist Legal Theory: Readings in Law and Gender*. Ed. Katharine T. Bartlett and Rosanne Kennedy. Boulder, CO: Westview Press, 1991. 95-123. Print.

3. Taking Back the Budget

Feminist Institutional, Gender-Based and Gender Budget Analysis

KATHLEEN LAHEY

IN THE LONG VIEW OF HISTORY, women have made stunning gains: no longer chattel, "civilly dead," banned from the public sphere, and embedded in male-controlled (re)productive institutions, women in Canada have gradually gained the right to own property, vote, hold public office, and pursue economic self-dependence. Even compared with women in the 1960s, women in twenty-first century Canada have made significant gains on key issues. [1]

In the shorter view, however, the strong gains made in the 1970s and 1980s have been replaced by virtually no progress toward economic or social equality, and this trend has become even more pronounced since 2006. According to Statistics Canada, by 2008, women's shares of market incomes remained almost exactly where they were in the late 1990s, and women still did 64 percent of unpaid work and 75 percent of part-time work, held less than a third of high elected offices, and faced growing gender income gaps when compared with men with the same education and training (Statistics Canada, *Women in Canada* 1985-2010).

These are significant changes. Formerly ranked first on the United Nations indices of human development (HDI) and gender-related development (GDI) (*Human Development 1995-1999*),[2] Canada's rankings fell rapidly during the 2000s to twentieth in 2012 (*Human Development 2011*). Various factors have been linked to these trends, including recessions, shifts in political discourse, a growing focus on economic efficiency and growth, and cultural expectations that women's primary roles should continue to be shaped around caregiving and secondary income earning (see Day and Brodsky; Donnelly; Scott; Freiler and Cerny; Zweibel). At the same time, courts have failed to hold governments accountable for implementing effective gender equality programs under the *Canadian Charter of Rights and Freedoms*, and since 2006, the federal government has repealed numerous equality laws and cancelled virtually all women's and Aboriginal programs (Lahey, *Gendered Budget* 20-23, 52-60).

To say that these developments reflect little empathy or concern for women or vulnerable groups in twenty-first century Canada is an understatement. The Canada that led the national and global movement to increased sex equality no longer exists, and within policy landscapes dominated by demands for "austerity" and "deficit reduction," the political and social space for articulating visions of equality is shrinking rapidly. To counter these trends, I advocate that women "take back the budget" in order to reinstate human priorities and human well-being as social and government priorities, and break with the exclusive concentration on economic development and growth.

The strategy of "taking back the budget" may sound odd, since most people tend to think of governmental "budgeting" as a dry, ultra-abstract accounting exercise that magically generates good government plans. Like many terms now in common usage, however, the word "budget" originally had a much richer meaning. In English usages, "to open one's budget" meant "to speak one's mind," and the antonyms "budget" and "mum[*mom*]budget" meant "to speak" and "to silence" (Quinion). Now "budget" is predominantly used to refer to the most exclusive realms of speech open only to the very top power holders in disembodied and seemingly genderless governments, business entities, and institutions. Vernacular references to the "budgets" of individuals and households persist, but with the connotation that ordinary people "budget" only when facing financial constraints. At the same time, "people" themselves are usually referred to in abstract terms in the lofty proclamations of government budgets.

Like women's "take back the night" movements, "taking back the budget" reclaims fiscal space and demands recognition that women have equal and undeniable interests in all aspects of governance, revenue production, and spending. This is not an abstract idea, but a demand that the full range of material, gendered realities shaping life on all levels be taken into consideration in policy analysis, and that the gender power relations that currently erase women from public finance discourses be exposed, dismantled, and rebuilt around standards of substantive sex equality.

This chapter outlines the legal and policy bases of gender-based policy analysis, and demonstrates how gender budget analysis can be used to take back the budget, ensuring that budgets speak for women's expectations of governments as well as for men's, and speak to, and of, women as equally deserving of government consideration. Providing examples of how both spending and tax items buried in national budgets can be examined for gender assumptions and effects, this chapter illustrates how analysts can use gender budgeting to uncover gendered misallocations of fiscal space, financial support, government recognition, and tax burdens, as well as a diagnostic tool to pinpoint transformative policies.

Canada's 2009 and 2010 budgets have been selected as the focus of this analysis because when the international financial crisis hit Canada in late 2008, the federal government used this "emergency" to reframe and deepen its business-first, neoliberal economic agenda in the guise of enacting new anti-recession policies. Making unprecedented changes in almost every category of budgetary action, the government broke with past Canadian budget practices and adopted approaches that have since then worked powerfully to reinforce male economic privilege and wealth. The very invisibility of the gender bias in these changes has added to their power, gender analysis being deflected by political appeals to "economic growth" in order to justify massive spending measures that favour men while at the same time emphasizing the need for "austerity" and "deficit reduction" to justify cutting programs of crucial importance to women. Looked at closely, these "crisis" measures also take a profoundly unempathic stance on economic issues, one that exemplifies the supposed gender "neutrality" of conventional economics (see Ferber and Nelson 17).

GENDER BUDGETING: THE BROAD THIRD PATH TO EQUALITY

Government obligations to carry out gender-based analysis of all matters within their scope of activities are grounded in the Convention on the Elimination of All Forms of Discrimination Against Women (CEDAW), which Canada ratified in 1981, and in the 1995 Platform for Action (PFA) adopted at the United Nation's Fourth World Convention on Women in Beijing. CEDAW requires states to use all their powers to routinize the production of equality in day-to-day governance. Both the general anti-discrimination clauses[3] and the specific clauses of CEDAW require substantive attention to the large and small details of women's lives, making empathic consciousness a prerequisite component of the production of new government policies.

The Platform provides detailed substantive directives on how governments are to empower women to speak on their own behalf and on behalf of their societies, and the many active steps they are to take to eliminate sex discrimination. Among the many specific actions are governance requirements designed to ensure that the raw materials of effective policy—sex-disaggregated statistics, gender experts, and effective monitoring and audit procedures—are also in place in every country. Thus the Platform requires all governments to ensure that data are collected at the individual as well as household levels, and include data on unpaid as well as paid work. Methods of analysis are to be wide and creative in nature, including sex-specific beneficiary assessment, public expenditure incidence analysis, consideration of the impact of gender relations on productivity and social needs, and tax incidence analysis when examining specific program elements of the budget (Beijing Platform, e.g., paras. 67-8, 104, 109, 206, 346).

As soon as the Beijing Platform for Action was adopted, Canada's *Federal Plan for Gender Equality (Setting the Stage for the 21st Century)* implemented Canada's commitments to carry out all these steps. This report confirmed that gender analysis would be mainstreamed in all federal policy areas—including tax, spending, and other fiscal policies (20, 65, 66, 69, 78, 86)—and that policy analysts in 23 other federal departments would be trained in the detailed techniques of gender-based analysis to carry out this work during the policy formation process. (See Status of Women Canada for detailed training materials and Auditor General of Canada 8-19, 24, 29, for examples of analytic techniques.)

As constituted in widely-accepted international treaties and in detailed international and domestic policy documents, gender budget analysis makes it possible to assess whether governments are willing to perceive women as economic actors, grant women's basic material and development needs the same importance as men's, and provide realistic budgetary support to implementing sex equality. The examples of gender budget analysis presented in the remainder of this paper begin with an overview of the entire budget, and then demonstrate how the gender impact of structural tax cuts, large spending programs (infrastructure spending) and special tax expenditures (home renovation tax credits) can be examined individually. These examples demonstrate why all aspects of government budgets must be considered, as Regina Frey suggests, in order to reveal how they affect the allocation of resources, opportunities, and well-being between women and men on a structural level as well as at the micro-level.

ASSESSING THE GENDER IMPACT OF BUDGETS AS A WHOLE

Table 1 summarizes the largest total budgetary changes made by the federal government for the 2010-11 fiscal year. Each of these budget changes is highly unusual. After years of relatively stable tax rates, the tax rates used in all three of Canada's major tax systems were cut dramatically. The large amounts spent on infrastructure funding (repairs to roads, buildings, trains) and on extra funds for the Employment Insurance (EI) system were also unusual, and were designed to help stabilize the economy overall during the recession. The infrastructure spending was aimed at creating jobs and work in the construction business, and the EI enhancements were to give unemployed workers more time on EI benefits while looking for new employment.

Even though each of these huge tax cut and spending items was said to be intended to help Canadians get through the recession, they produce structural fiscal changes that will inevitably affect women and

Table 1
Largest Budgetary Allocations and Universal Child Care Benefit (UCCB) Tax Cut by Sex, Canada, 2010-11

Item	Amount	Women's shares
GST tax cuts	$10.8 billion	38%
Corporate tax cuts	$10.5 billion	10% to 37%
Infrastructure spending	$9.6 billion	9% to 22%
Personal income tax cuts	$7.4 billion	40%
Employment insurance enhancements	$4.8 billion	36%
Single-parent UCCB tax cut	$0.005 billion	81% (max. $168 per child)
Total	$43.105 billion	

Source: Lahey, Kathleen A. "Women, Substantive Equality, and Fiscal Policy." Canadian Journal of Women and the Law 22. 1 (2010): 70, Table 4.

men differently. This is confirmed by Table 1, which shows that with the exception of the UCCB tax cut, well over 50 percent of each item in Table 1 went to men. Thus, on a purely financial level, men received larger shares of all these spending items than would be justified by allocating equal 50 percent shares to women and men.

In governmental budgeting, some budgetary items do give larger shares to women than to men. For example, low-income child benefits go mainly to single mothers, and thus men receive only small shares of those types of items. However, such items are rare, and tend to involve relatively small amounts. For example, the fact that 81 percent of $5 million for UCCB tax cuts went to women (Table 1) does not offset the unequal effects of leaving between 60 percent and 91 percent of the other $43.1 billion in men's hands. In addition, as discussed below, all of the large budget items listed in Table 1 will, at best, reinforce women's inequality, and, at worst, exacerbate it.

DISCOVERING THE GENDER IMPACT OF TAX CUTS

When budget items take the form of tax cuts, the effect such cuts have on women can be measured by comparing women's shares of tax cuts to their annual shares of net after-tax incomes. In 2010, women as a class received only 40 percent of all net after-tax incomes. (See Lahey, "Women" 68, Table 4; Federal-Provincial; Clark.)

The gender allocation of the $7.4 billion personal income tax cuts for 2010-11 in Table 1 shows how large budget items can reinforce women's existing inequality. Overall, women received 40 percent of that total benefit. Because that figure is the same as women's 40 percent pre-existing allocation of net after-tax incomes, keeping their share of new tax cuts at 40 percent reinforces women's existing inequality and keeps them locked more tightly into that unequal 40 percent share.

Some people might say, as did the government, that tax cuts will cut taxes proportionate to existing tax liability (Lahey "Women"). But that is not the real issue. The reality is that the federal government decided to provide new annual "bonuses" or new benefits to adults in the total amount of $7.4 billion for 2010-11. It could have distributed that economic power in many different ways; it had full choice as to how to structure those payments. Indeed, the tax experts in the Department of Finance knew that delivering that bonus or benefit by cutting personal income taxes would guarantee that the largest shares of those cuts would go to those with the largest incomes, and that no share would go to those with no income tax liability. Women's incomes are persistently much lower than men's, and many women do not even have any personal income tax liability to cut.[4] By deliberately choosing to distribute this bonus in an "upside down" pattern, the government knew full well that doing so would invisibly perpetuate women's inequality.

In the case of these personal income tax rate cuts, this policy choice meant that in 2010-11, men received approximately $0.8 billion more in tax cuts than women would have received if those tax bonuses had been allocated equally to women and men. Fifty percent of adults—men— ended up receiving 60 percent of that $7.4 billion, or $4.4 billion. If the other fifty percent of adults—women—had received 50 percent of that $7.4 billion instead of just 40 percent, women would have received $3.7 billion instead of the $2.9 billion they actually got. Men's extra $0.8 billion in this situation can be thought of as a sex discrimination bonus. Such bonuses are no less valuable because they are invisible. Indeed, their very invisibility makes them politically very useful, because they are so difficult to see and thus to criticize.

The same pattern can be seen in the allocation of the GST rate cuts the federal government used to leave an extra $10.8 billion in the hands of individuals in 2010-11 (and similar amounts in every year following). As seen in Table 1, women receive only 38 percent of the total value of the GST rate cut—two percent less than their current 40 percent share of after-tax incomes, and 12 percent less than their 50-50 percent share. If the $10.8 billion spent on this tax cut in that year had been distributed equally between women and men, women would have received $1.3 billion more in after-tax incomes. Even losing that extra two percent alone (compared with women's 40 percent shares of net after-tax incomes) cost women $0.2 billion.

The corporate income tax cuts have an even more dramatic effect, with men receiving between 63 percent and 90 percent more than women of this $10.5 billion tax benefit. Depending on assumptions about who receives the true economic benefit of corporate income tax rate cuts, these cuts left between $1.3 and $4.2 billion more in after-tax corporate-source income in men's hands than they would have received if these revenue cuts had been distributed to women and men equally.

These changes took place during the worst period of recession in Canada since the 1930s depression. Even though the government felt moved to spend a total of $28.9 billion in one year just on these three major tax cuts, it is evident that the federal government had little concern for women as it decided how to deliver these benefits.

MEASURING THE GENDER IMPACT OF INFRASTRUCTURE SPENDING

In response to the 2008 global economic crisis, the Canadian government included two expenditure items in its 2009 and 2010 budgets, providing some $9.6 billion for infrastructure projects and another $4.8 billion to extend unemployment insurance benefits. The infrastructure funding was designed to fund heavy construction projects: the construction or repair of roads, water facilities, and waste facilities; energy retrofits; brown field redevelopments; port and ship facilities; parks and trails; transit; municipal buildings; airports; and community centres.

It is not always easy to determine who actually benefits from project funding like this, in which the government provides funds to be spent within project guidelines. The most direct benefits go to the private companies that contract to carry out these projects, their suppliers and their employees, managers, owners, and subcontractors. Net profits will eventually end up in the hands of the owners of capital—shareholders of corporations, business partners, and owners of unincorporated businesses. Those who use the facilities or resources that are ultimately produced by the spending program can also be thought of as "beneficiaries," although their benefits will be indirect, deferred, and in kind rather than financial.

Since one of the most important goals of this "stimulus" infrastructure spending was to support workers against unemployment, and businesses against bankruptcy during the recession, women's pre-existing shares of market incomes form the most appropriate measure of whether women can be said to benefit from infrastructure spending. In 2009, women's pre-tax shares of market incomes—wages, salaries, and investment incomes—came to a total of 36 percent (Clark). Unlike tax cuts, which were to be permanent, the large infrastructure programs were to expire in 2011 and were only extended into 2012. Thus they were essentially one-time transfers of government support for specific employment and business sectors.

When compared with women's representation in the population as a whole, it can be seen that women's 36 percent share of market incomes is even smaller than women's 40 percent share of after-tax incomes. This is because one of the core causes of women's economic disadvantage is their lack of equal access to money incomes and assets. The tax-transfer system does redistribute a small share of income from men as a class to women as a class. In 2009, that gender redistribution was 4 percent. However, the total tax-transfer system as presently constituted does not redistribute enough economic power from high to middle and low incomes effectively enough to bring women to a 50 percent level. The remaining ten percent gap between women's and men's after-tax incomes has proven to be quite durable, and, in fact, is likely to grow in the wake of the recession and the fiscal policies implemented during that era.

Using women's 36 percent share of pre-tax market incomes as a measuring stick, it can be said that if women receive exactly 36 percent of infrastructure funding, then that allocation reinforces women's existing economic inequality. If they receive less than 36 percent, it will intensify women's inequality, and if they receive more than 36 percent, it can help them slowly inch toward a slightly larger share of market incomes overall.

Given the gender profiles of the industries that are involved in the areas of infrastructure construction and repair, it can be seen that comparatively little of the immediate benefit of Canada's infrastructure programs was likely to go to women, and that the allocations of benefits so heavily favour men that the programs are likely to deepen women's existing inequality. This is because occupations in Canada continue to be markedly gender-segregated by types of work activities (see Beijing Platform for Action Committee)[5] and by quality of workforce attachment (Statistics Canada, *Women in Canada* 124, table 5.8). And nowhere are these biases more deeply entrenched than in the heavy construction industries that are the typical focus of infrastructure stimulus programs. All of these labour force sectors continue to be "non-traditional" employment for women and unquestionably "traditional" jobs for men. At best, only 6.4 percent of those in the construction, trades, and transportation sectors are women, and the representation of women in engineering, natural sciences, and mathematics is just 22 percent, in primary industries just 20 percent, and in manufacturing, processing, and utilities workers, 30 percent (data are from 2009; see Canada, *Women in Canada* table 12, at 21). On these numbers alone, it appears highly unlikely that the infusion of nearly $10 billion into these sectors of the workforce will benefit women and men equally.

Even though the Employment Insurance program also received extra funding during the recession, nothing was done with any of that funding—or with federal sex discrimination laws—to improve women's access to these areas of training, education, work, management, and ownership. Between women's very restricted access to the trades and in-service training (see Cooke, Zeytinoglu, and Chowhan), and the fact that only eleven percent of those in the trade "pipeline"—in apprenticeships—are women, members of visible minority groups (5.6 percent), or Aboriginal persons (four percent), the gender figures in the trades are not likely to change without ambitious government support, despite skyrocketing demand for licensed tradespersons (see Menard *et al.* 38, table A.1.1.2). Nor did the $1.9 billion given to universities to support their engineering and technology programs help break down gender barriers to those professions. In fact, most of this funding was actually earmarked for heavy university construction projects, and only $440 million was allocated to educational operating expenses such as salaries and research costs (see Department of Finance, *Budget 2010*: 67-8, 77-87). Instead of using the direct educational funds to attract more women to engineering, sciences, mathematics, and technology programs, the $440 million has been used to recruit senior university researchers who will "create the economy of tomorrow" (*Budget 2010* 46). To date, all of these "star" senior academics have been male.[6] These trends are even more evident in the physical sciences, mathematics, engineering, and computer sciences and technology, where women's enrolments have grown more slowly, have stayed at quite low levels (a peak of 22 percent in engineering), and have resulted in even lower levels of women in graduate studies, the academic ranks, and funded projects.

Women are also under-represented in ownership, management, and employment positions in the industrial and business sectors that were singled out for this infrastructure spending. In recent years, the numbers of women in corporate management, board, and management pipeline positions have been falling (see "Catalyst 2005 Census"; Apostolidis and Ferguson), women MBA graduates continue to face gender differences in salaries, promotions, and layoffs at the management level ("Women MBAs"), and the substantial majority of corporate shareholders continue to be men (Canada Revenue Agency, *Income Statistics 2006,* Table 4, lines 11, 60).

In short, women are likely to benefit far less from any of the infrastructure stimulus than men simply because they make up relatively small proportions of workers in the sectors benefited by infrastructure spending. With fewer than 36 percent of women in any of the relevant occupations, men will gain economic ground faster than women from this spending even if there were no gender pay gaps in these occupations. In addition, new federal legislation prohibiting labour unions from bargaining over pay equity issues makes new progress on these issues even less likely. In fact, the sharp increase in demand for enough workers to complete all of the thousands of infrastructure construction projects that had to be completed by funding deadlines in 2011 and 2012 to qualify for payment is likely to lead to increased income disparities between women and men as competition for male personnel leads to increasing wages, yet women continue to be seen as unsuited to these types of work.[7] At the same time, racism continues to compound difficulties faced by women who may have entered this area of industry in other less discriminatory countries but who face sex barriers to employment in their professions in Canada (see Boyd and Shellenberg).

Nor does it appear that the federal government made any attempt to consider the gender impact of the types of projects that received infrastructure funding either. Some 43 percent of all project funding reported by the end of 2009 was for highway, regional transit, and local roads, and only 8.3 percent to public transit. With men driving more than twice as much as women (Statistics Canada *Canadian Vehicle Survey* 40, Table 2), and women relying heavily on public transport (Statistics Canada *Where Canadians Work*), this category of infrastructure spending substantially favoured men's needs and interests and only minimally addressed women's, though the inclusion of "cultural infrastructure" on the lists of qualifying projects might seem to indicate that new and expanded childcare facilities, women's shelters, and other resources for women could be funded under these programs. As administered, however, infrastructure funding was limited to projects involving government buildings, museums and other cultural buildings, and sports facilities. Social housing could only be built on brownfields (land previously used for industrial purposes), and only two women's shelters managed to get small amounts of funding—less than half of what was approved for local animal shelters (see Infrastructure Canada, *Creating Jobs*).

INTERSECTIONALITY-BASED GENDER ANALYSIS OF SPECIFIC TAX "EXPENDITURES"

"Tax expenditures" are types of budgetary measures that are intended to deliver financial "benefits" to selected groups, but are legally delivered not as direct government grants, but as tax benefits delivered through tax statutes. (For the classic description of tax expenditures, see Surrey; also Department of Finance Canada, *Tax Expenditures* for a variant of the Surrey-style tax expenditures budget published each year.) The big difference between tax expenditures and direct government benefits is that direct benefit programs will list their eligibility criteria and funding formulas right in the enabling statute or regulations authorizing the program. When government benefits are delivered in the form of tax expenditures, this information is buried in the fine print of tax legislation, and is generally poorly understood.

Tax expenditures affect women as a class differently than they do men because women's economic conditions are generally much more constrained than men's. But failure to examine the gender impact of such spending items prevents both technical policy analysts and ordinary people from seeing those gender effects. In effect, lack of empathy drives policy and undercuts gender equality.

Take, for example, the Home Renovation Tax Credit (HRTC), which was offered on a one-time basis during 2009 as part of the overall economic stimulus package. Individuals could claim tax credits of up to $1,350 for the 2009 tax year if they spent up to $9,000 on home renovation costs (Statistics Canada "Tax Measures" 336).

On its face, this home renovation tax credit seemed to be open to everyone, and of course it was described in strictly gender-neutral terms. The biggest limit was that it could only be claimed by homeowners, and not by renters. Also, they had to have enough tax liability to be able to legally claim the credit—to "cash it out"—so those with little or no income, and thus little or no tax liability, could not claim it. And of course they had to have enough cash or credit to be able to afford to make expensive renovations as well.

Each of these criteria, all implying some level of wealth, savings, and income tax liability, made it clear that women would have much less chance of obtaining a share of the $2.5 billion allocated to this special stimulus measure. Most women's incomes fall into the three lowest income quintiles, in which taxpayers are "net dis-savers"— ending every year with net debt, not with net savings. In contrast, men dominate the two top income quintiles, in which net savers are concentrated (Sauve 21, Table 1). Women trying to close the savings gap by borrowing money to pay for home renovations would have actually added to their net end-of-year debt. Worse, the tax credit they might have received after borrowing this money could easily end up being less than the interest paid on credit cards or bank loans (the federal credit is 15 percent of the cost of renovations; credit card interest rates can go as high as 19.5 percent to 24 percent). In addition, consumer durables such as new appliances did not qualify as "renovations"; renters who made otherwise qualifying renovations could not get this credit because they were not homeowners; and the short notice and program time frames excluded those who needed more time to save enough for special projects involving these amounts of money. And at least 40 percent of women who file income tax returns will have incomes so low that they cannot take full (or even partial) advantage of tax credits. (The comparable figure for male tax filers who are not taxpayers is 27 percent. See Department of Finance Canada, Taxation Year 2008.)

But there were other gender-specific requirements attached to this credit as well. The gender requirements were buried in the finest print, and stipulated that married and cohabiting couples were allowed to share each other's credit space and renovation expenses back and forth to make sure that they could use all possible credits. The gender requirements also spelled out that two unrelated taxpayers could each claim their own full $1,350 credit, even if they both owned shares in the same house. As the Canada Revenue Agency (*Homeowners*) itself demonstrated on its webpage with a fictitious taxpayer named "Mrs. Martin," however, single women with low incomes received no such consideration. The example of "Mrs. Martin" was poignant. Living on an income of $18,500, it was pointed out by the CRA that she could already claim the personal income tax credit on $10,320, an age amount of $6,408, and the pension income amount of $2,000, for a total of $18,728; therefore she had no income tax liability. She was too rich to qualify for the credit, even though she had spent a hypothetical $4,300 on qualifying renovations and would have received a tax credit of $495 if she had had more income tax liability (Canada Revenue Agency, *Homeowners*).

Not all those whose income taxes are so low they cannot "cash out" tax credits like the home renovation tax credit will be denied tax benefits in the same way that "Mrs. Martin" is. In income tax law, as in most social benefit laws, marital status can make a huge difference. In the example above, if "Mrs. Martin" had been married, or even cohabiting with an adult partner, then she could have spent her money on renovations and let her spouse or partner claim the credit—even if her own income was so low that she had no income tax liability herself.

While married couples and cohabiting partners can also lose out on nonrefundable tax credits like the HRTC if both spouses or partners have low incomes, it is single women who are most vulnerable to being denied valuable income tax credits due to their financial inability to "cash out" non-refundable credits. This is true for "average" single women, and it is even more true for unmarried/coupled women who are disabled, economically disadvantaged, racialized, or Aboriginal. The more multiple disadvantages women face, the more likely they are to fall into the lowest income ranges that can benefit from supposedly general tax measures.

Intersectionality-based gender analysis asks whether "the specific problems faced by different groups of women" are being adequately addressed by particular policies (Association for Women's Rights 2, 6). Income data are still useful in answering that question when fiscal measures are being examined. However, income data have to be disaggregated not just in relation to sex, but also by race, identity, and heritage characteristics to be of assistance in such analysis.

Using the data in Table 2, it can be seen that the gender impact of the HRTC will be affected by both racialization and marital or cohabitant status. Table 3 provides average male and female incomes in five racialized groups in Canada in 2005. With the exception of the category "All groups," which includes all racialized and non-racialized census groups, each group in this table is defined as a race/ethnic identity group by Statistics Canada. Not all the census groups are included in this table because the point of this example is to demonstrate that race/ethnic identity is critical to intersectionality-based gender analysis, and that racialization does not affect incomes and gender gaps in the same way for each group. There are very large variations between different racialized groups as well as in comparison with the averages for "All groups."

Although these data are themselves aggregates, they do show marked differences in how the intersection of racialization and gender affects both the incomes of women and men in each group and the size of the

Table 2

Average Incomes by Selected Racialized Census Groups and Gender, Canada, 2005

	Japanese	All Groups(a)	Black	Korean	First Nations on reserve
Men	$51,971	$45,000	$29,361	$25,543	$20,251
Women	$28,986	$27,000	$24,976	$17,682	$18,636
Gender gap(b)	44.3%	44.0%	14.9%	30.8%	8.0%

Sources: *Statistics Canada. 2006 Census. Ottawa: Service Canada, 2008; Canada Revenue Agency 2007, Table 16 ("all groups").*

(a) *Includes all racialized and non-racialized in census data, not just those listed in this table.*
(b) *The gender gap is the number of percentage points between women's average incomes expressed as a ratio of men's and 100%. For example, Japanese women's average incomes are 55.7% of those of Japanese men, leaving 44.3 percentage points difference between the two.*

gender gap between women and men in each group. The two groups with the highest average male and female incomes (Japanese and "All Groups") also have the largest gender gaps. This finding suggests that to the extent that partners and heterosexual couples are from the same groups (and they certainly are not, in reality), reduced economic pressure on women to contribute to family incomes might increase pressure on them to produce in-kind goods and services. At the same time, groups with lower male incomes have smaller gender gaps, which might suggest the opposite pressures on women—to contribute to cash production and to in-kind production.

While these are still group-based generalizations, it can be seen that, as in the Canada Revenue Agency example of "Mrs. Martin," some racialized women even in their peak-earning years are more likely to be shut out of tax benefits such as the home renovation credit more completely than others. For example, Korean women with average incomes of $17,682 will have, at best, maximum creditable renovation zones of $7,362 instead of the full $9,000 zone. Thus, on average, they can expect to be able to claim only partial credits ($1,104) instead of the full amount of the credit ($1,350).[8] At the same time, even though First Nations women on reserves have slightly higher average incomes than First Nations men on reserves, First Nations men and women will both be excluded completely from this tax credit because living on reserve takes status "Indian" persons outside the *Income Tax Act*: neither the liability nor the benefit provisions of income tax legislation apply to status "Indian" persons.

Membership in racialized groups with average incomes lower than the "All groups" averages in Canada intensifies the risk that both men and women in those groups will fall into the category of tax filers who are not taxpayers. Thus they face an increased risk that they will not have enough federal income tax liability to "cash out" any HRTC credits they might have. And in these income ranges, not only the "Mrs. Martins," retired senior women receiving low-income tax benefits aimed at pension and age issues, but also women who are already receiving other low-income tax benefits that would zero out their tax liability (such as disability or infirmity benefits), will be prevented from being able to cash out this benefit. At the same time, however, marital status will advantage such women with spouses or partners who have some tax liability with which to "cash out" the credit.

In tax policy literature, one of the many criticisms of tax expenditures has been their "upside down" effect. The "upside down" effect occurs when high-income taxpayers receive the largest financial benefits from tax expenditures because they have a greater financial capacity to "cash out" such benefits, credits, special rates, exemptions, and deductions. Intersectionality-based gender impact analysis demonstrates that the realities of women's lives routinely produce gender-specific "upside-down effects" on the basis of gender and all their other characteristics. In the example of the home renovation credits, the largest and most complete claims to this tax credit will be available to the men in each racialized group (except First Nations men on reserve), when compared with women in each group. Identifying and projecting these "upside down" distributions helps reveal in greater detail why the real-world gender allocation of the HRTC will incrementally reduce women's current 40 percent share of after-tax incomes and cannot possibly increase it. In 2009, women ended up receiving only 36 percent of this credit, so it incrementally pushed women's after-tax incomes lower than their 40 percent share at the same time that it incrementally pushed men's higher than their pre-existing 60 percent share (CRA *Income Statistics 2009*, Table 4).

Intersectionality-based gender impact analysis can provide forward-looking information that can be used to ensure that future policies do not discriminate on the basis of gender, income levels, and race/ethnic identity group characteristics. Requiring analysts to consider how particular programs will affect people by gender, incomes, and race/Aboriginality can disrupt the androcentric and Eurocentric frameworks within which fiscal policies continue to be formulated. Even if there is a real-world failure of empathy for those who are structurally excluded by many policies, the detailed guidelines used in gender-based analysis can bring these factors into the analysis even without genuine empathy on the part of analysts. If policy makers are required to address the impact of proposed policies on gendered low incomes, they are more likely to consider delivering credits like the home renovation credit in the form of fully refundable tax credits, which would ensure that these credits will reach all women as well as men and all members of racialized groups (except First Nations men and women) regardless of how low their incomes might be. If policy makers are required to consider the impact of such benefits on members of *all* racialized groups, then they are more likely to consider delivering home renovation benefits to people in the form of direct grants rather than in the form of income tax credits. If policy makers are required to address the impact of gender and racialization on access to home ownership in the process of making new policy on home renovations, they can legitimately ask why such benefits should go only to those who are "owners" of homes or recreational property and not to all those with "home" renovation needs regardless of their legal tenure or the nature of their dwelling.

INSTITUTIONALIZING GENDER MAINSTREAMING—THE FUTURE IS NOW

This chapter has examined how the Canadian government continues to privilege men in the exercise of its broad powers over economic relations, taxation, spending, and other fiscal issues despite its many domestic and international obligations to eradicate sex discrimination. The "politics of budgets" may seem far removed from women's lives, but the pervasive effects of tax laws and spending decisions are so closely woven into the fabric of everyday life that until they are addressed, further progress for women will be very difficult to attain.

Women around the world are now well equipped to take on national budgets and the concentration of wealth in men's hands in the ongoing search for genuine equality. Rikki Holtmaat has demonstrated that the language of Article 5(a) makes it impossible to read the CEDAW as anything but demanding that states engage in continuous dynamic transformative processes of replacing all policies, practices, laws, and "social and cultural patterns of conduct" perpetuating women's inequalities with those that promote substantive equality. These guarantees mean that women have every right to demand of their governments that they recognize women as equally worthy constitutors of the state whose well-being is just as urgent as men's.

When the Canadian Charter of Rights was enacted, the inclusion of sex equality clauses was in part required by CEDAW, which Canada had just ratified. Canada's ratification of CEDAW has not yet resulted in Charter sex equality decisions that eliminate systemic discrimination and bring about material and representational equality for all women. However, a number of developments suggest that sooner or later, the promises contained in CEDAW and the Beijing Platform for Action will be taken more seriously by Canadian governments and courts.

In 2000, Status of Women Canada appointed an expert panel to review women's progress toward sex equality in Canada, which concluded that not only was the progress to date not adequate in light of demonstrable needs in the country, but also that concrete legislation requiring the government to carry out gender-based analysis of all existing and proposed policies was urgently necessary (Steinsky-Schwartz *et al*). Citing legislation already in effect in Norway, Sweden, and the UK, the expert panel recommended that legislation and other binding steps for monitoring and implementing CEDAW and substantive constitutional and human rights guarantees be taken as a matter of urgency. Steinsky-Schwartz (Annex E) provides details of these measures and recommendations.

Nearly a decade later, these findings have been confirmed by the Auditor General of Canada, whose office sampled federal use of gender-based analysis in policy review and formation in 2009 in the first audit of this obligation. The published report, which detailed audit findings on 68 recent programs, policy initiatives, and acts of legislation developed in seven federal departments, found that only four departments appeared to have attempted to use gender-based analysis consistent with Canada's obligations under CEDAW and its own policies. Perhaps even more alarmingly, the report also found that there was no evidence of any attempt to do any type of gender-based analysis in nearly half the programs, and no effort in the core agencies (Treasury Board, Privy Council Office, Finance) or in the machinery (Status of Women Canada) to ensure that gender-based analysis be used (Auditor General 12-13).

Whenever the substantive equality provisions of CEDAW have been brought directly or indirectly into application, the result has been more equality-promoting decisions. Under the Optional Protocol to CEDAW, the UN Commission on the Status of Women (CSW) has begun issuing decisions that treat a country's failure to enact legislation which meets women's basic needs for security and equality as a breach of its obligations under CEDAW decisions that place pressure on states to bring their laws into compliance with their international obligations (see for instance *A.T. v. Hungary* 10-28). As the provisions of CEDAW have been brought directly to bear on state policies, court decisions have made it clear that nothing less than genuine and substantive equality will do. Alda Facio, for instance, holds that, under CEDAW, disproportionate gender representation on legislative committees violates state obligation to secure sex equality. UK civil society groups have taken heart from CEDAW—and have now initiated legal action seeking court orders compelling the government to carry out gender-based analysis of all fiscal policies on an ongoing basis (Fawcett Society), and women in Canada have been heartened by the Supreme Court of Canada's recent reference in *Khadr v. Canada* to the importance of "fundamental human rights protected by international law" formed by ratified treaties in applying the Charter to government action (par. 14, 16).

When the Beijing Platform for Action was adopted in 1995 and Canada simultaneously adopted its Federal Plan for Gender Equality, it titled that policy "Setting the Stage for the Next Century." We are now more than a decade into this new century, and to date, the most notable development regarding women's equality is that it has been more or less flat-lined on core indicators in Canada since the turn of the century, and has even gone into reverse on indicators like advanced education-earnings data.

The promises have all been made. Women are now living in this "next century." The stage is set and the time to implement genuine equality in Canada is here. Full-scale implementation of gender mainstreaming and all of Canada's promises under CEDAW and other constitutional and human rights instruments can only take place when women themselves begin to "open their budgets," rescue empathy from the forces of economic ideologies, and thereby take back the budget for everyone.

[1]According to Statistics Canada, when the Royal Commission on the Status of Women was struck in 1967, only 33 percent of women worked for pay, compared with 75 percent of men. By 2004, nearly 58 percent of women worked for pay, while men's labour force participation rate had fallen to 68 percent. Between 1967 and 2004, women's shares of market incomes rose from 20 percent to 36 percent, and their share of unpaid work fell from 80 percent to 66 percent. See Bird (1970) 21-3, par. 14, and 22, Table 1; Statistics Canada, SPSD/M, version 16.1 (2009) database and modeled variables. The assumptions and calculations underlying the SPSD/M simulation results in this article were specified by the author, and the responsibility for the use and interpretation of these data is entirely that of the author.

[2]The HDI and GDI are separate scales contained in each annual report. All years can be accessed through the UN website <hdr.undp.org/en/Statistics/data/hd_map/gdi>. The 1995 HDI and GDI rankings were based on data from 1990 to 1993 due to the time lag in reporting data on economic equality indicators.

[3]"For the purposes of the present Convention, the term "discrimination against women" shall mean any distinction, exclusion or restriction made on the basis of sex which has the effect or purpose of impairing or nullifying the recognition, enjoyment or exercise by women, irrespective of their marital status, on a basis of equality of men and women, of human rights and fundamental freedoms in the political, economic, social, cultural, civil or any other field" (CEDAW, Article 1).

[4]It is well known that women in different income classes will always be affected differently by the same tax cut. Approximately 40 percent of women's incomes are so low that they will receive no benefit from any personal income tax rate cuts at all. Women with low incomes who

do have some income tax liability will receive smaller total benefits than men in their income classes, because women's incomes are, on the average, lower than men's all the way up the income scale. Only women with the highest incomes will be able to receive the full benefit of these cuts, and they are a tiny number of all women.

[5]The largest majority of women in paid work are still concentrated in most of the same "top-10": "traditional female jobs" reported in Canada over a century ago, all associated with care giving, food preparation, and services.

[6]On the "discouragement" of female academics, see Rabson, as well as Side and Robbins. Chase and Church on "How Canada Poached Academic Stars" is also useful. For data on enrolments for 2006-2008, see Statistics Canada "University Enrolment."

[7]This type of labour market segmentation may be what lies behind the growing gaps between women and men in Alberta, where male wages are increasing, women's rates of education and wages are falling, and women's birth rates are increasing.

[8]This is because the first $10,320 for 2009 was completely tax-exempt as the result of the personal credit to which each taxpayer is entitled. With income of $17,682, the taxpayer would have had tax liability on $7,362 ($17,682 minus $10,320), and so only $7,362 of qualifying renovation costs could be used to calculate her tax credit. She would need to have income of at least $19,320 to be able to "cash in" the full $1,350 credit. (And this only if on that income she owned a home and had been able to spend $10,000 on qualifying renovations to get a tax credit on $9,000 of those expenses.)

WORKS CITED

A. T. v. Hungary. CEDAW Communication No. 2/2003, UN Doc. CEDAW/ C32/D/2.2003 (26 Jan. 2005). Web. 23. Aug. 2010

Apostolidis, Sylvia, and Rhonda Ferguson. *Catalyst's Report to Women in Capital Markets: Benchmarking 2008.* Toronto: Catalyst 189. Web. 14. Aug. 2012.

Association for Women's Rights in Development. "Intersectionality: A Tool for Gender and Economic Justice." *Women's Rights and Economic Change* 9, August 2004. Web. 14 Aug. 2012.

Bird, Florence. Chair, Royal Commission on the Status of Women. *Report.* Ottawa: Information Canada, 1970. Web. 14 Aug. 2012.

Beijing Declaration [Platform for Action]. Report of the Fourth World

Conference on Women. United Nations Doc. A/CONF. 177/20 Annex II, Chapter IV. Web. 14 Aug. 2012.

Beijing Platform for Action Committee. "Women in Paid Work." *Women and the Economy: A Project of UNPC.* Web. 14 Aug. 2012.

Boyd, Monica, and Grant Shellenberg. "Re-accreditation and the Occupations of Immigrant Doctors and Engineers." *Canadian Social Trends* Sept. 2007. Web. 22 Aug. 2012.

Canada. Auditor General. "Gender-Based Analysis." *Report of the Auditor General of Canada to the House of Commons.* Ottawa: Minister of Public Works, 2009. Web. 14 Aug. 2012.

Canada. Canada Revenue Agency. *Homeowners HRTC Calculating Your Credit Examples.* Web. 22 Aug 2012.

Canada. *Income Statistics 2007 [for the 2005 tax year].* Ottawa: Canada Revenue Agency. Web. 12 Aug. 2012.

Canada. *Income Statistics 2011 [for the 2009 tax year].* Ottawa: Canada Revenue Agency. Web. 12 Aug. 2012.

Canada. Department of Finance. *Budget 2010.* Ottawa: Department of Finance, 2010. Web. 14 Aug. 2012.

Canada. *Taxation Year 2008 Estimate.* Standing Committee on the Status of Women: Minutes of Hearing, May. 2008. Web. 14 Aug. 2012.

Canada. *Tax Expenditures and Evaluations.* 2009. Web. 14 Aug. 2012.

Canada. Infrastructure Canada. *Creating Jobs, Creating Communities: Ontario Infrastructure Projects,* 2010. Web. 14 Aug. 2012.

Canada. Statistics Canada. *2006 Census.* Ottawa: Service Canada, 2008; Canada Revenue Agency 2007. Web. 22 Aug. 2012.

Canada. *Canadian Vehicle Survey.* Ottawa: Statistics Canada, 2008. Web. 22 Aug. 2012.

Canada. *Social Policy Simulation Model and Database, version 16.1.* Ottawa: Statistics Canada, 2009. Web. 22. Aug. 2012.

Canada. "Tax Measures: Supplementary Information." Budget 2010: Annex 5: 313-15; "Notices of Ways and Means Motions." Web. 22 Aug. 2012.

Canada. "University Enrolment" *The Daily* (13 July 2009). Web. 22 Aug. 2012.

Canada. *Women in Canada: A Gender-Based Statistical Report.* 5th ed. Ottawa: Minister of Industry, 2006. Web. 14 Aug. 2012.

Canada. *Women in Canada: A Gender-Based Statistical Report.* 6th ed. Ottawa: Minister of Industry, 2010. Web. 14 Aug. 2012.

Canada. *Women in Canada: Work Chapter Updates.* Ottawa: Minister of Industry, 2007. Web. 14 Aug. 2012.

Canada. Status of Women Canada. *Economic Gender Equality Indicators*. Ottawa: Status of Women Canada, 1997. Web. 18 May. 2013.

Canada. *Gender-Based Analysis: A Guide for Policy-Making*. Ottawa: Status of Women Canada, 1998. Web. 14 Aug. 2012.

Canada. *Setting the Stage for the Next Century: The Federal Plan for Gender Equality*. Ottawa: Canada, 1995. Web. 22 Aug. 2012.

Canada (Prime Minister) v Khadr. 2010 SCC 3, Canada: Supreme Court, 29 January 2010. Web. 14 Aug. 2012.

Canadian Charter of Rights and Freedoms, s 2, Part I of the Constitution Act, 1982, being Schedule B to the *Canada Act* 1982 (UK), 1982, c.11. Web. Web. 22 Aug. 2012.

Cassin, Marguerite. "The Routine Production of Inequality: A Study in the Social Organization of Knowledge." Diss. University of Toronto, 1990. Print.

"Catalyst 2005 Census of Women Board Directors of the FP 500." Toronto: Catalyst 2006 (11). Web. 14 Aug. 2012.

Chase, Steven and Elizabeth Church. "How Canada Poached Academic Stars from around the Globe." *Globe and Mail* 18 May 2010. Web. 14 Aug. 2012.

Clark, Warren. *Economic Gender Equality Indicators 2000*. Ottawa: Status of Women Canada, 2001. Web. 23 Aug. 2012.

Cooke, Gordon B, Isik U. Zeytinoglu, and James Chowhan. "Barriers to Training Access." *Perspectives*. Web. 14 Aug. 2012.

Day, Shelagh, and Gwen Brodsky. *Women and the Equality Deficit: The Impact of Restructuring Canada's Social Programs*. Ottawa: Status of Women Canada, 1998. Print.

Donnelly, Maureen. "The Disparate Impact of Pension Reform on Women." *Canadian Journal of Women and the Law* 6 (1993): 419-454. Print.

Facio, Alda. "Gender Equality and International Human Rights in Costa Rican Constitutional Jurisprudence." *The Gender of Constitutional Jurisprudence*. Ed. Beverley Baines and Ruth Rubio-Marin. Cambridge: Cambridge University Press, 1999.109-13. Print.

Fawcett Society. Web. 14 Aug. 2012.

Ferber, Marianne A. and Julie A. Nelson, eds. *Feminist Economics Today: Beyond Economic Man*. Chicago: University of Chicago Press, 2003. Print.

Freiler, Christa and Judy Cerny. Benefiting Canada's Children: Perspectives on Gender and Social Responsibility. Ottawa: Status of Women Canada, 1998. Web. 14 Aug 2012.

Frey, Regina. "Paradoxes of Gender Budgeting." *Nordic-Baltic Network on Gender Responsive Budgeting."* Discussion paper 14. Genderbüro, Berlin: Vilnius, 2008. Web. 14 Aug. 2012.

Holtmaat, Rikki. *Towards Different Law and Public Policy: The Significance of Article 5a of* CEDAW *for the Elimination of Structural Gender Discrimination.* Netherlands: Ministry of Social Affairs, 2004. Print.

Lahey, Kathleen A. *Canada's Gendered Budget 2012: Impact of Bills C-38 and C-45 on Women.* Kingston, ON.: Feminist Legal Studies Queen's, 2012. Web. 10 Dec. 2012.

Lahey, Kathleen A. "Women, Substantive Equality, and Fiscal Policy." *Canadian Journal of Women and the Law* 22 (2010) 27-106. Print.

Menard, Merinka, Cindy K. Y. Chan, Frank Menezes and Merv Walker. *National Apprenticeship Survey: Canada Overview Report.* Ottawa: Statistics Canada, 2008. Web. 14 Aug. 2012.

Quinion. Michael. "Budget." *World Wide Words.* Web. 10 May. 2013.

Rabson. Mia. "Female Academics 'Discouraged' after Women Shut Out of Funding." *Winnipeg Free Press* 19 May 2010: 1. Print.

Sauve, Roger. *The Current State of Canadian Family Finances: 2007 Report.* Ottawa: Vanier Institute, 2008. Print.

Scott, Katherine. *Women and the* CHST: *A Profile of Women Receiving Social Assistance in 1994.* Ottawa: Status of Women Canada, 1998. Web. 14 Aug. 2012.

Side, Katherine and Wendy Robbins. "Institutionalizing Inequalities in Canadian Universities: The Canada Research Chairs Program." *National Women's Studies Association Journal* 19.3 (2007). 163-81. Print.

Steinsky-Schwartz, Georgina, Dorienne Rowan-Campbell, and Louise Longevin. *Equality for Women: Beyond the Illusion.* Final Report. Ottawa: Status of Women Canada, 2005. Web. 14 Aug. 2012.

Surrey, Stanley. *Pathways to Tax Reform: The Concept of Tax Expenditures.* Cambridge, MA: Harvard University Press, 1973. Print.

United Nations. Convention on the Elimination of All Forms of Discrimination Against Women (CEDAW). GA Res. 34/180, 34 UN GAOR Supp. (No. 46) at 193, UN, 1980. Doc. A/34/46; 1249 UNTS 13; 19 I.L.M. 33 (1980). Web. 14 Aug. 2012.

United Nations. Development Program. Gender Development Index. Web. 31 Mar. 2013.

United Nations. Development Program. Human Development Index. Web. 31 Mar. 2013.

United Nations. *United Nations Human Rights and Human*

Development Report. 1996-2000. Web. 14 Aug. 2012.

"Women MBAs." *Catalyst* 2012. Web. 14 Aug. 2012.

Zweibel, Ellen B. "Child Support Policy and Child Support Guidelines: Broadening the Agenda." *Canadian Journal of Women and the Law* 6 (1993): 371-401. Print.

4. Aboriginal Women on the Frontline of an Addiction Crisis

MARIE WADDEN

ABORIGINAL ISSUES FLEW TO THE FOREFRONT of Canadian public life in 2012 thanks to the creative activism of four First Nations women in Saskatchewan: Nina Wilson, Sheelah McLean, Sylvia McAdam, and Jessica Gordon. They were the first to coin the term "Idle No More" to launch a nationwide series of protests against Bill C-45, which will dismantle many of the protections that safeguard Canada's natural environment. Aboriginal people see themselves as stewards of the animals and freshwater resources that have sustained their people for thousands of years. It doesn't surprise me that Canadian Aboriginal women have created the "Idle No More" movement in their continuing commitment to improving the lives of their people.

In 2005, I met and interviewed many outstanding Aboriginal women working on the "frontline" of an addiction crisis. My work was funded by the Atkinson Fellowship, which selects a journalist each year to promote understanding of public policy issues. (The resulting research is published in the *Toronto Star.*) I had already learned that Aboriginal women in Labrador were involved in a social healing movement. The Atkinson Fellowship made it possible for me to travel across Canada— to Inuit, Métis and First Nations communities—where I discovered that social healing, led by Aboriginal women, is truly national and international in scope, and has been woven from heartbreak and grit. I felt, on many First Nation reserves (in northern Ontario and Manitoba in particular), an overpowering sense of grief and despair, caused by the high rates of youth suicide and unemployment. While I have never experienced the marginalization of these people, it was impossible not to empathize with them. Their willingness to trust me, not with their despair, but with their solutions, inspired me to communicate their needs, as best I can, to the Canadian public. It made me deeply committed to sharing what I learned with as many people as possible. The newspaper articles grew into a book (*Where the Pavement Ends: The Aboriginal Recovery Movement and the Urgent Need for Reconciliation*), and now, happily, a chapter in this collection.

I have selected ten of the groundbreaking women I met to profile. They have been pioneering techniques of social healing that may some day find their way into mainstream society (see, for instance, Rod McCormick's discussion of substance abuse treatment). That these women had to overcome tremendous personal odds to make the lives of future generations better, makes their struggles and successes that much more significant. And, as it turned out, they were to teach me a lot about the power of empathy as a motivating force for change.

Maggie Hodgson

In September 2010, Indigenous people from all over the world gathered in Hawaii for the sixth annual Healing Our Spirit Worldwide (HOSW) conference. As much a movement as a conference, it was founded by a Canadian First Nations woman, named (Marjorie) Maggie Hodgson. While her name is unknown in most Canadian households, she has received many honours; her low profile in public life reflects the marginalization of Aboriginal people. Hodgson is one of the most prominent names in the Indigenous social healing movement, which was instigated and continues to be supported by women, most of whom work without recognition outside Aboriginal society.

In 2009, Dr. Hodgson was named a Champion of mental health by the Canadian Alliance on Mental Illness and Mental Health, which cited her extensive involvement in Canadian Aboriginal health initiatives:

> As the Executive Director of the NECHI Institute on Alcohol and Drug Education, Dr. Hodgson has been the driving force behind many Aboriginal health initiatives, including mental health and addictions, family violence, sexual abuse, and residential schools. She is one of the main supporters of mental illness, addiction and support programs in the aboriginal community. (Canadian Alliance)

Outside Canada, Hodgson is best known to the international Indigenous community for her work organizing the HOSW conferences, which are part academic gatherings, part spiritual and cultural Olympics, and part AA meetings. More than anything, the movement is about going beyond staunching the horrendous wounds inflicted by identity brainwashing and cultural destruction. It is about stopping the plague of poverty, addiction, and dependency that began when colonial governments stole lands and imposed assimilation on the original peoples of the countries they took over.

Hodgson chaired a World Health Organization (WHO) committee that supported the development of WHO addictions projects in developing countries. She brings that expertise to the HOSW movement, which aims to cure the self-destructive pathologies common to many traumatized peoples around the world: addictions to alcohol, drugs, sex, and gambling. The goal is to bring those identities and societies back to their former vigour. Maggie Hodgson believes that if Indigenous people are to heal, traditional religious and cultural beliefs must be valued and honoured. "What better way to do that," she asks, "than to be part of a movement of faith and action with a belief in the human spirit?"

Western addiction treatment methods just do not work for a health crisis that has so targeted Indigenous people. Hodgson believes recovery requires a return to cultural and spiritual roots, as the HOSW covenant affirms:

> Remembering the devastation and confusion that colonization brought, including alcohol and disease; grieving for the land taken and the loss of communal life; we the Indigenous Peoples of the world, having come together as part of the Healing Our Spirit Worldwide movement, declare with one voice and heart our resolve to strengthen the Spirit of our Nations and Peoples, to clear from our hearts and minds the clouds of confusion and doubt.... We commit ourselves to work in unity and with resolve to strengthen and heal the spirit of our Peoples. (Healing)

My introduction to Hodgson and her work came long before I attended the fifth HOSW conference, which was held in Canada (in Edmonton) in 2006. I had heard about her from Innu women in two Labrador communities fifteen years before. In 1992, Hodgson had come to the aid of the Innu, who were grappling with an overwhelming wave of alcoholism that began in the 1960s, shortly after they were subjected to an enforced settlement, from a nomadic to a sedentary way of life. The massive industrial development built to harness the hydroelectric power of a huge falls on the Innu's Mistashipu River (Churchill River on Canadian maps), made the Innu way of life, as nomadic hunters and gatherers, thereafter unsustainable thereafter. A sense of powerlessness followed.

The Innu were not consulted over this development, even though their territory had never been legally ceded to Canada by any treaty or land claims agreement. The oldest grave found in the Innu homeland is 5,000 years old, yet Innu rights to their territory were ignored until 2011 when a number of court decisions forced governments to sign what is called "The New Dawn Agreement": it provides the basis for self-government and a land claims settlement, as well as financial compensation for the first Churchill Falls project.

By 1992, Hodgson was already a veteran of similar crises, having many times witnessed what happens when there is a sudden forced relocation or traumatic change in the life of an Indigenous community. Canada's Indian Residential School policy created a catastrophe for her Nadleh Whuten Carrier First Nation in central British Columbia. Her mother was among the first generation forced to attend a residential school. In these boarding schools, children were cut off from their parents and community for months at a time, and taught to feel ashamed of their language and customs. Her mother returned from school broken, and eventually became alcoholic. Hodgson might have ended her days in the same way had it not been for an act of violence. When she was a teenager she was raped. The investigating RCMP officer told her mother not to expect more for her daughter: "You're an alcoholic and an Indian, and so is she. She's there to be used."

A younger, less senior, officer followed the devastated teenager outside the police station, expressing sympathy and promising to make the rapist pay for what he had done. "He showed me I was a human being and deserved the same safety as other kids," she recalls today. "He gave me comfort within my spirit."

Hodgson resolved to stop her own slide into alcoholism by channelling her frustration and anger into action. She may have learned her determination from her French Canadian father, who was fired from his job at the LeJac residential school because he refused to lie to a public inquiry concerning the deaths of three children: he testified that they were beaten, fled the school, and froze to death. "The Principal had made an example of my dad," Hodgson says. Few others were willing to speak up because of the Principal's threat. "If you don't say what we want you to say," they were told, "you too will be fired."

In 1973, Hodgson worked at Alberta's national counselling services, and helped the province pioneer the country's first Aboriginal addiction recovery services. A First Nations man named Eric Shirt founded Poundmakers Lodge. From his initiatives, the NECHI Training, Research and Health Promotions Institute grew to become this country's preeminent training centre for front line workers in addictions. "When I took over NECHI in 1983, we had about 60 graduates," Hodgson says. "It swelled to about three hundred per year across Canada. Eric convinced the federal government to fund addictions programs."

Hodgson estimated that as many as 90 percent of the adults on reserves in western Canada had become alcoholics by the mid-1970s. She raged at the untrammelled suffering she witnessed, and at the contempt of those in the wider society who saw drunkenness as a natural state for an Indigenous person. NECHI sent trainers across the country to Aboriginal communities like those in Labrador, to teach counselling strategies and make suggestions on ways change could be brought about: one individual, one family, at a time.

NECHI had more credibility in these communities than the federal government's National Native Alcohol and Drug Abuse Prevention Program (NNADAP), created in 1981, which stationed one sober, but poorly trained, person in each community to run AA programs. NECHI went much further, building teamwork within a community development framework. It effectively encouraged each community to use its distinct spiritual and cultural traditions to create its own treatment programs.

"We effected change from the bottom up," Hodgson says. "We chose role models who were abstainers to be leaders, to set a standard. If they wanted to be elected, they understood that the community wanted to elect sober people."

Alcoholics Anonymous (AA) recognizes "a higher power" and is based on Christian traditions, whereas Aboriginal spiritual beliefs predate Christianity and were damaged by colonial policies. Hodgson believes healing requires taking people back to a time when their cultures were strongest.

I tried to set up an interview with Hodgson in 1992. At the time, video was circulating around the world, showing Innu children inhaling gasoline and threatening suicide in the Mushuau Innu community of Davis Inlet, Labrador. Hodgson rebuffed me, saying "I don't speak to white journalists," because, as she well knew, there were hundreds of other Davis Inlets in Canada that were not being talked about in the press, nor was there ever much discussion of the complex problems that had led the children of these reserves to resort to this dangerous "high." I knew I had lost access to an important and powerful conversation, so I waited, and tried again fifteen years later. By then, Hodgson had several other amazing accomplishments to her credit.

She was instrumental in helping to achieve justice for residential school students through the country's largest class action lawsuit. The

Residential School Settlement Agreement was reached out of court between former students and the Federal Government because Hodgson and others proved that a very great injustice had been done. Big problems never daunt this woman. "I set up the first national dialogues on residential school issues," Hodgson says, "with five hundred people, former students, and federal government departments. We went about developing the principles which any settlement agreement had to include." She then co-chaired the working caucus on residential school issues which included some of the people who were at the national dialogues. "We were strong on our position that there needed to be counselling support which would include traditional people," she says.

Canada made a commitment to compensate former students, and to hold a Truth and Reconciliation Commission, which is still underway in 2013, to air the issues raised by the destructive and racist government policy which created residential schools.

When I met Hodgson in Edmonton in 2006, she agreed to help my research. A book I had published on the Innu in 1991 (*Nitassinan: The Innu Struggle to Reclaim their Homeland*) helped establish my credibility as someone who was interested in telling the truth about the plight of Aboriginal people.

The Edmonton "Healing Our Spirit" conference attracted 3,000 delegates from as far away as New Zealand and Australia. Aborigines in Australia, the New Zealand Maori, the Navahjo, the Hopi, the Saami, Circumpolar Inuit, Japan's Enu and Thailand's Indigenous residents, to name just a few, are all to some extent grappling with the same destructive social pathologies created by extreme poverty and political oppression as Canada's First Nations, Métis, and Inuit. All ages were represented at the conference, with an especially high proportion of youth—as many as nine hundred. A special program was designed by the young adults who were part of the organizing committee. Hodgson describes the event as one that combines "research, social issues, healing, music, laughter, singing—a celebration of coming together to strengthen our international vision for our seventh generation, which is now in our midst."

Hodgson is in her sixties, a small fireball of a woman whose health has suffered because of the long days required to achieve all that she has. She has had one stroke, and has been told she is at risk of having another. "I was so excited last night that I just couldn't sleep," I overheard her telling some HOSW organizers who are gathered on the ground floor of Edmonton's Shaw Conference Centre. "I'd better pace myself this week."

The conference prospectus is more than 100 pages long. Participants sit through inspiring speeches and performances that emphasize the importance of sobriety, hard work, family unity and self-respect: values that colonial policies seem to have knocked out of the societies they tried to assimilate. Information is exchanged at hundreds of workshops. I attend one that Hodgson presents on her latest passion, the creation of a "National Day of Healing and Reconciliation (NDHR)" on May 26. (That day is called "Sorry Day" in Australia, following the apology for a policy similar to Canada's for Indian residential schools.) Hodgson believes sobriety and social healing will spread faster among her people if they engage in counselling services, avail of addiction and trauma treatment, attend traditional ceremonies, and work hard at parenting and community development. They also have to let go of their anger and hatred over what happened.

"The campaign's intent is not to impose guilt on Canadians," Hodgson explains. "Healing is not an Aboriginal issue, it's a Canadian issue. If we Aboriginal people want others to know and support us, it's going to happen when we get interested in Canadians."

Hodgson should have no trouble creating a special day of commemoration since she has already created a "week" in Canada. Thirteen years ago she was instrumental in creating National Addictions Awareness Week (NAAW) in November. For this she received the Canadian Substance Abuse Award for Excellence. "I finally clued into the fact that we needed to celebrate the successes, however small or large," Hodgson says today. "We had to move forward collectively. It was the first national week that was started by an Aboriginal."

In 2006, she was made an Officer of the Order of Canada, and was among 1000 women from around the world (ten of them Canadian) nominated for that year's Nobel Peace Prize. When she stepped down from the Healing our Spirit Worldwide committee, the International Indigenous Council presented her with an award of great personal significance to her: a soapstone carving of an eagle holding the Earth within its wings, and the title Vision Keeper. She continues her tireless advocacy while in retirement.

Rose Gregoire

When I interviewed Rose Gregoire in December 2005 about her important work, neither of us could have imagined that liver cancer would take her life less than two years later. She died within weeks of her diagnosis, in March, 2007, and few of us were prepared to lose a woman who, when she was alive, shared Maggie Hodgson's vision.

Gregoire's people are Innu, a First Nation closely related by language and culture to the eastern Cree. Rose grew up in Sheshatshiu, Labrador; but her people, who once travelled nomadically across the entire Quebec-Labrador peninsula, are now settled onto some fifteen reserves in those two provinces.

Rose (Nush) Gregoire was born in 1948, on an island once covered with birch trees which is now submerged in the huge reservoir that is the catch basin for the water diverted from the Mistashipu for the Churchill Falls hydroelectric project. Rose's passion for the issues facing her people made her often impatient with outsiders, but those lucky enough to get close to her found a very soft centre. Her father was a nomadic hunter whose family had been given the French surname Gregoire by a Roman Catholic missionary. Priests frequented the small trading posts that drew the Innu out from the interior each summer, and they bore gifts like donated clothing from the south, and copies of their prayer books. In 1956, Rose's parents bowed to the pressure of a priest at the North West River trading post, and left their youngest daughter behind in the fall, to attend school and learn the English language. The Innu were fast becoming a minority in their homeland and it was hard to resist the pressure to learn the language and ways of the outsiders. Rose once spoke to me of the abandonment she felt as she watched her parents and older siblings leave for the fall caribou hunt, which would keep them away from the village until Christmas. She always regretted not knowing how to do the things other Innu women, like her elder sister Tshaukuesh, could do because they had been raised in the hunting tradition.

Rose and some of her peers, including Ben Michel, Daniel Ashini, and Greg Penashue, learned English, religion, and mathematics from the resident priest and nun in Sheshatshiu, but their education seems to have come at a cost. All of these former students died in middle age, while many of their peers, raised in the bush, are still alive. In fact, the traditional diet and exercise seem to have made them stronger. Rose's elder sister, Tshaukuesh, aged 68 in March 2013, led a three-week trek into the bush that year, as she has done for decades, despite subarctic temperatures that, during the trek, frequently fell below minus 30 Celsius.

Rose's strengths were in the community, where she helped her people through the worst period of their history by acting as a go-between with government officials. By the mid-1960s, most Innu had been convinced to stay in the village during the months they would normally be hunting, so that their school-aged children could be educated. Very poorly built houses, shacks really, were constructed for them, and for a people not used to living in close proximity to others (Innu traveled in small family groups), it was a social experiment that went terribly wrong. The men had no work, there was no running water or waste disposal system, the new diet of convenience food was nutritionally inferior to the protein-rich country food, and the cash economy perverted traditional social values based on sharing. Widespread malaise and the enthusiastic sales pitch of bootleggers (some of them Provincial employees) led to widespread alcohol consumption and an epidemic of alcoholism. All this, coupled with the indignity of being cut off from their land base by the Churchill Falls hydroelectric project, created profound anomie.

Gregoire graduated from grade nine and trained to be a nursing assistant. She had four children with her non non-Innu husband Richard Adams. For most of her adult life she worked as a mediator between Innu families and the English-speaking social workers who were sent in to staunch the flood of personal tragedies that accompany an epidemic of addiction. Rose was indispensable to the young social workers who came and went with the seasons. She translated, explained kinship relationships, and advised on which families were best able to care for others' neglected children. Because Rose lacked formal training for the job she was doing, she was never paid adequately, or recognized by the social work profession. She was never offered the opportunity to get further training either. In contrast, the formally trained social workers were not required to speak the Innu language, nor did they live in the community where they could have learned how to help. Though well-intentioned, they could not develop empathic awareness under these conditions.

Rose was the person her people turned to for support. She found ways to thwart a system that tried to dismantle the culture's traditional adoption practices. She knew that when children at risk were taken from the community instead of being placed with extended family, a strong web connecting Innu families was destroyed. Rose worked as a sort of double agent, saying one thing to the social worker, another to families she was helping, by keeping familial connections as strong and intact as possible. She kept her ear to the ground, ready to respond at a moment's notice to a child and a family in need. Her home became an informal shelter for the vulnerable of her community. She never turned anyone away. By the time she died at the age of 59, Rose had become a hardened cynic concerning the Canadian social work establishment. She found it to be distant, bureaucratic, and heartless. But to any individual who sincerely wanted to ease her people's suffering, she extended her appreciation and support.

In the mid-1980s, Rose was among a group of Innu who organized protests against Canada's plan to allow European bombers to train for combat over her homeland. She hiked to the bombing range that was already in use, risking her life to protest the militarization of her beloved country. The threat died a natural death when NATO realized its low-level jet bombing strategy was too dangerous to be widely applied in combat.

By 2005, the Innu obtained more control over their health services, and Rose became case manager for the Family Treatment centre in Sheshatshiu, where she also worked as an addictions counsellor. The NECHI Institute was brought in to train community counsellors. Of the graduates, one became a lawyer, another a social worker with credentials, and others furthered their studies in other disciplines. Rose arranged for one person to travel to Alberta to attend NECHI full time for a year, and he came back to support her in the development of a land-based treatment program. She worked with men at the Labrador Correctional Facility in Happy Valley-Goose Bay, encouraging inmates to confront underlying problems—often involving childhood neglect—that led them to commit crimes. She was also interested in justice reform and became a proponent of Aboriginal sentencing circles.

Gregoire's youngest son took his life in 2006, a tragedy from which she never fully recovered. It was a cruel blow to a woman who had helped so many other families avoid similar disaster. She feared she had failed her own. Of course she had not. Suicide is tragically common in Canada's First Nations communities. Her son was a victim of his time and place.

Rose's memory has been kept alive in a very tangible way. A few months after she died, a shelter was opened in her name to help troubled adolescents, particularly those under the influence of solvents and drugs. The Rose Gregoire Safe House in Sheshatshiu can accommodate three youths at a time. Counselling is available at an adjacent group home. On the day the centre opened, Mary Mae Osmond, the former director of social health for the Sheshatshiu band council, credited Gregoire with leading the way. "I think Rose is here in spirit smiling down today," Osmond said. "This was her vision—for youth to be in a safe place."

Jack Penashue, Gregoire's nephew, said his aunt's dream was to see the Labrador Innu stand on their own. She was the person who encouraged him to go to NECHI, and then to university where he obtained a degree in social work. Rose's daughter, Janet, was present when the First Nations and the Inuit Suicide Prevention Association posthumously presented her mother with a lifetime achievement award.

"I felt like my mom was looking down and thanking us," Janet said after the ceremony, attended by 550 people. "My mom would always say 'In the future, things will change. People will get healthier, people will get stronger.' That was what my mom wanted. And I think that's what's happening."

Her mother's caring response to her community has paved the way.

Tshaukuesh Penashue

Rose was very close to her eldest sister, Tshaukuesh (Elizabeth) Gregoire Penashue, despite having been brought up apart from her. The fact that Tshaukuesh kept her Innu name, whereas Rose was known by an English one, underscores the difference in their upbringings. The sisters, though raised apart, loved one another and brought different gifts to the cause of healing their people. Tshaukuesh, raised by her parents in the bush, nudged her sister out of the comfort of working for a salary within the Provincial Government's Department of Social Services, and into the realm of political action. This happened in the mid-1980s when Canada invited NATO to create a training centre for jet bombers at Goose Bay; and to use Labrador airspace for air-to-air combat training, and its pristine land for bombing ranges. Both women knew this project would frighten families from going into the bush, cutting them off from cultural practices and the better nutrition of country foods. If Nitassinan became a playground for military air forces from around the world, caribou migration would be disrupted by the noise of bombers flying less than 30 metres above the ground.

Tshaukuesh was undaunted by the powerful forces against her as she coaxed her people towards civil disobedience. The North Atlantic Treaty Organization meant little to her. Pointing out how young Innu women with low self-esteem were already being sexually exploited by personnel at the Goose Bay military base (created by the U.S. during the second world war), she succeeded in convincing Rose that her hard work keeping Innu families together would be for naught if the government plan went ahead. The sisters rallied other women in Sheshatshiu, and later on, their men. They camped on the airport runways, putting their bodies in front of menacing jet bombers to prevent takeoff. They put up tents on bombing ranges that were already being used for live-weapons testing, making themselves human targets, and successfully disrupted flight training. Tshaukuesh was motivated by a passionate desire to protect the environment. She saw the jets, already training at

Goose Bay, as powerful assault weapons against the living creatures of her beloved homeland, Nitassinan. As her sister's empathy was for her people, Tshauskuesh's was for the animals.

In contrast to her sister's upbringing, Tshaukuesh's childhood was imbued with the spiritual practices that included showing respect for bear, caribou, porcupine. She feels a strong connection with the natural world, and communicates with the animals when she's on the land, in "nutshimit." When accepting an honorary degree from Memorial University of Newfoundland and Labrador in 2005, she made reference to this ability, while also expressing fear for how bears, beaver, muskrat and other species will suffer if more land is flooded in Labrador. These concerns certainly set her speech apart from most convocation discourse, springing as they do from historic and complex sources, bound up in the Innu cosmology of being at one with nature. Tshaukuesh's relationship with the land feeds her soul and spirit. When children began gas sniffing in her community, she started to lead an annual winter walk into the Labrador interior, bringing some of them with her, pulling a heavily laden toboggan as her parents had, setting up camp every night, and catching food along the way. She keeps Innu culture alive by telling stories in her tent and encouraging her younger companions to stay strong, as their people have always done.

Tshaukuesh also leads a summer canoe trip down what is left of the once powerful Mistashipu. Tshaukuesh has been outspoken in her opposition to a second hydro project planned for the river, a project that will flood more Innu land, kill more animals and foul more waterways. She works outside the Canadian system, using Innu culture and traditions to create change, and her arguments have been respected in her community despite agreement by a small majority to allow the development. Tshaukuesh believes her people will heal when they learn to respect their historical connection to the traditional way of life, and to the land, as exercise, good food, and a return to cultural practices prove to cure the malaise that has alienated her people from themselves. She thinks formal education is important too, but not at the expense of the Innu way of life.

Tshaukuesh has worked at the community school in various informal roles, for instance as cook, to maintain contact with the children, whom she loves to talk to about Innu traditions and their own responsibilities in the continuum of life. She is warm, maternal, and funny, so the children look forward to these interactions. The crisis of the past with widespread gas sniffing among youth has abated somewhat, but Tshaukuesh would be the first to say that it is too soon to speak of a "cure." Rapid cultural change continues to pose a challenge for her people.

Now in her late sixties, Tshaukuesh continues her political activism, persuasive still, but challenged as never before because there are more and more newcomers with hearts and minds to win over. She invites visitors to her tent, sometimes pitched on the side of the road near Sheshatshiu, or further inland while she is walking or canoeing. Inside the tent, Innu culture is brought alive in the fragrant boughs that Tshaukuesh has skilfully woven into a comfortable insulated carpet; and in the Innu language and the customs she still observes. She offers a meal of caribou, porcupine, beaver or goose, kept hot in iron frying pans set over the small wood stove, with freshly made soda bread at the ready to soak up the rich gravy. Tshaukuesh's tent is also a confessional at times, where women from the community come to talk, to purge the emotional wounds of colonialism, and to connect once again with the unique values that make the Innu distinct in Canada's mosaic. She listens with understanding, never with judgment.

Sharon Clarke

Sharon Clarke, like Rose Gregoire, has spent a lifetime working inside the help "system," but working to change it, to better serve her people. This Cree woman from Saskatchewan had been executive director of the National Native Addiction Partnership Foundation for six years when I met her in 2006. Prior to taking over the Aboriginal-run service, Clarke worked for Health Canada, visiting National Native Alcohol and Drug Abuse Prevention (NNADAP) workers and doing her best to support them. The NNADAP program employs a small retinue of 1500, mostly Aboriginal, frontline addiction workers paid by Health Canada. They work in their remote home communities, trying their best to help, despite limited training and resources. "What I learned is that there are a lot of NNADAP workers out there, putting in long hours, doing all kinds of jobs, not just working for addictions and referring people to treatment, but they're doing counselling, crisis response, corrections, looking after people on parole and not getting much money for it," Clarke told me when we spoke.

Clarke began by changing Health Canada's practice of providing programs that targeted only males aged eighteen to thirty-five. She advocated for the needs of women and younger teens. "I got involved quite a while and became interested in looking at things from a larger picture," she told me over coffee at an Edmonton Tim Horton's during a break from the HOSW conference in the summer of 2006. "I know there's a lot that needs to be done at the community level, but if you don't have supportive systems and structures in place, it's very difficult to make changes, long lasting change."

Clarke left the security of a well-paying job at Health Canada to help set up the Native Addiction Partnership Foundation. She has become a successful lobbyist at Health Canada, Canada's largest bureaucracy, because she has earned respect for saving money, and producing results.

"In a lot of ways I'm very proud of what we've done. We've managed to inspire a movement in each of the provinces for people to do something to improve NNADAP and not just in the provinces, but within Health Canada. Since we've been around, Health Canada has done more to improve NNADAP than it's done in the years before. About three years ago we began a project called 'Re-profiling Treatment Centres.' We said our treatment programs are outmoded, our treatment plans are old, and we need to inspire some renewal. We need to provide people with money so they can redesign their programs, train their staff to do the new programs, and we need to talk about the services they need in the regions. That was two years ago. We got funding for one year, then two years, and they cut the funding, but in at least three of those regions, people are re-profiling their centres with the assistance of Health Canada, so the idea has moved forward and they're doing it now."

Clarke has her own five-point plan for changing the tragic dynamics in many Aboriginal communities:

- "One: people need to feel ownership of the response—that is key," she says.
- "Two: the response has to be appropriate for the community in terms of their culture and traditions."
- Her third point is that the response has to be a multi-level one. "If you have all those agencies but they do not support what the communities are doing, "she explains, "you might as well forget it."
- Her fourth point is that training has to be appropriate. "I don't mean dumbed-down training. I mean training for people with a potential to work up to a degree. And credit for their traditional cultural knowledge."
- And the fifth: "We're also developing traditional cultural modules so that anybody who wants to work in our communities has to have that module before they go in. Health Canada employees would have to have it."

Sharon Clarke and her partners at the NNAPF have found that they are more effective working outside traditional government structures, and they do so, even though this does not pay nearly as well.

"A lot of the work that we've been doing is not funded," she told me, "but it's got us further than a lot of our funded projects, because our funded projects have very limited scope in them."

Clarke says things are improving in First Nations communities, and addiction levels are going down. But there's a lot left to do. "The partnership foundation has always felt that health goes beyond the physical. For Aboriginal people, talking about being healthy individuals means not only being alcohol and drug free, but also that we're physically and spiritually healthy," Clarke says. "We have to have that, otherwise I think that we fail in our quest, or our journey."

Sharon Clarke has left the National Native Addiction Partnership Foundation in good hands and now continues her advocacy work within the health care system, as lead consultant on Aboriginal health for the Saskatoon Health Region.

Cornelia Wieman

Dr. Cornelia Wieman is Canada's first female Aboriginal psychiatrist. She is Co-Director of the Indigenous Health Research Development Program and an Assistant Professor at the University of Toronto. These positions enable her to advocate and educate on the need for improved mental health services for Aboriginals. She is a member of the Little Grand Rapids First Nation in Manitoba, but never had the opportunity to grow up there. She was brought into the custody of the Children's Aid Society and raised by a Dutch family in Thunder Bay, Ontario. Her biological mother died of alcohol-related causes.

Wieman credits her success to the fact that her outside adoption gave her access to the same educational opportunities as most other children in Canada. The fact that children on her reserve didn't have those same opportunities deeply troubles her. "Just think of the lost potential," she tells me as we drive through the Six Nations reserve near her Ontario home. "Children on Canada's First Nations reserves receive less funding per capita for education than other children." This situation persists, despite the universal agreement that better education is key to raising the standard of life in Aboriginal communities.

"Nel" Wieman's CV underscores the point that given educational opportunities equal to those of other Canadian children, youth on First Nations reserves can go far. She completed her first year of medicine at McMaster University in 1991, finished her MD in 1993, and served as the elected President of the Medical Residents' Association in 1996. Later, she took a master's degree in biomechanics and then undertook special training in the field of psychiatry. Wieman has also studied kinesiology at the University of Waterloo and, in 1997, was elected Chair of the Native Mental Health Section of the Canadian Psychiatric Association. As an active member of the Native Physicians Association in Canada, Wieman devotes much of her time to community outreach programs in Aboriginal communities, and has played a major part in developing the Six Nations Mental Health Services in Ohsweken, Ontario, serving the Six Nations of the Grand River. She is the only licensed Aboriginal psychiatrist in Canada.

If, for Wieman, professionalization and empathy with her people ever seemed at odds, she overcame any sense of estrangement. When she was first practising community psychiatry on the Six Nations Reserve in Ontario, she recognized a mentor in Roberta Jamieson, a Mohawk lawyer, who has spent a lifetime working to advance the recognition of the rights of First Nations. Wieman's friendship with Jamieson enabled her to deepen her understanding of her Indigenous identity.

Wieman has committed herself to the cause of First Nations students. "Why do Aboriginal children drop out of school?" she asked me, from the driver's seat of her truck as we continued the tour of Six Nations, which has become her second home. "Where do kids get this attitude that, 'Well, I'll just drop out of school and I'll go on welfare'? Like to me, that's unacceptable, for kids to even think like that. They should stay in school. They should be in school. "

Wieman says support for the education of Aboriginal children is falling behind at a time when more investment than ever is required, especially in the area of health care. "I mean, the Royal Commission on Aboriginal people (1995) recommended 10,000 Aboriginal health professionals be trained in 10 years. The infrastructure to train that many health professionals just doesn't exist. There are very few schools in Canada that have answered that challenge."

Wieman's empathy is best expressed in the duty she feels to make her life and experience count towards her people's future: "I see myself as a product of seven generations past.... Things have happened that have allowed me to become who I am today. The full impact of what I accomplish in my life, in terms of Aboriginal health, will not be realized for seven generations. I clearly won't be around to see the impact of my work. I mean in some ways that's a huge responsibility—to realize that you have to work hard on behalf of future generations. You know what I mean? And I truly hope that there is a much more positive status quo for Indigenous people, not just in Canada but all over the world, in seven generations."

What better expression of caring is there than this statement of conviction? "We have been given certain gifts and we're taught that we need to use them as best we can, and work as hard as we can over the course of our lifetime, to make things better for our young people especially," Weiman told me. "I want to see improved mental and physical health status for our people. I want to see that gap closed. I would like to see much lower rates of suicide. I would like to be part of the solution."

Nympha Byrne

Nympha Byrne is a beautiful and feisty middle-aged Innu woman who has dedicated her life to fighting the scourge of addiction among her people. The empathy that drives her was apparent to me one day as we sat in a sunlit window of her house in Natuashish, Labrador. A stooped man walked past the window, with the gait of someone facing the gallows. "Poor Andrew," she said. "He doesn't realize how much of his pain is internal, and could be healed."

Byrne grew up in Davis Inlet, Labrador, a shanty town created in 1967 to house the Mushuau Innu, one of North America's last nomadic hunter-gatherer populations. Alcohol was sold from a Government-subsidized coastal boat service, and when that alcohol ran out, people made homebrew. Nothing in "Utshimassit," the Innu name for Davis Inlet (literally: "the place of the boss"), made sense to the Mushuau Innu. They were settled on an island that cut them off from the vast Labrador interior that provided their traditional diet of caribou, porcupine, beaver, arctic hare etc. Now they depended on meagre rations provided by a store that was stocked in the summertime only, with preserved foods, most of it junk, that could last over the winter. Watching her parents decline into depression and addiction led her to dedicate her working life to effecting change. Like Rose Gregoire, she worked primarily inside the system, and fought hard for services that would create internal healing on an individual by individual basis. Government departments seek big solutions that will show results in the short term, but Byrne knows that approach is not realistic. Pushing back against this agenda has been frustrating and painful for her, but she persists.

Empowering a community that no longer believes in itself is a big job. Byrne tackled it with gusto after a fire in Davis Inlet in 1992 killed 6 children, waking people up to the danger that widespread alcohol abuse posed for their children. Byrne helped lead "the people's inquiry" that encouraged the Mushuau Innu of Davis Inlet to reflect on what caused widespread alcohol abuse, and on what changes were needed to make people better. This inquiry created the local and national impetus that resulted in the more successful relocation of Byrne's people to a mainland Labrador community called Natuashish. In 1993, she joined Chief Katie Rich, and another woman, the native constable, in disrupting district court proceedings to demand that the Newfoundland judge and his officials leave town. These strong women, who stood on the airstrip when the plane carrying court officials was preparing to land, believed that jailing their troubled youth, which is all the court system was doing, was just damaging them, and failing to advance the community's health and social development. This action and the disruption of court proceedings led to jail time for Byrne and the other women ("I Followed"), but also to the awareness that reform of the province's justice system was needed, to make it fairer and more culturally appropriate for Aboriginals. The women believed a restorative justice model would do more good by offering help rather than punishment for perpetrators who committed most crimes while under the influence of alcohol.

Byrne's creative abilities, and love of her culture, are demonstrated in a book she co-edited with St. John's-based writer and editor, Camille Fouillard entitled *It's Like the Legend: Innu Women's Voices*. Here she describes the years she spent with her parents and grandparents, living in tents, cleaning and preparing animals for food and clothing, listening to Innu legends, and feeling cared for and secure with the adults around her. The prevailing social order was thousands of years old. With the move to Davis Inlet, that social order fell apart and it seemed to her that her parents turned on their children whenever they were drinking ("I Am").

Despite incidents of binge drinking and gas sniffing during her teenage years, Byrne avoided becoming addicted (233-4). Alcoholism has resulted in some terrifying events for Byrne's extended family. In the winter of 2005 her cousin, Debbie Rich, died from exposure to the extreme cold (minus 30C). Rich passed out while binge drinking and by the time she was missed from home, it was too late to save her. Byrne says that grief from losses like this and the many suicides that have occurred in her community, contributes to increasing alcohol and drug use. Even empathy can be ineffectual in the face of hopelessness.

"They go back over the 'I'll never forget that,' 'This is what's happening to me,'" she says. "And a lot of times we don't go to the future and think about the future. Like we don't deal with grief. People started drinking because they didn't deal with the loss of a loved one. Another thing: when you were abused physically or sexually in the past, you were too ashamed to talk about it. And I think that it does take a long time for people to get well in those situations."

Byrne, now the mother of four grown children, fought all odds to get an education and training in addictions while raising her family, but with the help of the NECHI institute, has become a fully-trained addiction counsellor employed by Health Canada as part of the Labrador Innu Comprehensive Healing Strategy. This multi-million dollar ten-year plan was created by the Federal Government to help the Innu of Sheshatshiu and Davis Inlet. It included a commitment to relocate the Mushuau Innu to Natuashish, closer to their hunting territory, and should have served as a template for healing other communities similarly affected. But it became a template for something else. The largely non-Aboriginal Health Canada staff based themselves first in Halifax; then, after opposition from Byrne and others, they relocated to Goose Bay, but refused to get closer to the Aboriginal communities they were supposed to be serving. Byrne found herself shoe-horned into a very rigid bureaucratic model that was big on form, but small on substance. She was the only Innu-speaking staff member, yet she was not allowed to work on the ground in Natuashish where she was known and trusted. It seemed that the institution was threatened by the possibilities of her identification with clients and promoted a kind of professionalism that precluded closeness.

"Everything I try to do, it seems like there's red tape at Health Canada," she told me, "and that frustrates me. When you have all the training, you want to be able to use that training. A lot of times I'm ashamed to say that I'm a Health Canada worker because I see kids on the road [sniffing gas] outside my house, and I'm not allowed to counsel people. Yes, I can do presentations, but there are times when people who trust you just need to talk to you and you can't talk to them. I find that really painful. I find that really hard."

Fortunately, Byrne did not always follow the rules. One evening while she was on a visit home to Natuashish, a young man came to her door in the wee hours of the morning, drunk and distraught. He had broken up with his girlfriend and was threatening suicide. Byrne knew that in a community where emotional resilience is threadbare, this was no idle threat. After some reflection, she decided this was the test of whether she could do better by being "unprofessional" and letting empathy be her guide. Through the rest of the night, she talked with the young man.

All the while, she tried to get him to dream of a future. After exploring his dreams and the possibilities for realizing them, he left her house more sober than he had been in years. "When I see him now," she tells me smiling, "he always nods at me and never speaks of that night, but I know I helped him, because he's not drinking now. He went back to school. I think he's happy."

Nympha Byrne knows there are no easy fixes. "We can't change people. They have to want to do it themselves—quit drinking or drugs or sniffing. We can't do it for them. Like sometimes I see social workers telling someone to go to treatment so they can bring their kids home. That's the wrong kind of pressure. You're pushing them, but if they're not ready it's just not going to work."

Things have improved a lot for the Mushuau Innu since Byrne's family moved to Davis Inlet in 1967. Alcohol is now banned in her community. The ban isn't a solution, but it will provide a reprieve while people come to terms with their future. "Well, it's going to take a long time," Byrne says. "It's not going to happen tomorrow or next month or next year. It's a long process to get well. We have to understand where they're coming from. When you're working with people you can't just say quit. You can't do that."

She explains her relationship with Health Canada in this way: "They say they'll walk with us and hold our hand. I say walk with us, but don't hold our hand. We're not helpless." Byrne's respect and understanding work to strengthen, not to subject.

Berma Bushie

You have only to take supper with someone like Berma Bushie, as I did one evening, to know that these frontline women making social change in Aboriginal communities are anything but helpless. She and I sat on the balcony of a restaurant overlooking the Saskatchewan river in Edmonton, and between courses, she told me about her work, and her life, in such a way that I began to feel I was in the presence of someone holy. People like Bushie, I've learned, get their strength and commitment from empathy, which is a quality highly valued in Aboriginal society. Bushie needed both strength and commitment when she set out, with others, to eradicate incest from her traumatized community. The Community Holistic Circle Healing (CHCH) approach was developed by Bushie and friends on the Anishinabe reserve of Wanipigow ("Hollow Water" in English), a First Nations reserve on the eastern shores of Lake Winnipeg.

"Community Holistic Circle Healing is a movement that will take us back to reclaiming the traditional structures of the Anishinabe people," she told me, "and will put each individual family and the whole community back in balance. By that, I mean that we will be responsible and accountable to each other for the wellness of each individual and each child in that community."

The idea was born from crisis. In the mid 1970s, a group of women on the reserve, through heart to heart conversations, discovered a harrowing fact: each of them had been the victim of incest. They invited other women to open up, and soon realized the full extent of child sexual abuse in their community. Bushie's own experience was typical.

"My grandfather played a game when he was alone with me," she says, "a game that left him with an erection after he tricked me into fondling him. It left me with a great deal of shame and guilt. My grandfather learned this game at residential school. I was unable to develop appropriate boundaries around men and this put me at great risk when I was a teenager and a young woman."

Bushie and her friends strategized, and then invited some trusted men to their meetings, small circles at first, then the meetings grew larger and larger until it was clear that this history of intergenerational sexual abuse was contributing to a lot of suicides and substance abuse in their community.

As we sat on a terrace overlooking the picturesque Saskatchewan river, I asked Bushie what she meant when she told me, "We have come out of the darkness."

"Well if you had seen my community back in the seventies, where there was so much chaos, and visible chaos," she told me, "you would have written us off. And we have come out of that. We have made change in the community. We are able to protect our children once again and we can protect the women. We can hold the abusers, both male and female, accountable for their actions. It was a long hard struggle, but we did it. And it continues to be a struggle. It's not linear from A to B. It's not like a straight line. It's more like a cycle. The chaos is just at our doorsteps. It's always something we have to work at, all the time. The whole community has to do its part in making sure children are protected and women are protected."

In a nutshell, what happens in the CHCH approach Bushie and her colleagues created is that an accusation of sexual abuse is taken to police. The accused must then plead guilty or not guilty. A not-guilty plea means the accusation will be brought to court. If the accused pleads guilty and agrees to take part in the CHCH approach, there is a five-year grace period from the courts before criminal charges are laid. During this grace period, the accused must participate in a number of circles involving community members, as well as receiving one-on-one therapy with a professional counsellor. The first circle is with immediate family of the accused, where an acknowledgement of the crime is made, and: Bushie says this step is lot harder for the accused than facing a judge in a courtroom. At each step of the way, the circle widens until the abuser is ready to face the entire community in an open meeting and speak of his or her actions, the hurt caused, and the proposed remedy.

Meanwhile the victim has also been encircled by loved ones and professionals. When he or she is ready to face the abuser, who must be ready to make a sincere apology, an important part of the process has been achieved. It takes five years to treat the abuser. Any backsliding will trigger criminal charges. Once the professionals are satisfied rehabilitation is complete, the abuser is accepted back into the community, with a formal feast, and a release from criminal charges. Besides showing compassion for offenders caught up in intergenerational dysfunction, the "outing" of the offender helps prevent repeat offences because the whole community is now aware of the risk. This is a highly simplified account of a very complex and ingenious process.

Bushie wants people to understand how the cycle of sexual abuse got its start: "At one time our nation was self-sustaining. Totally responsible for itself. We had no expectations of being cared for by the outside. And now with the impact of colonization, assimilative practices, residential schools—all those processes that came into play to eliminate our people, that's part of our history. No one else is going to make things right for us. That's something that we have to do for ourselves, regardless of how it was done, when it was done. The fact is, today we have no choice but to go back to our traditional ways and our traditional structures. We have to bring the lodges back. We have to bring the languages back. So there's a lot of work. Really it is a lot of work. Every one of us is responsible for making sure that the next generation is given the opportunity to live a full life."

"What do you want Canadian people to understand?" I asked her.

"I think the Canadian public needs to understand the long term impacts of colonization. They need to understand the practices used by government, and by churches, to totally wipe out the Aboriginal nations. And I think that people need to understand that we've come a long way, and that our struggle should be celebrated, and not be ridiculed. Just that kind of acceptance, and that kind of acknowledgement, I think, would go a long way to make the struggle less painful. Because we all recognize that this is our fight, and we will do it. We are up for the challenge, and we will do it, and that's all I ask for, and I think that's all a lot of Aboriginal people ask for."

"The Hollow Water program was the first study done in Canada, on the econnomic benefits of treating sexual abuse," Maggie Hodgson says. "The study is touted across Canada and internationally." Despite proving the economic and social benefits of such a program, CHCH has barely been funded adequately for its own community, let alone as a model to be replicated in other Canadian Aboriginal communities. Bushie and Hodgson see this as a tragic oversight. "A traditionally based treatment program for sex offenders and their families like CHCH can save lives and taxpayers the costs of prison incarceration," Bushie says.

But who is listening?

Mary Sillett

The first Inuit woman in Canada to receive a university degree is also firmly committed to helping her people, even if it meant leaving the bright lights of the nation's capital, Ottawa, for the isolation of a tiny Labrador hamlet called Hopedale. When I visited Mary Sillett in 2006, she was Hopedale's mayor. She had come home after a career in Ottawa that culminated with her work as a commissioner for the Royal Commission on Aboriginal Peoples in 1995. Before that, Sillett worked in Ottawa for Pauktuutit, the national Inuit women's organization, and with the Inuit Tapirissat of Canada, the political organization representing Canada's 50,000 Inuit.

Sillett's university degree was, not surprisingly, in social work, a field of study that generally attracts empathic people. Her parents couldn't look after her because they were alcoholic, so she was raised by her grandparents from infancy. Her grandfather had small jobs working on the former U.S. base, CFB Goose Bay. Her grandparents also drank heavily at times, neglecting her. She knew she was cherished, but as the eldest of a growing family, she became caretaker of the younger children. She credits the mentorship of the local Moravian Church (Moravian) minister, William Peacock, with helping her soar to the top of her classes once she had mastered the English language. Sillett says getting an education gave her the edge she needed to break out of the addiction cycle that plagued her elders. She now wants to help as many children as possible get that same chance. She also wants more investment in early childhood education.

"If you ever go to the daycare centre, that's a really positive place. It's warm there, it's colourful. You have day-care workers who have been trained to really respect the children, who are professional on the job, and I've always thought this prepares the children for a more positive experience at school. It's important to create very positive environments for children who aren't doing well at home." Sillett continues: "I think that if children receive an education, then they can make other choices. I lived in that kind of a home, everyone in there was drunk except the kids, and I was the oldest girl."

Understanding adults outside the home were a lifeline for the young Inuit girl. "I remember the thing that saved me is that ever since I was very young, there have been people outside of my home who were extremely strong and they were influential in the community and they were always there for me.... We have to understand if a child is not doing well at home, at least you can be kind to them sometimes. Teachers can encourage the students. I mean they don't realize what an impact they can have later on. If those kids do well, it was because of all the kindnesses they met on the way."

Mary Sillett reflects on the testimonies she heard while serving on the Royal Commission: "One of the issues that affected me personally were the stories of children who went to residential schools. Those were heartbreaking, heart-wrenching stories and you hear a lot about that still."

Sillett puts her social work degree to good use in Hopedale, working to ensure the children of her community get the best education possible, without having to leave. The political sphere is also important. Labrador Inuit signed a self-government agreement with the Federal and Provincial Governments in 2005, creating a territory called Nunatsiavut. As Clerk of the Nunatsiavut Assembly, Sillett is helping her people move forward politically towards the independence that made them strong and self-sufficient in the past. Meanwhile, Canada's Truth and Reconciliation Commission on Indian Residential Schools is holding public hearings across the country over the next few years, hoping to engage the rest of Canada in the healing efforts. Sillett hopes that non-Aboriginal Canadians will become more engaged in the process.

Phyllis Chelsea

Phyllis Chelsea will probably attend a Truth and Reconciliation hearing when the Commission holds a special event in British Columbia in 2013. She is a survivor of a residential school and the experience haunts her till this day. Sadly, her educational experiences were not as positive as Mary Sillett's. All the same, empathy has helped her to turn a childhood nightmare into motivation to help others.

Chelsea, a Shuswap woman in her late sixties from Alkali Lake, British Columbia, is the co-star of a film that is widely shown at addiction recovery centres throughout North America, and even at the Betty Ford Centre in California, but she is little known in Canada. It is not an exaggeration to say she and her husband Andy are the most famous people in North America's Aboriginal sobriety movement, but they have done their work with very little financial support from mainstream Canadian society. When I met Phyllis in the summer of 2006, she had just been diagnosed with severe osteoporosis. She could not afford to follow her doctor's orders. "He told me to drink orange juice and milk," she says, "and eat lots of cheese. I can't afford those things." It is a shock for anyone who knows the story of the contribution the Chelseas have made, to find them living in such poverty.

Phyllis has a harsh dry cough that she believes is a result of the moulds growing in her small bungalow on the outskirts of her reserve, Alkali Lake, now known by its Shuswap name, Estemec. The Chelseas' home has been condemned because of the mould, but they cannot move because they have paid off the mortgage on their house, and it has no resale value. It was constructed in a substandard way, like so many houses on reserves, by contractors paid for by Canada's Central Mortgage and Housing Corporation.

The film that made the Chelseas famous is called *For the Honour of All* (1985). It is a docudrama based on the true story of what Phyllis did in 1972 after her daughter Ivy decided she preferred staying with her grandmother, who did not drink alcohol, to staying with her partying parents. Love for her child encouraged Phyllis to stop drinking, and her husband soon followed. The couple then made sobriety in Aboriginal communities their life's work. They began with their own reserve. Phyllis seized authority from the social worker with her husband's help. Andy was Chief at the time, and threatened the government agent with force after he insulted Phyllis, saying she was too stupid to put in place her plan to divert social welfare payments into store credit so families would use the money more responsibly. This is exactly what Phyllis did, and it worked. Before long, the couple had thrown a corrupt priest, and a shopkeeper who continued to bootleg alcohol after it was banned, out of the community. Phyllis replaced welfare money with food vouchers to help enforce the ban since people then had no cash to buy bootlegged alcohol. The couple confronted drinking parents at parties that went long into the night, asking why they were not with their children. They personally alerted family and friends of children at risk, asking for help to protect them.

The Chelseas' tough love approach, coupled with the control they had of over reserve services, eventually led to a sobriety ethic that informs life on the Estemec reserve today. What was accomplished is a source of pride, but serious problems remain: dire poverty, mouldy houses, and a great deal of anger at the "DIA," the Department of Indian Affairs (an older name for the government department now known as Aboriginal Affairs and Northern Development Canada) which the people feel keeps them in a state of dependence.

Phyllis has received public acknowledgement for many of her other achievements. She has an Order of Canada, and in 2005 The University of British Columbia presented her with an Honorary Doctor of Laws degree, citing the following contributions:

> Phyllis fostered abused and underprivileged children. Her home became a haven for dozens of children seeking respite from dangerous home environments. She instituted local services to replace those provided by agencies unfamiliar with local traditions. She had the previously forbidden Shuswap language revived and recognized as a credit for university entrance at the University of British Columbia. And she was the moving force behind the development of an Elementary School on the Alkali Lake Reserve. Because of her efforts, Alkali Lake is now a model for other native communities across Canada. Her work is recognized not only in Canada but also in the United States and Australia. Phyllis Chelsea's commitment as a mother, grandmother and community leader, has given inspiration, hope and support to all who have known her. (Order of British Columbia, 1990).

Phyllis did not find it at all strange that a young Innu man I know wanted me to bring back some sweet-grass and sage, wild plants common where she lives, but foreign to the Innu homeland. She gets many such requests. They are part of the cleansing ceremonies that have become integral to the Aboriginal addiction recovery movement. I was also asked to bring back Phyllis Chelsea's autograph, which I did, making sure I had a copy for myself.

Katie Rich

Nympha Byrne has dedicated a poem to her cousin Katie Rich in *It's Like the Legend*. It is called "Almighty Woman" and is a tribute that could apply to so many of the empathic and empowered women I met during the course of this research. Rich is an Innu woman capable of incredible strength but also incredible tenderness, especially for the most vulnerable. Her tenderness is best seen in the hand-sewn moccasins that wrap around the feet of a brain-damaged child named Preston whom she began to raise when he was left behind in hospital by his immature teenage mother. The mom had been told Preston was damaged before he was born by the alcohol she consumed during pregnancy, but Katie believes Preston's damage is genetic because she remembers a similar child born before the scourge of alcohol came upon her people. She took Preston home and cared for him, as she had done for her own seven children (Jack, Rich and Byrne 258).

The Presentation nuns ran a mission in Davis Inlet in the 1970s, and seeing Katie's potential, encouraged her to go to St. John's at the age of thirteen to finish school. The results were mixed. Katie learned to be more comfortable in an English-speaking world, but felt horribly out of place with her classmates. "No matter how much mascara, blush or lipstick I put on my face, I didn't look right," she writes in *It's Like the Legend*. "Realizing that I couldn't be a White person, I had to accept the way I was" (Jack, Rich and Byrne 258).

The relative affluence of St. John's showed Rich just how far she had to go to put her people on an equal footing. In 1992, she was the first woman to be elected chief of Davis Inlet. She led the People's Inquiry that brought the community together after the deadly fire that killed six children, and made recommendations that began community change. In December 1993, she led the group (including Nympha Byrne) that evicted Judge Robert Hyslop from the community because his court only incarcerated Innu youth; it didn't help them to heal. Her actions and those of the other women stimulated reform of the justice system for Labrador's Aboriginal communities. Rich was also instrumental in persuading the federal government to relocate her people to the more suitable site, called Natuashish. She was given a Woman of Courage Award by the National Action Committee on the Status of Women in 1995, and is currently band manager in Natuashish. She was responsible for the campaign that led to a plebiscite making Natuashish a dry community (one where alcohol is banned). Rich, like Berma Bushie, knows that recovery is not a straight line, and that there is a great deal more to be done before Innu youth have a positive vision of the future.

Nympha Byrne's tribute poem to Katie, called "Almighty Woman," could equally be addressed to many other Aboriginal women in Canada. Fittingly too, it encompasses what empathy means to the women whose will to effect change is celebrated in this chapter.

You are the strength for your people
And your land...
you've been crying for so long,
you've washed your face with your tears,
letting your hair grow
for your strength,
braiding your hair
for your proudness,
sharing your spirit for kindness.
You will be a legend
to your people.
You will empower your community...
you free your spirit for your beliefs. (252-3)

[1]Not to be confused with Inuit, a people whose language is unrelated to that of Innu and other First Nations people. First Nation is an umbrella term for a myriad of cultures that are indigenous to Canada, but are not Inuit or Métis.

WORKS CITED

Byrne, Nympha. "Almighty Woman." *It's Like the Legend: Innu Women's Voices*. Eds. Camille Fouillard and Nympha Byrne. Charlottetown, PEI: Gynergy Books, 2000. 252-53 . Print.

Nympha Byrne. "I Am." *It's Like the Legend: Innu Women's Voices*. Eds. Camille Fouillard and Nympha Byrne. Charlottetown, PEI: Gynergy Books, 2000. 219-23 . Print.

Nympha Byrne. "I Followed." *It's Like the Legend: Innu Women's Voices*. Eds. Camille Fouillard and Nympha Byrne. Charlottetown, PEI: Gynergy Books, 2000. 246-51 . Print.

Canadian Alliance on Mental Illness and Mental Health. Web. 24 Nov. 2010.

Community Holistic Healing Circle (CHCH). Web. 24 Nov. 2010.

First Nations and Inuit Suicide Prevention Association of Québec and Labrador. Web. 24 Nov. 2010.

For the Honour of All: The People of Alkali Lake. P. Chelsea and A. Chelsea. 1985. Video. British Columbia, Canada.

Fouillard, Camille and Nympha Byrne, eds. *It's Like the Legend: Innu Women's Voices*. Charlottetown, PEI: Gynergy Books, 2000. Print.

Healing Our Spirit Worldwide. Web. 24 Nov. 2010.

Jack, Justine Noah, Katie Rich, and Nympha Byrne. "In Our Culture We Don't Sign Papers." *It's Like the Legend: Innu Women's Voices.* Eds. Camille Fouillard and Nympha Byrne. Charlottetown, PEI: Gynergy Books, 2000. 254-63. Print.

McCormick, Rod M. "Aboriginal Traditions in the Treatment of Substance Abuse." *Canadian Journal of Counselling and Psychotherapy* 34.1 (2000): 25-32. Print.

National Action Committee on the Status of Women. Web. 24 Nov. 2010.

National Native Addictions Partnership Foundation. Web. 24 Nov. 2010.

National Native Alcohol and Drug Abuse Program (NNADAP). Web. 24 Nov. 2010.

NECHI Training, Research, Health Promotions Institute. Web. 24 Nov. 2010.

Order of British Columbia. Web. 24 Nov. 2010.

Wadden, Marie. *Nitassinan: The Innu Struggle to Reclaim their Homeland.* Vancouver: Douglas and McIntyre, 1991. Print.

Wadden, Marie. *Where the Pavement Ends: The Aboriginal Recovery Movement and the Urgent Need for Reconciliation.* Vancouver: Douglas and McIntyre, 2008. Print.

5. The Presence of Motherhood in the Absence of Children

Negotiating Infertility in Ireland

JILL ALLISON

> *That my agency is riven with paradox does not mean it is*
> *impossible. It means only that paradox is the condition of its*
> *possibility.* —Judith Butler (*Undoing Gender* 3)

THE "PRESENCE OF ABSENCE" is embodied paradox: through these words I came to understand a contradictory sense of loss that accompanies infertility, particularly for women.[1] The simple but powerful turn of phrase was used creatively by one woman who generously shared her story with me, about trying, and failing, to conceive a child. Even in an era of increasingly complex biomedical technologies aimed at assisting reproduction, the meaning of *being* a mother remains linked to some relationship with a child. It is the range of possible permutations in that relationship—social and/or physiological—that are subject to constant revision and re-organization under rubrics of biological, social, adoptive, genetic, foster, and surrogate among others. However, for women in Ireland, motherhood has also become part of a subjective sense of political and social personhood which exists prior to *becoming* a mother.

Women who experience infertility do not only grapple with the implications of a physiological inability to conceive children; they also experience a profound sense of loss around the inability to perform a motherhood identity they feel is already part of themselves as women. This sensation of conjoined loss, of the ideals of both motherhood and womanhood, is expressed by many as an embodied absence: a constant presence of something that is not. For some infertile women, the presence of absence also provides a means of laying claim to an ideal, resisting the perception that they have failed as women, and resisting that sense of disorder and embodied revulsion that Julia Kristeva calls "abjection." Their claims to a motherhood identity are creative and pragmatic but still rooted in the social merger between the subjective identity of woman and the reproductive body of mother effected through political, bio-medical, scientific and religious discourses in Ireland.

This chapter maps out the historical evolution of this conflation of "woman" and "mother" in Ireland and a history in which fertility, procreativity and maternity come to be embodied in the subjectivity of womanhood. I will describe how the "presence of absence," as an aesthetic sensation of complex loss, provides a space in which those who are struggling with infertility can articulate or resist medical, social, and subjective meanings in light of the privilege accorded to fertility and motherhood.[2] Motherhood is always bound to social and moral ideals but these have intensified in their political meaning in Ireland where gender has been employed in the service of defining nationalist identity and constructing the borderlines of nationhood itself. For those who have embodied an ideal that they cannot realize, there is a compelling need to acknowledge loss from within a construction of motherhood they have embraced.

Over the course of eighteen months in Ireland, I conducted extensive, unstructured interviews with forty women (sometimes with their partners), and in some cases met with them several times. The narratives I collected between 2004 and 2005 form the basis of the research on which this chapter is based. Many of the women I met, spoke to, and interviewed used their experiences with infertility as a means of challenging the normative expectations of Irish social and political life. But for some, I will argue, this challenge comes in the form of resistance, not to the social expectations or ideals themselves, but to the failure of others to acknowledge that infertile women experience and embody the role, identity and subjectivity of motherhood, albeit in an unconventional way.

The presence of absence thus provides an opportunity to examine the significance accorded to conception, pregnancy, and motherhood in Ireland's present in spite of recent social and economic changes. Infertility draws into sharp relief the often conflicted and complex origins of empathy. The difficulty arises most acutely, Ruth Behar suggests, in distinguishing among empathy, pity, and self-awareness in the effort to understand and represent the pain of others (21-22). The stories of women who struggle to conceive are produced and narrated from a complex set of experiences in which empathy fosters creativity and a wider interpretive frame for defining motherhood. And yet, as I will show, the merging of motherhood and womanhood in Ireland has left little, if any, space for empathy toward women who do not conceive. But how can the sensations women feel be represented accurately and fully? The presence of absence has provided a means to develop the ethnographic empathy necessary to foster an understanding.

The medicalization of infertility is also steeped in paradox. The classic definition used by medical practitioners is a failure to conceive after a year of unprotected sexual intercourse. Thus its very meaning employs a kind of paradox since infertility, as a medical diagnosis or condition, is not defined by something that occurs in the body, but rather by something that does not. As a disease phenomenon, infertility has been effectively constituted by the very medical treatments that are now available to address the physiological challenges that can (and often do) occur in human reproduction (Sandelowski and de Lacey 34-35). One in six couples in Ireland will fall under the classic definition of infertility, and while not all will require medical intervention, all will have become aware of the social symptoms and contradictory meanings of their inability to conceive.

During the research period, there were nine clinics in Ireland providing a variety of services aimed at assisting conception. For those who seek fertility treatment, the intensity with which infertility is medicalized objectifies the corporeal while failing to address the embodied social suffering and loss. The experiences of my participants paralleled those described in other studies in the U.S. and Europe. People felt swept up or overwhelmed by medical and scientific rhetoric, described by Sarah Franklin as that of "helping nature" (96), or being "proactive" and feeling obligated to try or to continue treatment (Becker 212; Franklin 170). Medicalization and the use of assisted reproduction technologies (ART) perpetuate the ideal of fertility, conception and birth as a norm for all women, offering no challenges to the construct of the ideal family and its relationship to political and social stability in Ireland. This point is particularly profound when contextualized against the fact that the clinical success rate for *in vitro* fertilization (IVF) runs only at about 15-20 percent in most clinics (CAHR 106).

The roots of a moral ideal embodied in motherhood are also bound to the historical importance of motherhood as a site for the inculcation of Catholic values in the family (Inglis 192-99). A contested but nonetheless influential moral, pro-life, and Catholic national identity has been forged on the basis of pronatalist reproductive politics (Conrad 72; Smyth 2). At the same time, the Catholic Church's position against IVF seems to work against the prospects of conceiving for infertile couples, and it contributes to the virtual stonewalling of attempts to regulate access to assisted reproduction technology (McDonnell and Allison 824-828).

Against this backdrop, I explore how subjectivity and the embodiment of moral and political ideals frame the social logic and norms of reproduction in Ireland. I begin with a brief historical description of the social, religious, and political underpinnings of both subjectivation and embodied values in Ireland that constitute the "presence of absence." This affords a way into the conceptual paradox by which infertile women can embody social ideals and values while resisting the need to define those ideals in traditional or conventional terms. I will argue that this kind of agency and resistance emerges from within the norms generated by the Irish social and political framework, in such a way that reproductive ideals are both affirmed and reshaped to accommodate an inability to conceive.

I draw on several examples beginning with "Elsa's"[3] artwork around the embodied ideals of motherhood and then incorporate other representations of a presence of absence. These examples illustrate a need for some women to "produce" something tangible, concrete, and enduring from the presence of absence in their lives. While their stories of infertility can be read as examples of the presence of embodied disability and dysfunction, loss and grief, social exclusion, moral contradiction and political ambiguity, they are also stories of reflexive and reflective action and powerful insight. Through their own explorations of the sensation of loss, they often construct an alternative meaning of motherhood, thus contributing to the wave of social change in the current definition of the ideal family in Ireland.

AESTHETICS AND THE EMBODIED SUBJECT: RESISTANCE FROM WITHIN

Any discussion of the subject identity that merges motherhood and womanhood must also include the significance of the body since it is through the body that fertility and infertility are defined and experienced. Michel Foucault's emphasis on the body as an object of disciplinary discourses has been taken up and extended in feminist and post-structuralist literature to include the production of particular bodies in relation to subjectivity and difference. João Guilherme Biehl, Byron Good, and Arthur Kleinman note that while "modes of subjectivation" are produced through institutional relations and discourses that shape the subject, "subjectivity is not just the outcome of social control or the unconscious; it also provides the ground for subjects to think through their circumstances and feel through their contradictions... [as] the means of shaping sensibility" (14). Saba Mahmood follows Foucault's analysis of the "paradox of subjectivation" in which "the very processes and conditions that secure a subject's subordination are also the means by which she becomes a self-conscious identity and agent" (17). Similarly, Judith Butler draws on Foucault's work in her own feminist analysis, in which she locates the capacity for agency within the workings of power rather than outside them. Butler argues that "agency does not consist in denying the condition of [one's] constitution" but rather " is opened up by the fact that [we] are constituted by a social world [we] never chose" (3). Our sense of ourselves as subjects then, is always in tension with its origins.

Equally significant, our capacity for engaging critically with the world around us is impacted by the sensations connected to inhabiting a body we did not choose, particularly in relation to health and well-being or illness and disease. Subjectivity and subjectivation are further complicated by the significance of the body as a fundamental interface which is "the very grounds of subjectivity or experience in the world"; at the same time, illness and pain make it "a disordered agent of experience" (Good 116). This becomes especially significant when political and social values are embodied and subjectivity is condensed in the bodily or "biological" capacity associated with health and function, as is the case with womanhood, motherhood, and conception in Ireland. Julia Kristeva describes another kind of disorder related to the body in "the abject,"[4] where there are uncertainties around boundaries and "what disturbs identity, system, order," when a subject "finds that the impossible constitutes its very *being*" (232, Kristeva's emphasis). An inability to conceive constitutes a threat of abjection in which women experience the body as liminal, out of order, and frightening in its failure to perform what is biologically fundamental and socially anticipated and expected.

Seeing illness itself as an "aesthetic object," Byron Good explores "the disjuncture between disease as an object or condition of a physical body, as it is popularly (and medically) conceived, and disease as a presence in a life or in a social world" (166). He emphasizes that illness and disability are not only experiences of the body as a scientific or political object; experiences of illness both produce and provide the grounds for social, political, spiritual, and gendered notions of self. Following Good, I use aesthetics to describe the complex link between sensation and response that is bound to the embodiment of cultural, social, religious, and political values. As it applies to health, Good (169) suggests this link shapes not only the experience and perception of bodily well- being or illness but also their expression. I draw on work in medical anthropology that incorporates "common graces and embodied values" with "sensibilities that contribute to the sensory ground" in which bodily well-being or illness is experienced" (Desjarlais 14). Desjarlais emphasizes the importance of the "aesthetics of everyday life" which govern the way the body expresses, moves, and feels; and he argues that "[s]ince these ways of being are not free floating but are driven by social dynamics that influence the very marrow of experience, their political underpinnings must be assessed" (14).

A growing feminist and medical social science literature takes up the relationship between embodiment and aesthetics often associated with altering or "producing" particular types of bodies that reflect a cultural, spiritual, or political ideal. Susan Bordo describes how slimness as an aesthetic representation of a feminine ideal is embodied in anorexia nervosa while Janice Boddy describes genital infibulation, in *Wombs and Alien Spirits*, as the embodiment of cultural values that emphasize enclosed or bounded spaces as safe and moral among Northern Sudanese women (55-60; 252). Boddy argues that aesthetic changes in bodies in conjunction with "continuous monitoring" ensure that "women become the embodiments of morality and local tradition" (Spirits 8). In both these cases the body is a site of production as well as a very material and aesthetic representation of social values.

In the stories that follow, the body is the medium through which material and aesthetic aspects of a reproductive or motherhood identity are felt and expressed: infertility disrupts the perception of order in the body, as constituted through medical, religious and state discourses. This disorder is part of a productive dynamic of social failure experienced as interrupted subjectivity in the woman/mother imperative that is a constant and enduring presence. The extent to which the socially constituted norms of fertility and conception are embodied is thus most evident in the stories of those who understand their failure to conceive as a function of disorder in their reproductive bodies, not simply as an objective medical or scientific fact but as a social disorder as well. As one woman describes it, becoming a mother through conception, pregnancy and birth, "was not something she had to do, it was something she had to *be*." So powerful is the sense of *being* for women that it is the loss of a sense of self as much as the loss of "conceptualized" (rather than conceived) children that is profoundly painful. An understanding of the power of this subject position requires us to engage with the meaning of reproductive bodies in shaping political, social, and individual selves. The depth and meaning of such sensations can be apprehended only through empathy—a deeper conceptualization of the presence of absence.

CONSTITUTING THE WOMAN/MOTHER PARADIGM IN IRELAND

Jane: *Okay. So I grew up I suppose in a sort of typical Catholic family.... And probably what has become obvious to me in the last year is that it was always assumed that you would become a mother. It was just there. It was never questioned and the biggest thing I have recognized is I can't remember anybody ever saying there was a choice about it. It was just a fact that you understood that you would become a mother.* (2005 Interview)

Embodiment can also embrace and reflect elements of a nationalist or cultural identity. Angela Martin describes how a kind of mimesis is at work in Ireland through which "embodied cultural aesthetics" are shaped by the importance of the Virgin Mary as a feminine ideal through imitative social practices (69). By enacting this ideal, Martin argues, women have been made to perform the "labor of representation" in Irish nationalism (67). Such representations exist in "the metonymic and metaphoric associations between women and Mary constructed through local familial and devotional practices [and] ... [n]otions of ideal motherhood and the discursive regulation of feminine bodies"(69). She suggests that women are conditioned, through bodies, spaces, and the responsibility for representation, by symbolism perpetuated by the Marian cults and apparitions of the Virgin Mary which continue to convey powerful messages of the ideals of motherhood. Indeed in many stories that follow, women have incorporated the iconic representations of the Virgin Mary and other biblical references to motherhood and/or infertility into their narratives.

Women's reproductive bodies have become the site for many claims of moral identity and political autonomy in the Irish nation and state. Multiple debates have centered on the issue of choice with respect to fertility control. Access to contraception, abortion, and even divorce have been the regulatory gateposts that feminist scholars such as Katherine Conrad and Emily Martin argue have made Irish women unequally responsible for representing the ideals of a nationalist identity based on morality (Conrad 70; Martin 67). The many references to a feminine "Mother Ireland" in historical and literary writings lead Martin to argue that "women have symbolically represented the purity and tradition of the country" (67). The political and social meanings around fertility control in the context of the ideal Irish family also resonate for infertile women whose struggles for reproductive choice run against the grain of popular understandings (and some feminist debates). The political banter about choice often fails to recognize the struggles of infertile women and men who are seeking the means to engage with conception rather than prevent it.

The meanings associated with fertility, birth, and motherhood were elaborated in powerful representations of women in Irish mythology and Goddess worship in pre-Celtic times (Condren xix). These meanings yielded to the rise of patriarchy, coincidental with early Christianity, when fertility and reproduction constituted a social power that must be contained, rationalized, and ultimately dominated. In more recent history, the Irish state, post-independence, incorporated Catholic social teaching in an "approach whereby the State, even if not acting strictly at the behest of church elites, came to legislate in a way that is extremely mindful of the requirements of Catholic tenets of morality" (Byrne *et al.* xi). Reproduction and sexuality became the focus of this regulatory program and the ideal of women as mothers became increasingly central to its implementation.[5]

The Constitution of 1937 establishes the fundamental significance of the family as a social and political unit in Ireland, and Article 41 in particular sets the tone for the position of women in Irish social, economic, and political life.

> The State recognizes that by her life within the home, woman gives to the State a support without which the common good cannot be achieved.... The State shall endeavor to ensure that mothers shall not be obligated by economic necessity to engage in labor to the neglect of their duties in the home.

The virtual conflation of "woman" and "mother" in passages of the Constitution (Conrad 73) suggests that while the Constitution is not the origin, it has consolidated the political meaning of a motherhood imperative in the identity of women in Ireland.

The addition of Article 40.3.3, which enshrined the "right to life of the unborn" in the Constitution in 1983, was preceded by socially and politically divisive debates on the need to enact this kind of protection in order to prevent legislative or legal changes that might permit abortion in some circumstances in the future. The debate around this amendment was re-opened twice during two subsequent referenda in order to clarify more succinctly the circumstances in which the state could exercise its duty to "protect" the unborn by regulating the bodies of women citizens. The issues that were put to referendum in 1992 and 2002 were the right to access information about abortion services abroad and the right of women to travel to seek an abortion.[6] These debates highlight the salience of the meanings associated with reproductive choice in the imagination of a national identity. Many scholars argue that aligning restrictive politics of reproduction with the tenets of Catholicism provided the moral distinction between "Irishness" and the "otherness" of Britain and later the EU (Conrad 79; Martin 71; Smyth 9). The ideal of a "pro-life nation" emerges in national and international politics as Ireland continues to negotiate protection of the constitutionally enshrined "right to life of the unborn" from any threat by broader legislative authority in the EU (Smyth 62-66).[7] Most recently this distinction has been argued in debates around the regulation of embryonic stem cell research in the EU.

The conservative pro-life lobby that mounted the campaign to foreclose demands for access to abortion in Ireland could not have anticipated the impact of new reproductive technologies that create and preserve embryos *in vitro*. Such technologies have created new ways of *being* unborn—circumstances that remain contested and indeterminate in both the courts and the Irish legislature. For infertile couples, this complexity resonates in the present as the Irish state has been unable to reconcile embryos in vitro with the meaning of the Constitutional protection of the unborn in attempts to produce legislation governing the use of assisted reproduction technology.[8] For many couples, the lack of certainty and legal protection, particularly for people who obtain reproductive services abroad, is a concern as they grapple with the realities of both family formation and dissolution.

The Catholic Church, in Ireland and elsewhere, has been at the forefront of arguments against IVF on the basis of a perceived interference in the procreative commitment in marriage and an affront to the dignity of the person when embryos are created in a laboratory rather than in the body of a woman (Doran; Jacobus 20).[9] What is most painful for women struggling with infertility, however, is the Church's exclusion of the conjoined losses of identity and imagined children from recognition in spite of its continued promotion of the ideal of motherhood. Although Tom Inglis describes a recent decline in the "moral monopoly" previously held by the Catholic Church in Ireland (203-242), my interviews with people struggling to meet the ideal of motherhood perpetuated by the Catholic ethos suggest that such changes are unevenly experienced in day-to-day life. Moreover, the sense that the Church lacks empathy for women who embody the very values that the institution espouses creates a great deal of angst and uncertainty for those who seek a moral compass for their reproductive decision-making.

AN AESTHETIC REPRESENTATION OF INFERTILITY: A CASE FOR THE PRESENCE OF ABSENCE

Elsa's art engages the embodied aesthetics of both a physical and a *sensed* awareness of bodily disorder and conflicted identity for someone who cannot conceive. She portrays the multiple moral and social imperatives signified by and inscribed on women's bodies when they are made into objects of beauty and sexuality, sites of reproductive nurturing, and spaces of biological functioning. Elsa renders the social and moral expectations apparent by juxtaposing a fertile, reproductive, and aesthetically normative woman's body with one that is biologically or naturally limited, flawed, and incapable of sustaining the aesthetics of youthful proportions.[10] She challenges contradictory expectations and constructions of female bodies at the point of the valorization of motherhood and with reference to the embodied social suffering and sacrifice that conception, pregnancy and birth represent, particularly in the ethos of the Catholic Church.

Elsa was someone I really wanted to meet. I had been introduced to some of her art work already when several pieces were featured in a National Infertility Support and Information Group (NISIG) newsletter. I was intrigued by the originality of her challenge to the fetishizing of motherhood and conception through her art. Moreover, I was drawn to her use of a simple, elegant, yet powerful trope for exploring and analyzing the experience of infertility. This theme was already the title of a major work, a handmade book she called *The Presence of Absence*. It seemed that this woman had explored artistically many of the same questions I was pursuing from an academic perspective. Our first meeting provided rich context for an analysis that explores the presence of absence in relation to changing places. In other words, the experiences of infertility that have constituted the subjects with whom I spoke were also embedded in a changing social milieu in Ireland that afforded new opportunities for questions and criticism.

Elsa lived in a modest older bungalow with a lovely private garden in the back. Like many people I had met through the course of the research, Elsa and her husband have dogs, and as she welcomed me into her kitchen the two dogs barked excitedly. Somewhat exasperated, she finally pushed them out into the back garden where they watched us through the windows of the patio doors. She cleared some newspapers from the table and we drank our cappuccinos while the rain intermittently splashed on the glass sunroom windows over our heads and the dogs peered in at us until, resigned to their exclusion and disappointment, they went to sleep on the patio.

Elsa grew up in Germany but married an Irish man, and has made her life in Ireland for the past decade. Approaching age forty-one when I met her, she describes a typical Catholic upbringing culminating in a sense of longing and a feeling of responsibility to reproduce within the sanctified institution of marriage. It was a great sadness and disappointment that in their marriage of more than twelve years she and her husband had produced no children. She pursued medical treatment for a time but stopped short of trying *in vitro* fertilization (IVF) because of her own ethical concerns over the process.

Elsa had recently begun to explore her latent creativity through courses at a local art college. Somewhat reluctantly at first, she had decided to use her experiences with infertility as a source of inspiration for her art. Her work had received high praise from both teachers and the public in a recent show at the college and one of her major pieces, the handmade book entitled *The Presence of Absence*, had been purchased for the permanent collection of the art college. Shy and self-effacing as she shared some of her art pieces with me, she conveyed a definite reticence to cross a public and private divide when talking about infertility. Elsa was inspired by artistic passion to "get it out in the open" while still very much aware of the social forces that conspire to keep infertility part of a secret world of shame, guilt, and misunderstanding that are the lot of those who feel marginalized by their inability to conceive.

Part of the paradox of this marginalization is that there is nothing obvious about couples who are infertile. Their inability, or "disability" as Elsa described it, is invisible. They look and act like everyone else. There is little to draw attention or public recognition to the problem of infertility, and yet this lack of visibility merely serves to amplify the embodied guilt and sense of inadequacy that couples feel in a social world that often revolves around family life. Elsa made a conscious decision to expose her own inability to conceive in order to foster public discussion and promote awareness of the issue of infertility.

Elsa: *With all the artwork I dealt with it (infertility) and did put it out there. It's a very strange feeling with the paintings. I*

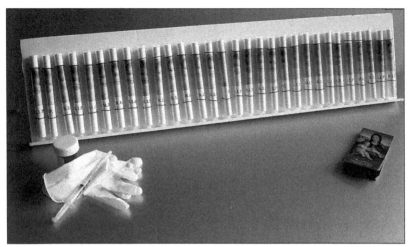

Figure 1: Display, "'Test-tube'" babies," © Ilona Madden, 2007.

just kind of put it out and you're standing there and exposing yourself to the world. It's often something, you know, that's hard to deal with.

The first piece she showed me was a metre-long board with dozens of test tubes mounted side by side (see Figure 1). Each test tube contained a photograph of Elsa as an infant photocopied on different colored paper with "R.I.P." inscribed beneath. The work plays on the popular description of IVF as producing "test-tube babies."

Seeing herself critically as a product of a highly technological world and yet unable to reproduce herself even with technological assistance provides a powerful sense of Elsa's conflicted subjectivity. The tombstone inscription is a stark reminder of her feeling that the "products" of her own reproductive dreams were in fact dead.

> Elsa: *I mean my children haven't been born or died for whatever reason, but I feel they are still very much there. And so how can it be? I think that makes a lot of people think....*

Beside the main board, Elsa placed surgical gloves and syringes and a stack of small cards the size of a book-mark. The cards bore a copy of a famous image of the Virgin Mary with the baby Jesus in her arms; underneath she added the caption "Thou shallst not conceive your own biological child [*sic*]." Elsa said she made these cards as a kind of challenge to the teachings of the Catholic Church that make Mary, the Madonna, an ideal for women. She wanted to play with the idea of the "immaculate conception" juxtaposing the scriptural explanations of a supernatural intervention through which Mary conceived to the idea of conceiving through *in vitro* fertilization, also without sexual intercourse.

Elsa's work plays powerfully with the symbolism of the miracle associated with conception and birth. The juxtaposition also challenges the paradox that emerges in religious opposition to IVF: While Mary conceived without the biological necessity of sex through a miraculous intervention, many other women, without the miraculous intervention of IVF, will be denied the opportunity to fulfill the iconic ideal of motherhood the Church has established in the Virgin Mary.

> Elsa: *I have taken on a lot you know, the Catholic Church, the Immaculate Conception, you know, and in a way I'm asking how did Mary get away with it (laughing). And there are other issues. I have a serious problem with the Catholic Church that they put so much emphasis on [the idea] that sex is dirty. The biggest issue I have with the Catholic Church is that on the one hand they are so pro-family and on the other hand they condemn IVF. This is something that I … [pausing]. You know, I have a brain and I can see certain points that they condemn in IVF but … [pausing].*

> Jill: *So it's almost like it's [IVF is] … a challenge to that idea that Immaculate Conception can only happen if God intervenes.*

> Elsa: *That kind of ties to this (pointing to the cards). But it's something like "Thou shalt not conceive naturally." And she didn't. That's exactly what it is you are saying—in a way she didn't conceive naturally. It was not natural.*

At the art show, to her surprise, people began taking the cards away with them and Elsa wondered what people were thinking as they picked them up. A contradiction embedded in the cards was effected through the use of the familiar image of Mary as the "birth mother" of Jesus holding her child in her arms even as a parody of God's words commanded that she should not have her own biological child. The infant Jesus is thus constructed as a product of non-biological processes and his birth symbolizes Mary's transcending of the biological limits of fertility and procreation. Such contradictions

---

about the nature and social significance of biological motherhood and the significance of the origins of genetic material become part of the dilemma of decision-making when couples struggle with options for conceiving beyond the usual procreative process. The body that conceives is imagined as the site of miracles and the body that fails to conceive remains constrained within the realm of human frailty. At the same time, where women are conceptualized as mothers simply by virtue of being women, the relationship between material conception and identity is tightly drawn. Even a miraculous conception becomes a material one, reinforcing the iconic power of the motherhood ideal in the Virgin Mary and her child.

Elsa said that until that moment she had not really thought of the potential impact of the Madonna image as the foundation for a more critical conceptual work on the contradictions experienced by infertile couples in Ireland. This connection proved the pivotal point for development of another idea; the next project involved hand-painting over reproductions of old masters' works to paint out the baby Jesus.

> Elsa: *You know ... even people who had children came up with stories they knew about [IVF].... The first time I did get a reaction. So then I kept thinking, well what else can I do. And what is the ultimate image of motherhood and that's where the Madonna image came in. And how can I work with that? And then I decided ... just out of, I don't know, like a habit, seeing the Madonna, you know I photocopied it.... And I just took a brush and painted over the baby, you know sort of very quickly. Then I said, hang on now, if I do that so that you can't see the baby anymore but she still has the clothes and everything, if I keep painting over that.... And my tutors really loved the idea from an art conceptual point, that I'm using painting which normally creates something, but I'm actually using it the reverse way and I'm taking it out. And it was very important that one was a photocopy and the other was an original painting.... Well it was just very powerful. I mean in the exhibition with the paintings on the wall a lot of people didn't even cop on that the child was missing, even though my painting is very obvious, you know? I mean I left it obvious so you could see. But it wasn't to them. Apparently, even a priest didn't notice. It kind of seemed to work on a level that I could explain it on our terms [from the perspective of those who are infertile].*

Figure 2: From the collection "Presence of Absence," Madonna and [Absent] Child,"
© Ilona Madden, 2007.

As Elsa notes, people did not notice the missing infant, seeing the scenes only as iconic representations of the perfect family. But embedded in the work, highlighted by the failure of so many people to see what was missing, is Elsa's representation of how the powerful motherhood ideal transcends an inability to conceive. Motherhood as an identity and an ideal takes on a life of its own in her work, separated from conception and birth as defining elements when people perceive the presence of motherhood in the Madonna even in the absence of a child.

Elsa extended this idea, creating a set of Christmas cards based on images of the Madonna and Child or manger scenes in which she used digital techniques to remove the infant Jesus, leaving Mary with empty arms or a crib with no child. The Christmas cards were taken up as a fund-raiser by the National Infertility Support and Information Group

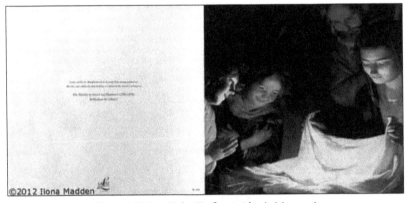

Figure 3: National Infertility Support fundraising card.

(NISIG). Many people relayed stories of the pain they felt when they received the classic iconic images of Mother and child on holiday cards. Hence people found in these cards a means of conveying the emptiness they felt and a way to subvert the imagery, taking it for their own and reinventing its meaning. The result is an expression of resistance. For members of NISIG, the cards challenged received notions of universal fertility and the ideal of the Madonna, but also the idea that as women, they had failed to meet the ideal themselves.

Another powerful and critical piece again incorporated the use of photographs. Elsa took a photo of her own torso in a pair of low-cut jeans with her shirt raised to reveal a slim figure and flat belly. She copied the photo multiple times and mounted the copies in a mural that ran the length of the corridor at the art college. As you look at the mural you become aware that the photographs gradually fade so that end to end there is a significant difference in the intensity of the images.

Elsa: *I had done a series of photographs that represented every month since we got married… Of my belly. Same photograph over and over and it was very long. It was a whole corridor long. And the photos faded. And I included a little statement there that this represents how every month my belly doesn't change.... It might be accepted that I didn't put on weight and I'm healthy (laughing). But it's not accepted that I never had children. And I kind of used the fading to say that there's a desire but that my ability to have children is fading. So I used that as my statement and that said it very blatantly. It was out there. Everybody knew and people came up to me and it was just amazing the reactions I got.*

As Elsa suggests, this mural highlights a number of issues around the social expectations that overlay the physiological or material bodies of women in post-industrial European society. Like Bordo's work on the embodiment of ideals of slimness in anorexia, Elsa notes that on one hand her flat belly would garner praise for her maintenance of a slim figure and unchanging shape over time, signs of good health and success in sustaining the requisite thinness equated with being attractive. Women's bodies are objects of aesthetic criticism even as they are expected to be essentially reproductive. But at the same time her belly never changed in all those months she was trying to conceive. For Elsa the failure to change, in this context, signifies the failure to embody both physically and socially, the ideal of pregnancy by growing a big round belly that becomes the public declaration of one's fertility.

The mural suggests that the validation of women in Ireland comes directly out of an embodiment of the importance of conception, birth, and motherhood and the power of a pregnant belly to represent the kind of embodiment of a social ideal that Boddy and Bordo both emphasize as "productive." This mural also represents the sense of paradox that is the body, described by Byron Good above as a "disordered agent," as part of the experience of infertility. Elsa plays on the order and (sometimes) regularity that is a normal menstrual cycle, a regularity that becomes a sign of disorder for women who are trying to conceive as each passing month and each onset of a menstrual period signals a failure.

GIVING ABSENCE A PRESENCE

Women who have failed to conceive often engage with their experiences by organizing support networks or counseling others. Sarah Franklin situates this kind of project in the context of "women's work" as nurturers and caregivers, suggesting that for many this provides a "means of coming to terms with the end of treatment" (123). However, for many women I spoke to, such projects were unrelated to treatment, but rather embedded in acknowledging a "presence of absence." The caregiving associated with women's work and nurturing is also reconfigured when the continuity of their own narratives of isolation, loss, and pain becomes the source, rather than closure, of caring for others in the same situation. This is the basis for the National Infertility Support and Information Group, formed in an attempt to address the feeling of isolation associated with infertility. The network was organized by a group of women from Cork who had been left childless by infertility. Some of them had not undergone any kind of infertility treatment; others had tried a number of courses of IVF. The group organized meetings in a few cities and sponsored a telephone support line. While the meetings were reportedly sparsely attended at times, the potential for individual contact and support on the telephone was crucial to the organization and mandate of the group. In conversations with the NISIG Executive, the executive were adamant that their purpose had never been political action and advocacy, but rather individual support (personal communication 2005).

One of the most profound examples of the National Infertility Support and Information Group's engagements with the presence of absence is an annual memorial service held to formalize—materialize even—the recognition of loss and sorrow for couples who have been unable to conceive. The idea of a memorial service began with one woman who held a Mass for her own unborn children—a boy and girl that she had named and wanted to introduce to her family and friends in order to make her loss tangible for others to share.

Catherine: *The priest was saying the Mass and I felt, perhaps maybe that they don't understand me and don't understand that there might be people like me in the congregation. Missing something. Because they don't understand that you would have had a loss.*

Jill: *It's a hard thing for people to conceptualize a loss.*

Catherine: *Of something that hasn't ever been. Yeah, yeah, even though in one's heart you would have conceived them. That's what Father Jim said to me. You know, he said they were all conceived in your heart. They were conceived [....] I decided to hold a Mass. Because I felt where am I to grieve? I'd like to have a Mass for my unforgotten dreams and for all the unforgotten dreams in my family. It was just absolutely amazing. And that became more important to me.... This was huge. And then at the Mass and we were singing and I had picked out all the hymns and it was just beautiful.*

Jill: *How many people came?*

Catherine: *Eighty something. I dropped them all an invitation. Two hundred and some people. They probably all thought I was mad ... I didn't care. I felt that they deserved ... my children deserved to be known. By their names. The fact that they [the children] didn't come didn't mean that they weren't wanted. So everybody who was important to me knew and knows their names now.*

This event was subsequently taken up by NISIG and formed the basis for interdenominational memorials that have been held annually since 2003. I attended the Memorial to Unforgotten Dreams in May of 2005, held in a garden called the Leanbh[11] Memorial behind St. Benedict's Priory at Cobh, County Cork. In years past it had been held in a church and presided over by clergy from several denominations, but when attendance began to fall the NISIG executive decided to make the event self-directed; the Leanbh seemed an ideal space for a memorial. Walled off from the rest of the cemetery, the Leanbh is essentially a peaceful garden designed as a place where stillborn and miscarried children could be memorialized with flowers and shrubs. We all left flowers and spent time in quiet reflection and were encouraged to contribute personal thoughts or prayers to a book kept by NISIG for this purpose.

NISIG sought permission from the Church to offer the garden as a place to remember children who were not conceived (in a material sense) or embryos lost after treatment, and asked that these entities— what NISIG calls their "unforgotten dreams"—be formally included in the mandate of the Leanbh. This inclusion of the loss and grief associated with infertility was important to the membership of NISIG as it accorded for the first time, not only a space of mourning for infertility, but recognition that such loss could be tangible. It was a way of reconciling the duality of grief in infertility, providing a space where the absence of motherhood was recontextualized by the presence of children as "unforgotten dreams"—material recognition of what had been the intangible.

CONCEPTIONS OF FAILURE

Another very powerful public expression of "presence of absence" appears in a book by well-known Irish novelist Martina Devlin. Her memoir *The Hollow Heart* was published in the summer of 2005. After reading the book, I had an opportunity to ask the author herself why she chose to divulge her own painful history of infertility, failed IVF treatments, and the ultimate loss of her marriage, rather than tell the story through the medium of her usual genre, fiction. It was her view that infertility cannot be understood in its entirety unless you experience it yourself. She wanted the story of her infertility to be a real story and to carry the weight of a genuine experience. Devlin also sought to "produce" a space in the loneliness and isolation couples feel by resisting secrecy and challenging silence. Devlin was featured in a number of newspaper articles and on the very popular Late Late Show, an Irish current events television program.

Devlin describes her profoundly passionate desire to have children as a kind of "baby hunger" (206). Like many women who undertook IVF as a means of overcoming their fertility challenges, she gave her embryos names and imagined them as children. Her acknowledgment of a presence of absence took the form of a stained glass window in her home as a memorial, and she still associates nasturtiums in her garden with commemoration of the "the ones [she] never gave birth to, for the ten embryos [she] loved —still love[s], can't forget and [doesn't] want to..." (255). She has difficulty reconciling her own failure to meet the social ideal of motherhood, drawing on biblical images by describing herself as "a barren, unnatural woman" in her failure to do what woman are supposed to do naturally (146). An illustration of Kristeva's abjection, Devlin's invoking of biblical reference to barren women (many of whom ultimately conceive through miraculous intervention) links disorder, betrayal, and a kind of abhorrence for a body that fails to perform as it should. This sensation has its roots in the discursive power of the Church, medicine, and the state to constitute women's bodies as ideally and normatively reproductive.

Medical institutions perpetuate the unequal weight of responsibility women feel for reproduction, sustaining the gendered hegemony of the iconic Irish family. While her book is a story of personal loss and difficulty in reconciling "the presence of absence" in her own life, she is critical of medical institutions that deal only with the reproductive bodies of women rather than embodied longing for motherhood. The dissonance is reflected in the language of warning to those who would undertake assisted reproduction with the kind of naïve optimism that she and her partner felt. Devlin is critical of the clinical constructions of hope and what she sees as a failure on the part of the medical profession to adequately prepare women and their partners for the emotional trauma of fertility treatment. Like virtually every woman or couple I spoke to about using IVF, her first round of treatment was undertaken with sheer belief in science and biomedicine, while subsequent treatments were a blur of fear and highly tempered optimism. In her work on IVF in the UK, Sarah Franklin describes the ambivalent place of hope as "double edged, both enabling women to continue and disabling them from reaching an endpoint of treatment" (192).

Devlin's critique highlights another subtle undercurrent in many of the stories I heard: when there is no conception after IVF, the optimism of medical practitioners left women feeling it that it was the women who had failed, not the treatment. The difficulties are greater if the infertility resides with the male partner and successful conception still depends on the rigors of IVF for women. For couples who seek refuge in a medicalized explanation for their infertility, a failure that is situated and then reiterated in women's bodies does little to validate their own subjectivity, firmly attached as it is to the motherhood ideal. In fact some women refer to themselves immediately after IVF as "pregnant until proven otherwise," an attempt to experience, however briefly, the sensation of being a mother, seeking the needed validation of that identity.

Devlin situates her feelings of loss very clearly in the subjective and embodied identity of motherhood that she felt was always a part of herself. Echoing many of my participants, her book presents a challenge to the fact that there is little recognition of the *maternal* for those who are not mothers. Alexis, whose embryos "died off" before they could be transferred back to her, also encountered a lack of understanding for the need to embody motherhood in a material way during IVF treatment.

Alexis: *I've never had the embryos back. I've had the egg collection but I've never had the transfer.... But psychologically I'm expecting a miracle by having them inside me, whereas I've never had them inside me and I'm missing out on that bit. I feel like ... I know some of the girls would be on the IVF websites saying something about their embryos and I would be thinking god, you're so lucky to even have them inside.... And I was saying, surely, the best place for the embryos is your womb and the embryologist said, no, the conditions in the lab are just as good, if not better.*

The embryologist here dissociates the powerful subjective experience of nurturing in motherhood from the bodily function of providing an environment for an embryo when he suggests that the lab might be a better place for this process. Clearly Alexis is looking for a way to embody the sensation of performing motherhood by housing and nurturing an embryo herself, however briefly.

Like Devlin, several women I spoke to noted their experiences with infertility would provide the focus for "helping others" with infertility; some contemplated a career change in this regard. Among many women, like those who started the support network and another who has developed an internet forum for infertility support in Ireland, there is an embodied sense of empathy and understanding identified as something always a part of themselves as a result of infertility.

Carol Ann: *The only good thing I suppose that has come out of it, is that it has helped me down the road if I don't get pregnant and maybe if I do.... I have made up my mind that I kind of want to change careers at some stage. I'd love to go into psychotherapy, counseling couples.... And who better to counsel somebody that can't have children than somebody who's been through the thing themselves, who can identify with what the person is going through because you've been through it yourself. I definitely would like to do that....*

Jill: *What do you think are the main things you have to work through in seeking out counseling?*

Carol Ann: *I suppose the first two times the treatment failed, feeling a failure as a woman. That you can't have children naturally, and that you tried treatment and that even then you still failed to, you know, the embryo failed to implant.... Because if you believe in conception being the beginning of life then you have a life within you. A woman normally, the only way they know they're pregnant is if they miss a period or they start feeling sick. Whereas you know from the very beginning that there's an embryo in there that could turn into a human being and you feel like you're pregnant right from the start. So that when it fails it's like having a miscarriage because you feel there was something in there that was growing and it just died. So it's like bereavement.*

Carol Ann describes succinctly the contingent loss of both her embryo and her identity as a woman. While she feels she can contextualize the lost embryos as bereavement, it is more complex to work out her own lost identity. The capacity to turn the sensation of a presence of absence into productive energy by sharing the weight of stories of other women and their partners reflects a kind of pragmatism in agency and resistance to the domain of the professional counselors who may not have shared such experiences.[12] In fact, out of three dozen women I interviewed, six indicated such an interest in using the experiences in their interrupted life narratives and identities, employing the empathic sense of a presence of absence in their own lives and offering support as therapists or counselors.

CONCLUSION

In this chapter I have tried to situate the struggles and experiences of infertile women against a complex social dynamic that perpetuates or reasserts a number of politically utilitarian meanings around reproduction. These meanings have sustained the relations of power among church, state, and medicine in Ireland, and while there has been a shift in the moral authority wielded by the Catholic Church in recent decades, the site of reproduction and family formation has been one of enduring conservative values.

I began with the suggestion that the presence of absence creates a conceptual space in which women who experience an inability to conceive can materialize their grief as a kind of resistance to constructions of social and biological failure, and abjection. Inverting Foucault's relational concept of power and resistance to create an expository lens, Lila Abu-Lughod argues that "where there is resistance, there is power" (42). Like Butler, Abu-Lughod draws from Foucault the recognition that resistance and agency are facets of relations of power, possible only within rather than outside those relations. I suggest that these are stories of women who have created a space for their grief and materialized their sense of loss as examples of resistance not to an ideal of motherhood, but to the centralizing of conception and birth as the foundation of identity for women. In this light, stories of infertility are signs of the enduring power of ideals such as motherhood, fertility, birth, and family in Ireland.

Motherhood and fertility are central to the stability and order of the medical, social, moral, spiritual, and political domains in which the politics of reproduction and the meanings of fertility are engaged. The politics of reproduction in Ireland has been altered by the shifting logic of planning families and the declining moral grip of Catholic ethos, but the representational power of a moral and stable nation remains with the ideals of motherhood and the nuclear family. The meanings of reproduction shape the subjective corporeal identities of women and men as gendered and moral citizens. As Elsa's artwork reveals, the reproductive bodies of women are sites of multiple contradictions and uncertainties. Her work addresses the continuing insistence that conception, "nature," and the body are morally connected and how the connection is ruptured when replicated by science in "un-natural" circumstances. She tackles the complex meaning of conception, "immaculate" (without sex) or otherwise, and its reconfiguration as both virtue and sin.

A kind of paradox or contradiction in itself, the presence of absence incorporates the embodied sensations of women in Ireland who find themselves overwhelmed by the tide of social expectation and the pressure to conform to those social ideals of family and parenthood. This ideal remains so powerful in daily life in Ireland that virtually all the women I spoke with viewed themselves as "mothers to be" even before thinking about conception and pregnancy. Underscored by a need to evoke empathy, these stories illustrate the need for tangibility and the need to acknowledge a loss of something that has not become— to grieve for children that were *conceived of* but not conceived. This materiality affords a means of resisting the abjection that attends failure as an ideal woman. When fertility fails and conception is not "materialized" some women seek alternate ways of reproducing a commitment to the motherhood ideal and providing a way for others to empathize with their sensations of loss. The stories are also examples of strategies of production in the absence of reproduction–production of narratives and aesthetic representations by women who experience infertility and thus cannot meet an ideal that they continue to embody and value as part of their own subjective identity. What becomes evident is the enduring significance of fertility and family and the perpetual presence of the woman/mother ideal in Ireland.

The author gratefully acknowledges support for this research by the

Social Sciences and Humanities Research council (SSHRC) and the Wenner Gren Foundation. I also thank the editors for their helpful comments. I thank Ilona Madden for generously and bravely sharing her artwork with me and allowing me to use it in this publication.

[1] I make no claim to originality in this expression, which has been given to me by my informant. Other scholars like Chris Shilling have discussed the need to recuperate the body in social theory describing it as an "absent presence" in many works of sociology (see, for instance, Shilling 16).

[2] This is in fact an inversion or play on words drawn from the title of an essay on art and photography by Victor Burgin called "the Absence of Presence" (qtd. in Harrison and Wood 1068-72). The pseudonymous artist Elsa (see below) thought the essay was a valuable insight into the technique of merging painting and photography that she later incorporated into her own work.

[3] Elsa is a pseudonym. Her artwork is in the public domain and she situates her work as a bridge between her own personal story and a public acknowledgment of her experiences. She has given me express permission to credit her work and released her story from anonymous protection but I prefer to shelter her interview-based narratives with a pseudonym.

[4] Kristeva's abjection draws on psychoanalysis; she identifies the maternal body as the site of abjection since the boundaries between mother and child in pregnancy are less distinct, resulting in "the primary experience of both horror and fascination" (229).

[5] Changes to land tenure and inheritance of family farms coincided with a pronatalist paradox in which late marriage and low birth rates accompanied high rates of emigration and celibacy. A kind of "biopower" exercised by church and state was aimed at controlling the population and increasing the standard of living while, at the same time, promoting Church doctrine by valorizing motherhood and promoting marital fertility, as Tom Inglis suggests. Fertility and family were encouraged, yet the structural constraints on family formation meant fewer people would have large numbers of children.

[6] The X Case (1992) and the more recent Miss D case (2007) involved adolescent girls who were denied the right to travel for the purpose of terminating a pregnancy in tragic circumstances. In 1992, a fourteen-year-old victim of rape wound up before the court after she threatened to commit suicide; she was ultimately given leave to travel (see Hug;

Smyth). In May of 2007, a seventeen-year-old ward of the state, who was carrying a foetus that would not survive, was refused the necessary documents to travel to the UK for an abortion by the Health Authority ("Ms. D abortion"; "Teenager seeking abortion").

[7]In signing the Maastricht Treaty (1991), Ireland inserted a special Protocol guaranteeing the primacy of Article 40.3.3 of the Constitution over any EU policies which might guarantee access to abortion or other services contradictory to a "pro-life" ethos (Conrad 107; Smyth 11-12).

[8]Discussion of state regulation is currently stalled at the level of an all-party committee by the difficulty in reconciling the arguments of elected representatives who oppose IVF as a moral transgression or risk to the life of the "unborn" and those who depend on it for any hope of conceiving a child.

[9]See also the encyclical "Donum Vitae: The Instruction on Respect for Human Life" (1987), an address given at the plenary session of the Congregation for the Doctrine of the Faith by then-Cardinal Joseph Ratzinger.

[10]For a detailed discussion on the discursive shaping of women's reproductive bodies as failing or abnormal see Emily Martin's The Woman in the Body and Margaret Lock's Encounters with Aging.

[11]Leanbh means "child" in Irish Gaelic.

[12]Margaret Lock and Patricia Kaufert both give examples of pragmatic agency and resistance among women who are dealing with complex reproductive health issues.

WORKS CITED

Abu-Lughod, Lila. "The Romance of Resistance: Tracing Transformations of Power through Bedouin Women." *American Ethnologist* 17.1 (1990): 41-55. Print.

Behar, Ruth. *The Vulnerable Observer: Anthropology that Breaks Your Heart*. Boston: Beacon Press, c1996. Print.

Biehl, João Guilherme, Byron Good and Arthur Kleinman. *Subjectivity: Ethnographic Investigations*. Berkeley: University of California Press, 2007. Print.

Boddy, Janice. *Wombs and Alien Spirits: Women, Men and the Zar Cult in Northern Sudan*. Madison: University of Wisconsin Press, 1989. Print.

Boddy, Janice. "Spirits and Selves in Northern Sudan: The Cultural Therapeutics of Possession and Trance." *American Ethnologist* 15.1 (Feb. 1988): 4-27. Print.

Bordo, Susan. *Unbearable Weight: Feminism, Culture and the Body.* Berkeley: University of California Press, 2003 [1995]. Print.

Butler, Judith. *Bodies That Matter: On the Discursive Limits of Sex.* New York Routledge, 1993. Print.

Butler, Judith. *Gender Trouble: Feminism and the Subversion of Identity.* New York: Routledge, 1999 [1990]. Print.

Butler, Judith. *Undoing Gender.* Boca Raton, Florida: Routledge, 2004. Print.

Byrne, Anne, Ricca Edmondson, and Tony Varley. "Introduction." *Family and Community in Ireland.* 3rd ed. Ennis: Clasp Press. 2001. Print.

Commission on Assisted Human Reproduction (CAHR). *Report of the Commission on Assisted Human Reproduction.* 2005. Web. 6 May 2005.

Condren, Mary. *The Serpent and the Goddess: Women, Religion and Power in Celtic Ireland.* Dublin: New Island Books. 2004. Print

Conrad, Katherine. *Locked in the Family Cell.* Madison: University of Wisconsin Press, 2004. Print.

Curtin, Nancy J. "'A Nation of Abortive Men': Gendered Citizenship and Early Irish Republicanism." *Reclaiming Gender: Transgressive Identities in Modern Ireland.* Ed. Marilyn Cohen and Nancy J. Curtin. New York: St. Martin's Press, 1999. 133-54. Print.

Desjarlais, Robert. *Body and Emotion: the Aesthetics of Illness and Healing in the Nepal Himalayas.* Philadelphia: University of Philadelphia Press, 1992.

Devlin, Martina. *The Hollow Heart.* Dublin: Penguin Ireland, 2005. Print.

Doran, Kevin. "Personhood: A Key Concept for Ethics." Irish Catholic Bishops' Committee for Bioethics, 1989. Web. 7 November, 2004.

Foucault, Michel. *History of Sexuality, Vol. 1.* 1978. Trans. Robert Hurley. New York: Vintage Books, 1990. Print.

Foucault, Michel. *Discipline and Punish.* Trans. Alan Sheridan. New York: Vintage Books, 1995. Print.

Franklin, Sarah. *Embodied Progress: A Cultural Account of Assisted Reproduction.* London: Routledge, 1997. Print.

Good, Byron. *Medicine, Rationality and Experience: An Anthropological Perspective.* Cambridge: Cambridge University Press, 1994. Print.

Harrison, Charles, and Paul Wood, eds. *Art in Theory 1900-2000: An Anthology of Changing Ideas.* 1984. Rev. ed. Oxford: Blackwell, 2003.

Hug, Chrystel. *The Politics of Sexual Morality in Ireland.* London:

MacMillan, 1999. Print.

Inglis, Tom. *Lessons in Irish Sexuality*. Dublin: University College of Dublin Press, 1998. Print.

Jacobus, Mary. "In Parenthesis: Immaculate Conceptions and Feminine Desire." *Body/Politics: Women and the Discourses of Science*. Ed. Mary Jacobus, Evelyn Fox Keller and Sally Shuttleworth. London: Routledge, 1990. 229-63. Print.

Kristeva, Julia. "Powers of Horror." *The Portable Kristeva*. Ed. Kelly Oliver. New York: Columbia University Press, 1997. Print.

Lock, Margaret. *Encounters with Aging*. Berkeley: University of California Press, 1993. Print.

Lock, Margaret and Patricia Kaufert. *Pragmatic Women and Body Politics*. Cambridge: Cambridge University Press, 1998. Print.

Mahmood, Saba. *The Politics of Piety: The Islamic Revival and the Feminist Subject*. Princeton: Princeton University Press, 2005. Print.

Martin, Angela. "Death of a Nation: Transnationalism, Bodies and Abortion in Late Twentieth-Century Ireland." *Gender Ironies of Nationalism*. Ed. Tamar Mayer. London: Routledge, 2000. 65-88. Print.

Martin, Emily. *The Woman in the Body: A Cultural Analysis of Reproduction*. Boston: Beacon Press, 1987. Print.

McDonnell, Oral and Jill Allison. "From Biopolitics to Bioethics: Church, State, Medicine and Assisted Reproductive Technology in Ireland." *Sociology of Health & Illness* 28.6 (2006): 817-837. Print.

"Miss D abortion travel case may be abandoned." *Irish Examiner* 7 May 2007. Web. 7 May, 2007.

Ratzinger, Joseph. "*Donum Vitae:* Instruction on Respect for Human Life in its Origin and on the Dignity of Procreation: Replies to Certain Questions of the Day." Congregation for the Doctrine of the Faith, Rome, 22 February 1987. Web. 1 Nov. 2004. Address.

Sandelowski, Margarete and Sheryl de Lacey. "The Uses of a 'Disease': Infertility as Rhetorical Vehicle." *Infertility Around the Globe: New Thinking on Childlessness, Gender, and Reproductive Technologies* Ed. Marcia Inhorn and Frank van Balen. Berkeley: University of California Press, 2002. 33-51. Print.

Shilling, Chris. *The Body and Social Theory*. 2nd ed. London: Sage Publications, 2003.

Smyth, Lisa. *Abortion and Nation: The Politics of Reproduction in Contemporary Ireland*. Aldershot, Hants.: Ashgate Publishing, 2005. Print.

"Teenager seeking abortion at no risk to suicide." *Irish Examiner* 4

May 2007. Web. 7 May 2007.

Whyte, J. H. *Church and State in Modern Ireland 1923-1979.* Dublin: Gill and MacMillan, 1984. Print.

6. The Humour of Lynn Johnston, *For Better or For Worse*

FAITH BALISCH

THIS CHAPTER DISCUSSES THE SIGNIFICANCE of the humour created by Lynn Johnston in her daily comic strip *For Better or For Worse*.[1] This may seem a strange endeavour, for the daily comic strip is among the most ephemeral of all popular forms, outside the realm of most academic analysis.[2] Yet this study has a place in a volume of essays which argues that gender awareness can and must contribute to "changing places" and changing lives. What seems ephemeral may merit serious academic attention and, more to the present purpose, humour, the humour of a woman, offers a singular form of social commentary which aims to create empathy by encouraging identification with the struggles of her characters rather than laughter at their expense.

Johnston's *For Better or For Worse* challenges any perception of women's humour as a passive response to the world by progressively questioning conformity to domestic paradigms established in earlier cartoon series. The strip's Canadian origin may have something to do with the traditional values it both presents respectfully and smiles at. But, whatever its genesis, Johnston's work is known worldwide. Its exploration of the vicissitudes of daily small-town life shows a familiarity with feminist aspirations and values, and an understanding that changes are under way and are needed. It is far from firing off satirical polemic on the decay of the family and "family" values in the late twentieth and early twenty-first centuries. But the strip frequently challenges assumptions concerning both the problems of our time and their perceived solutions, by depicting intimate domestic relations and their larger significance, in many voices and from many points of view. These qualities are among the reasons Johnston is one of the most important Canadian humorists living today.

That this paper can make the last assertion is in itself a tribute to the work done by the feminist critics of the latter half of the twentieth century who refused any longer to accept the prevailing view, inherited from the nineteenth century, that humour may be *about* women but is created primarily by men. Regina Barreca quotes early twentieth-century writer Minna Antrim: "Man forgives a woman anything save the wit to outwit him" (*Snow White* 36); she also notes that the belief that women do not have a sense of humour has meant there has been little interest in women's humour.

> Women's humor has not so much been ignored as it has been unrecognized, passed over, or misread as tragic. Because literary critics, analysts, novelists, and academics can all supply reasons why the creation of comedy by women is impossible, it does not follow that women have not created comedy. It is similar to the situation in which experts in physics and aeronautics have explained to their own satisfaction that the bumblebee cannot possibly fly given its weight and wingspan, even as they dash about hoping not to be stung. (*Untamed* 17)

Although she is speaking here not of women cartoonists, but of women as humorists generally, Barreca's point is well taken. Furthermore, even in the late twentieth century, women's humour was regularly unrecognized and passed over. In her 1990 article, "Social Cognition, Gender Roles and Women's Humour," Alice Sheppard cites the following anecdote to illustrate that as late as the 1990s, women and men differed in their judgements as to what constitutes humour, with men's judgment prevailing:

> A couple of years ago, *Esquire* decided to put out an issue on women edited by women. One of the women in charge asked me [Elizabeth Janeway] to contribute a piece responding to the familiar query, "Why Does the Women's Movement Have No Sense of Humor?" I did so. The woman editor called me to say it was fine. Two weeks passed. One morning the mail brought the article back, with a note explaining that while the women doing the job enjoyed it, masculine top brass didn't feel that it was the thing at all—distinctly not funny. (39)

While this anecdote refers to attitudes in the U.S., the humour of women in Canada is even more undervalued and ignored because, in Canada, we have a rather ambivalent attitude to Canadian humour. We do not generally write learned articles about our popular humorists, and only reluctantly, it seems to me, do we write about our "literary" humorists. As the creator of a weekly comic strip, Lynn Johnston would be excluded as a matter of course: even popular humorists write columns or short pieces, and significant cartoonists produce recognizably "political" cartoons. Lynn Johnston is Canada's only long-standing syndicated woman cartoonist, and although she has retired from regular publication, her comic strips continue to appear in many newspapers for the delight of a new generation of readers, offering them renewed opportunities for empathy through the longitudinal development of the characters.

Lynn Johnston launched *For Better or For Worse* in September 1979, and it went on to appear in more than 2000 newspapers in eight languages worldwide. Beginning in 1981, her comic strips were collected and published in annual volumes. The final volume, *Just a Simple Wedding*, appeared in 2009. In addition to three earlier volumes of discrete cartoons, Lynn Johnston has published more than thirty books including twenty-nine annual collections of these daily and weekly strips, four special anniversary volumes—two of which, *A Look Inside For Better or For Worse* (1989) and *It's the Thought That Counts* (1994), contain that year's annual collection—and two special collections detailing the lives of specific characters: April, the unexpected late-in-life baby, and Farley, the family sheep dog. Since the daily strip ceased in 2008, she has taken another unprecedented step in the history of cartooning by reusing the former plotlines as starting points for new ones. To date she has issued two new "treasuries": *Something Old, Something New*, which includes strips from the first three volumes of her work, and *In the Beginning There Was Chaos*, which includes material from volumes two through six. In addition to the older material she has added new strips (identified by an asterisk), as well as commentary, newspaper clippings, and photographs which contextualize the earlier strips while giving her present perspective on the material presented.

The significance of her work has been well recognized in the United States. Johnston is the first woman, the first Canadian, and the youngest artist ever to win the National Cartoonists Society's Reuben Award for Outstanding Cartoonist of the Year (1985); her work won the Society's Best Syndicated Comic Strip Award in 1992, and the designation Comic Creator of the Year from *Editor and Publisher* in 2001. She was also nominated for a Pulitzer Prize (one of only two cartoonists in the history of this prize). In 1992, she received the Order of Canada.

Years earlier, the Order of Mariposa was bestowed upon her by her colleagues in humour "for her contrubtions [sic] to Canadian humour" (Harris 1). Other recognitions include her induction in 1997 into the International Museum of Cartoon Art's Hall of Fame in Boca Raton, Florida; honorary degrees from McMaster, Nipissing, the Emily Carr Institute of Art and Design, and the University of Winnipeg; being named Comic of the Year by *Editor and Publisher,* and her induction in 2008 into the Canadian Cartoonists Hall of Fame as well as the National Cartoon Museum Hall of Fame. In 2004 the union of Ontario Indians, which represents forty-two communities of the Anishinabek Nation, awarded her the Debwewin Citation for excellence in Aboriginal issues journalism.

In its usual format of a weekly four-frame comic strip plus a weekend colour supplement of up to nine frames, *For Better or For Worse* is a continuity strip, which means that, while any given strip may end with a punch line, all feature an established group of characters and carry the story forward to the next installment. Many continuity strips (such as *Peanuts* or *Blondie* or *Cathy*) rely largely on single-episode "gag" humour, in contrast to comic books or the increasingly popular graphic novel. The characters in most continuity strips do not change in age: the *Peanuts* gang are forever children; Cathy, technically an adult, remains childlike in attitude and action, preoccupied with fashion, figure, and her seemingly voracious appetite. Although Nancy Walker suggests that *Cathy* "confronts issues central to women's lives without disparaging either women or the issues" ("Toward Solidarity" 76), Cathy the character is not designed to register emotional or social growth.

David Carrier points out that "To understand comics, we need to analyse the institutional framework within which they are seen," since "[t]hey are read so casually that often their highly original features are taken for granted" (88). Lynn Johnston has situated her comic strip in small-town Canada, and has grounded it in contemporary realities. In depicting the lives of a fairly privileged middle-class family and its interactions with the community, she deploys both sensitivity and a wry wit that have kept the strip from incurring the accusation of sentimentality often directed at women's humour, or the kinds of condescension addressed to the humour of such noted women as Jean Kerr, Erma Bombeck, and Betty MacDonald (see for example Spacks 282). It is rare for a comic strip to tap in as acutely as Johnston to the everyday lives of quite ordinary people and it is equally rare for so-called women's humour to portray women, particularly housewives, with any degree of empathy or respect.

Traditional women's humour has not usually been kind to women, as Suzanne L. Bunkers suggests: "If women have been perceived as having any sense of humour at all, it has been self-deprecatory humour; that is, humour characterized by the joke teller laughing at herself and putting herself down" (83). It is for this reason, primarily, that feminist critics in the 1970s found so little of value in this domestic or "housewife" humour, and contrasted it with the newer feminist humour that was emerging. Even in 2001, in *The Great Women Cartoonists,* Trina Robbins dismisses Johnston's comic strip for not being overtly feminist, characterizing it as somewhat outdated for the late twentieth century: "today's family strips are about single working mothers and non-traditional families, and their creators are not afraid of the F word: feminism" (140). Making a similar distinction in *Pulling Our Own Strings,* Gloria Kaufman says: "Feminist humour tends to be a humor of hope, female humor of hopelessness" (13-14). She describes feminist humour as "the pick-up, an obvious reversal of the put-down," and "a healthy contrast to mainstream humor, most of which seems to knock people down—or to laugh at people who are already down. Laughs come from a perceived superiority of the hearer or reader to the character ridiculed." She distinguishes this from what she calls "pickup humor," which has its roots in empathy: "Through it, we do not laugh *at* people, we bond *with* them" (16). In these definitions, she constructs "female" humour as one form of "mainstream" humour.

Any negative attitude towards domestic humour on the part of critics, particularly feminist critics, however, has not deterred readers from enjoying Johnston's comic strip which, at least in terms of its subject matter, has its genesis in the domestic sphere, and can at times be more feminist than many critics recognize. A small group of "feminist critics" do not necessarily define feminism or humour for everyone else. However, the perception that Johnston's work is mainly "domestic," combined with its obviously Canadian origin, has meant that *For Better or For Worse* is usually omitted from critical surveys such as Trina Robbins' *From Girls to Grrlzs* (1999), and Robert C. Harvey's *The Art of the Funnies: An Aesthetic History* (1994). Furthermore, the assumption that "domestic" humour must be self-deprecatory has blinded many critics to the subtlety, originality, and the subversive nature of Johnston's work. She often invites us to consider how places might be changed.

In her 2003 essay "Gender and Humour in Social Context," Mary Crawford reports on conversations in which gender and humour intersect. She points out that when gender and humour were first linked in research, studies looked for differences between men's and women's discourse in general, and humour in particular. Not surprisingly, these studies then discovered such differences. Crawford and others have questioned that approach and the assumptions embedded in it: that men and women are opposites; that gender is a fixed attribute; and that issues of power and dominance can be separated from the language in which they are coded. In short, she regards both "gender" and "humour" as contested categories:

> Gender is conceived as a system of meanings that influences access to power, status, and material resources. Humour is conceived as a mode of discourse and a strategy for social interaction.... [I]ndividuals use humour in gendered ways, thereby performing and producing the gender system. (1414)

Crawford points out that this kind of *performance* includes the deconstruction of gender, its prescriptions and/or its expectations —*through humour* (1414). It is precisely this overlap between the performance of gender and the deconstruction of gender performance that Lynn Johnston's work suggests.

In the comics from its first years, the number of characters in *For Better or For Worse* is relatively small and the setting is either the home or the neighbourhood. The strip focuses on the family life of John and Elly Patterson, their two children, Michael, a son reaching kindergarten age, his baby sister Elizabeth (Lizzie) who is about a year old, and their friends. The daily strips are quite unrelated to one another except for their focus on the same characters. As with many continuity strips, its narrative basis is, for the most part, underdeveloped and oversimplified, while the drawings offer minimal detail—just enough to give the reader a sense of where things are happening. These early strips in *For Better or For Worse* might *prima facie* seem to rely on a fairly standard version of the type of domestic humour that Zita Dresner hypothesizes "developed during [the period from 1946-1960], for it is in many ways another by-product of the 'bewilderment' that was generated by post-war antifeminist sentiment, another response to the confusion that existed about woman's identity, purpose and place.... [Such] [d]omestic humour tended to provide women with a temporary tool for coping with those negative feelings about themselves and their lives" (93). This humour often contains disappointment.

Johnston herself recognizes the emotions of those early years. In the

Figure 1: *"I didn't know you had any talent."* (Something Old, Something New) *93*

most recent collection, she comments on a strip in which John, having read something Elly was writing, walks away saying, "I didn't know you had any talent." Under this strip she writes, "This was a mean comment and not something Rod [her real-life husband] would have said. I guess I was in a negative mood when I wrote this one. I think he put up with a lot of this kind of thing in the early years" (*Something Old* 93).

In *Suddenly Silver*, she comments: "*For Better or For Worse* began with hesitant lines, disjointed ideas, and a rather dour attitude, but it was funny"(4). What she calls "dour" some would call feminist: the dawning of the realization that, educated as she was, Elly was suddenly confined to the domestic sphere. She was not the one putting on her public face, interacting with adults, earning a salary, building a career. In the first year, for example, Elly's frustration with her lonely role as a housewife with a degree is apparent in a strip in which, having failed to tempt baby Lizzie to use the potty ("Nizzie big girl. Big girls sittum on poe"), she exclaims in frustration: "And for this I majored in English" (*Washload* 13).

In another, Elly yearns to be out in the workforce, and envies John his job "escaping to the air-conditioned office, meeting new people … accomplishing things" (10). But John, conscious only of pressure, oblivious of his status, salary, and daily contact with the professional world, envies Elly what he sees as the flexibility of her day. Johnston, it seems, is quite aware of the contradictions of the late twentieth century with which the Women's Movement of the second wave was grappling. In the same volume, she shows Elly's understanding that she is somewhat out of step with the larger world: in one strip, while John has gone to a conference, Elly is pictured feeling lonely in the double bed; listening to the night sounds, she thinks to herself: "I wonder how many feminists are afraid of the dark?" (70). The comment suggests that feminists offer a standard, at least notional, by which she evaluates herself, her life, *and* feminists: are they as confident as they seem?

Figure 2: *"For this I majored in English. (I've Got the One More Washload Blues) 13.*

Figure 3: *"How Many Feminists are Afraid of the Dark?"*
(I've Got the One More Washload Blues) 70.

Although some of the early strips do invite that "An't it the truth" and Poor me" way of looking at life that Betty Swords suggests characterizes women's point of view and the oppression they suffer (Swords 79), Johnston takes the humour beyond dissatisfaction and suppressed anger into ironic recognition by incorporating various points of view and offering readers alternative perspectives on domestic events. She includes, for example, the children's perspective, as when Michael teases baby Lizzie by slowly eating a cookie in front of her, then calls out in joyous excitement to his mother, "I taught Lizzie a new word!!" while she in tearful frustration yells, "Uh Uh Uh Gookie" at him (*Washload* 67). The incident can also be seen from a feminist viewpoint: Big Brother knows he can get away with it, because he's "teaching," a helpful activity, while actually teasing, testing his power, intending to enrage.

Later, we may find ourselves empathizing initially with John when Michael asks the following series of unanswerable questions: "If there was a bomb dropped on us daddy, would we go to heaven?" and "Would heaven get filled up? Would everyone turn into angels?" and "What about the people who dropped the bomb? Would they be alone in the whole earth?" John, who is depicted with drops of sweat coming off his forehead after his final set of tennis, can only grab his five year old son in a tight hug and exclaim: "Mike...can we go back to 'why is the sky blue?'" (101; see Fig 4). In this recognizable domestic situation, the male perspective seeks understanding: John recognizes that he is unequal to the challenge of the child's questions and gives him a big hug. But another reading is that he ducks, albeit gently, his responsibility: when the child is asking about serious issues, John reacts, if not without empathy, certainly evasively, not engaging the child's fears; and he has had the luxury of a tennis game, while Elly has been on duty. Johnston is already finding methods to shift domestic affairs away from self-deprecation and create a more complicated, inclusive kind of humour—with feminist possibilities, whether intended or not. Johnston herself often seems to work in a self-reflexive zone, watching herself watch Elly struggle with the illogical unfairness of life. Perhaps some readers miss the implicit feminist angles of the series because Elly does not rage against her lot in life; she comes across as reflecting on it, the better to engage the reader's empathy and trust. It is often her silence, for example after the tennis match or when Michael teases Lizzie, that motivates the reader to deconstruct the gender performances of these domestic moments.

Johnston has always stepped around the pitfalls of traditional women's humour by shifting perspectives so that readers' responses change as they see through the eyes and minds of various characters, giving a rich sense of the ironies involved. By the second year of *For Better or For Worse,* Lynn Johnston took another original turn. It rapidly became clear that she was moving beyond the almost universal characteristic of the comic strip—the evasion of a narrative structure in which a character recognizes that his/her destiny and condition are based on time. In his 1972 essay "The Myth of Superman" Umberto Eco points to the absence of entropy in comic strips, noting that they show the characters existing in "a kind of [static or immobile] climate—of which the reader is not aware at all [and so has no sense of] what has happened before and what has happened after" (153). Instead Johnston presents the routine of Elly's days, which feel *long,* often spent in isolation from friends, tending to young children and doing chores, then usually a woman's experience, in order to develop a new type of cartoon. "Women's work," unpaid of course, was often assumed to be easy and somehow mindless; men's work to be more interesting and challenging as well as lucrative. From the first volume Elly longs for such work, even as she cherishes her children. Observing

Figure 4: "Back to 'Why is the Sky Blue'" (I've Got the One More Washload Blues) *101.*

the passing days at close range may have appealed to Johnston the artist as a way to outsmart entropy in her own life. By witnessing small significant changes, the wisdom of the young, or the comic potential of misunderstandings, she tracks and questions the clash of contradictions yielded by domestic life in all its daily minutiae (as in the example above of Elly's and John's differing perspectives on the other's working day).

Embracing entropy also gives Johnston the opportunity to write the history of the characters and their/her world. Depicting characters as they are born, grow up, marry, age, fall ill, and even die, yet remain recognizably themselves, is rare in comic writing, but in managing it successfully for over 30 years, Johnston has given us a document of the times. The second volume of the strip, *Is This One of Those Days, Daddy?* sees the start of extended narratives which signal that the strip is now in "real time" with Lizzie having her second birthday and Michael in grade two.

Not that Johnston has held herself to daily or weekly reports or continuous histories. Among the many narrative threads, there are interruptions, and she mingles gags, wordless humour, puns and "quickies" with extended story lines. She may follow a specific character over days or weeks, focusing on one perspective, that of a family member or a friend, in contrast to the weekend panel which is usually complete in itself, and often of the "gag" variety. But the aging of the characters always proceeds at the same rate in both formats, as does that of their friends, relatives, and pets. Thus Johnston can respond to social change, through the shifting perspectives of her characters and the ironies that emerge from the intersections between them—because the characters are not "stuck" forever in childhood, or in young adulthood, or in domesticity for that matter. They can and do act to realize their dreams and hopes, though they experience their fair share of bumps and setbacks along the way. By the second volume, Elly is depicted as filling in when John's receptionist is away, and starting courses at night school before she begins unpaid work for the community paper three mornings a week (*It Must be Nice to be Little* 75). Shortly thereafter she accepts a paid part-time position in charge of children's programs for the town library. For many readers the open acknowledgement of her guilt at leaving her children to the care of others brings instant recognition. But assumptions change, and in later strips she shows no guilt in leaving young April with a baby sitter or in day care. By the time *For Better or For Worse* ends in 2009, the family has come full circle, with some significant changes. Michael is the parent of two children, one ready to start school. His wife is working outside the home to support the family while Michael writes fiction and starts publishing. And Elly has owned, and retired from the ownership of, her own bookstore.

While Johnston has claimed that her strip is not political, the politics of the everyday certainly emerge as the characters evolve. Nancy Walker has said that "the tradition of women's humour [in American culture] is a record of women's conscious denial of inferiority and subordination, and a testament to their spirit of survival in sexist culture" (183). At one level Johnston's strip can be read as Elly's memoir of surviving domesticity and establishing a vocational identity, but Johnston is not fixated on one theme or character: in her portrayal of perspectives that differ, she identifies and deconstructs binaries based on age, race, ability, and class, as well as on sex; her narratives feature unfaithfulness, homosexuality, domestic violence, bullying at school, the fall-outs of divorce, and the lives of single parents. She also explores life's stages from birth to death: toddlerhood, elementary and high school, teenage angst, leaving home, the world of college, the search for love, starting a professional life, menopause—as well as illness, aging, remarriage late in life, and sexual feelings in old age.

Nor is Johnston's humour of the assertive kind that Walker seems to have in mind. It is closer to Michael Mulkay's description of humour as "defined by its acceptance of ambiguity, paradox, multiple interpretations of reality, and partially resolved incongruity" (qtd. in Crawford 1420). Three sequences in particular show Johnston's sensitivity to others' struggles and her strategy of highlighting egocentric perspectives through ironic contrast.

In *Things Are Looking Up*, Elizabeth (in her teens) feels frustrated at home because her parents have installed various gates to protect her baby sister. Elizabeth appears in the first frame naively confiding to her favourite teacher, Miss Edwards, who is paraplegic, "Boy you don't know what it is like being in a place with barriers everywhere" (75). The perspective then opens onto a detailed wide-angle drawing of Elizabeth

Figure 5: "Boy, you don't know what it's like." (Things are Looking Up 73).

and Miss Edwards in a school corridor. Elizabeth is blissfully unaware of the two sets of stairs, the height of the drinking fountain, and the narrowness of the doorways leading off the hallway (one of them to a ladies' washroom). All of these are barriers for Miss Edwards, who says nothing about them in deference to Elizabeth's obvious frustration. The rapid shift in perspective, in this case achieved through the detailed drawing, has the effect of "making strange" the familiar and, in so doing, revealing the irony often inherent in everyday assumptions. Johnston offers such revelations to draw attention to what needs to change in order to accommodate varied needs. Miss Edwards' dignified silence, if anything, increases the reader's awareness of the unfairness of her situation, and also of her forbearance towards the teenager who is not yet seeing the world in the round, with empathy.

One of the first, and eventually most controversial, of the non-family characters to appear in the strip is Lawrence Poirier, Michael's best friend in the early days of the comic. When, in his mid-teens, Lawrence recognizes that he is gay, he confides in Michael (*There Goes My Baby* 111-19). In presenting Lawrence's dilemma, Johnston incorporates four different points of view: Lawrence's, Michael's, Lawrence's mother Connie's, and his step-father's. Reactions range from shock (Michael), to anger (the step-father), hurt and denial (Connie), rejection (everybody, initially), defensiveness (Lawrence), loss (Connie), pain (Lawrence), and eventually to guarded, then less reserved acceptance—and Lawrence gets on with his life as best he can. The reactions of his schoolmates are not shown. Johnston perhaps wanted to avoid giving reinforcement to any teenage homophobia when "Lawrence" was at school every day in the "real time" present; but she does include the moment of celebration (and surprise) when Lawrence brings the great love of his young life, Ben, to the school's graduation prom. In later strips his sexual orientation is respected, or in his mother's case accepted with reservations: when Connie regrets that she is never going to be a grandmother, Johnston is documenting how far she has travelled from explosive disbelief.

Sue Lafky and Bonnie Brennan praise the sensitivity of this narrative sequence of twenty-three strips extending more than three weeks, maintaining that it both "resisted and reinforced traditional family values" (23). They also recognize the surprise value of this particular revelation: "while it is not unusual to find controversial topics addressed on the funnies page, most of these controversies have stemmed from self-conscious political positions taken by the artist (and articulated by a character within the strip) rather than [from cases in which] the storyline has dealt with issues encountered in everyday life" (27). The public outcry in opposition to this introduction of a gay teenager into *For Better or For Worse* was huge, with the result that many American papers cancelled the strip, something that did not happen in Canada. Lafky and Brennan find the controversy illuminating as it "provides insight into how market-oriented censorship and ideological constraints frame the social construction of the private and public spheres in a way that leads to some comic strips being allocated to the editorial pages, others to the funnies pages, and still others to be never published" (24). If Johnston was holding to the liberal view that the individual and the family are entirely responsible for the conduct of their lives, this statement may have come as a surprise. The very visible hand of the U.S. market cancelled potential debate on gay rights and reduced her income.[3]

Lawrence is depicted encountering homophobia years later when, in *With This Ring*, Michael chooses him as best man for his wedding to Deanna Sobinsky. Deanna's mother does not approve: "I don't want a gay person in the wedding party" (104). She appears to have the function in the strip of voicing the most reactionary and bigoted attitudes—a female Archie Bunker whose role is to reveal prejudice for the life-denying force it is. But Michael and Deanna's decision prevails and, at the wedding dinner, comedy and perspective return when Lawrence, as best man, offers a very traditional (and very touching) toast to the "gride and broom"(109). Clearly the stress of the occasion has affected him and Johnston invites our understanding; but with the Spoonerism Johnston also mocks the absurd binary categories Lawrence has had to negotiate.

One of the final sequences involves April's blossoming friendship with Shannon, a student with a disability at her high school. This narrative in many ways demonstrates Johnston's capacity to use a combination of narrative, art, and humour to influence readers' attitudes by dramatizing empowerment. April's friends are not pleased when "special needs" students are integrated into one of their classes, and for several years their treatment of these young people is cruel and offensive. April, now lead guitarist for her popular band, has sufficient social clout that she can afford to ignore her peers. Through her friendship with Shannon she gains understanding of Shannon's capabilities, dreams, and sensitivities. April's support reinforces Shannon's confidence and sense of self-worth. When, one day, matters come to a head, it is Shannon, not April, who acts to face down her detractors. Normally shy and self-effacing, Shannon suddenly climbs onto a table in the school cafeteria and yells: "I …want … to say … stop! Stop … ma … king … fun of us. We're dif'rent from … you … but … So What?!!" And in the next strip she adds: "I can't … change … the way … I … talk … But … you … can change … the … way … you…. Listen!!" The teens are so taken aback they do listen and they give her a rousing cheer (*Home Sweat Home* 100). In her halting speech, Shannon has changed the politics of her school.

As Elizabeth matures, she sets out to become a teacher and follow in the footsteps of Miss Edwards, her favourite grade school teacher, but perhaps differently from what readers might expect. First, she chooses to attend Nipissing University in Canada's North, where the student body includes both Aboriginal and non-Aboriginal students. Later she begins her teaching career in the fictional village of Mtigwaki much further north, where many of her students are Aboriginal. In the series of strips

Figure 6: "You Can Change the Way You Listen." (Home Sweat Home 100).

featuring Elizabeth as both student and young teacher, Johnston, in the words of (then) Chief Phil Goulais of the Nipissing Nation, "helped to sensitize mainstream journalism and larger society to the Aboriginal community" (Tombs). She does so by portraying First Nations citizens without stereotyping. For example, when Elizabeth offers her romantic vision of teaching in the very far North in a remote village "where there's a one room school house, where people still speak their own language and live off the land," her friend Greta's Uncle Denny says, "There's places like that ... with internet and cable access" (*Striking a Chord* 106).

These vignettes begin to capture the empathic dimension of *For Better or For Worse*. Johnston shows without criticism the experience of the young as they learn to learn. And she leaves the statements, and silences, of wisdom to those who have wisdom. Along the way, Johnston's humor uncovers resistance to changing attitudes in Canadian society, and hesitations, and breakthroughs. Through her irony and her manipulation of multiple perspectives—highlighting one character, then another even within a single strip, Johnston exposes insensitive assumptions and practices, while maintaining a generous perspective.

Johnston's description of herself as apolitical does not apply to the strips concerned with power imbalances and cruelties, but she does not attack. While the cartoonist may not have marched or demonstrated, her 30-year epic has recorded how over that period, a major change has been brought about by women like her, whose energies and causes have removed some of the barriers between private and public life. Women sharing their stories with other women over coffee; networking at the gym; being elected to municipal and school committees; in Elly's case, starting a business which becomes a meeting place. If not activism as usually constructed, these are steps in community building, where *community* is not simple, not a given. Where the differences that divide sometimes arise from the kinds of inequities noted in *For Better or For Worse*, Johnston suggests that above all *community* is about changing places for the better.

[1]The cartoons reproduced in this chapter are used by permission of Universal Uclick. All rights reserved

[2]For studies of Canadian political cartoons and cartoonists, see Peter Desbarats and Terry Mosher's *The Hecklers: A History of Canadian Political Cartooning and A Cartoonists' History of Canada* (1979), Douglas Fetherling's edition of J. W. Bengough's 1886 *A Caricature*

History of Canadian Politics (1974), and Carman Cumming's *Sketches from a Young Country: The Images of Grip Magazine* (1997).
[3]My local newspaper did not discontinue the strip, but for several years afterwards moved it from the comics page to the social pages.

WORKS CITED

Balisch, Faith. "Lynn Johnston's 'Theratoons': Extending the Limits of the Comic Strip." *Images and Imagery: Frames, Borders, Limits: Interdisciplinary Perspectives.* Ed. Corrado Federici. New York: Peter Lang, 2005. 241-54. Print.

Barreca, Regina. *They Used to Call Me Snow White ... But Then I Drifted: Women's Strategic Use of Humor.* New York: Viking, 1991. Print.

Barreca, Regina, ed. "Making Trouble: An Introduction." *New Perspectives on Women and Comedy.* Philadelphia: Gordon and Breach, 1992. 1-11. Print.

Barreca, Regina. *Untamed and Unabashed: Essays on Women and Humor in British Literature.* Detroit, MI: Wayne State University Press, 1993. Print.

Bengough, J. W. *A Caricature History of Canadian Politics* (1886). Ed. Douglas Fetherling. Toronto: Peter Martin Associates, 1974. Print.

Bunkers, Suzanne L. "Why Are These Women Laughing? The Power and Politics of Women's Humor." *Studies in American Humor* [New Series] 4.1,2 (Spring/Summer 1985): 82-93. Print.

Carrier, David. *The Aesthetics of Comics.* University Park, PA: Pennsylvania University Press 2000. Print.

Crawford, Mary. "Gender and Humour in Social Context." *Journal of Pragmatics* 35 (2003): 1413-30. Web. 10 Feb. 2011.

Cumming, Carman. *Sketches from a Young Country: The Images of Grip Magazine.* Toronto: University of Toronto Press, 1997. Print.

Dresner, Zita. "Domestic Comic Writers." Sochen. 93-114. Print.

Eco, Umberto. "The Myth of Superman." *Arguing Comics: Literary Masters on a Popular Medium.* Eds. Jeet Heer and Kent Worcester. Jackson, MS: University Press of Mississippi. 2004. 146-64. Print.

Groensteen, Thierry. "Why Are Comics Still in Search of Cultural Legitimization?" *Comics/Culture: Analytical and Theoretical Approaches to Comics.* Eds. Anne Magnussen and Hans-Christian Christiansen. University of Copenhagen: Museum Tusculanum Press, 2000. 29-41. Print.

Desbarats, Peter and Terry Mosher. *The Hecklers: A History of Canadian*

Political Cartooning and A Cartoonists' History of Canada. Toronto: McClelland and Stewart, 1979. Print.

Harris, Jim. "Johnston and Johnston or The Bestowing of the Order of Mariposa on Lynn Johnston by President Dick Johnston." *Newspacket* 29.1 (2002): 1, 8. Print.

Harvey, Robert C. *The Art of the Funnies: An Aesthetic History*. Jackson MS: University Press of Mississippi, 1994. Print.

Heer, Jeet and Kent Worcester, eds. *Arguing Comics: Literary Masters on a Popular Medium*. Jackson, MS: University Press of Mississippi. 2004. Print.

Johnston, Lynn. *Home Sweat Home*. Kansas City: Andrews McMeel, 2008. Print.

Johnston, Lynn. *In the Beginning, There Was Chaos*. Kansas City: Andrews McMeel, 2011. Print.

Johnston, Lynn. *I've Got the One-More-Washload Blues*. Kansas City: Andrews McMeel, 1981.

Johnston, Lynn. *Is This One of Those Days, Daddy?* Kansas City: Andrews McMeel, 1982. Print.

Johnston, Lynn. *It Must Be Nice to Be Little*. Kansas City: Andrews McMeel, 1983. Print.

Johnston, Lynn. *It's the Thought That Counts: For Better or For Worse Fifteenth Anniversary Collection*. Kansas City: Andrews McMeel, 1994. Print.

Johnston, Lynn. *Just A Simple Wedding*. Kansas City: Andrews McMeel, 2009. Print.

Johnston, Lynn. *A Look Inside For Better or For Worse. The 10th Anniversary Collection*. Kansas City: Andrews and McMeel, 1989. Print.

Johnston, Lynn. *Something Old, Something New*. Kansas City: Andrews McMeel, 2011. Print.

Johnston, Lynn. *Suddenly Silver: Celebrating 25 Years of For Better or for Worse*. Kansas City,: Andrews McMeel, 2004. Print.

Johnston, Lynn. *There Goes My Baby!* Kansas City,S: Andrews McMeel, 1993. Print.

Johnston, Lynn. *Things Are Looking Up...* Kansas City: Andrews McMeel, 1992. Print.

Johnston, Lynn. *With This Ring*. Kansas City: Andrews McMeel, 2003. Print.

Kaufman, Gloria and Mary Kay Blakely, eds. *Pulling Our Own Strings. Feminist Humor and Satire*. Bloomington: Indiana University Press, 1980. Print.

Lafky, Sue A. and Bonnie Brennan. "For Better or For Worse: Coming Out in the Funny Pages." *Studies in Popular Culture* 18 (Oct. 1995): 24-47. Print.

Magnussen, Anne and Hans-Christian Christiansen, eds. *Comics/ Culture: Analytical and Theoretical Approaches to Comics*. University of Copenhagen: Museum Tusculanum Press, 2000.

Mulkay, Michael. *On Humour*. New York: Basil Blackwell, 1988. Print.

Robbins, Trina. *From Girls to Grrrlz: A History of Comics from Teens to Zines*. San Francisco: Chronicle Books, 1999. Print.

Robbins, Trina. *The Great Women Cartoonists*. New York: Watson-Guptill Publications, 2001. Print.

Sheppard, Alice. "Social Cognition, Gender Roles, and Women's Humour." *Women's Comic Visions*. Ed. June Sochen. Detroit: Wayne State University Press, 1991. 57-81. Print.

Sochen, June, ed. *Women's Comic Visions*. Detroit: Wayne State University Press, 1991. Print.

Swords, Betty. "Why Women Cartoonists Are Rare and Why That's Important." *New Perspectives on Women and Comedy*. Ed. Regina Barreca. Philadelphia: Gordon and Breach, 1992. 65-84. Print.

Spacks, Patricia Meyer. *The Female Imagination*. New York: Alfred A. Knopf, 1975.Print.

Tombs, Deirdre. "Cartoonists's Ordinary Native People Celebrated." *Windspeaker* 22.10 (2005): 20. Web. 9 Aug. 2012.

Walker, Nancy. *A Very Serious Thing: Women's Humour and American Culture*. Minneapolis: University of Minnesota Press, 1988. Print.

Walker, Nancy. "Toward Solidarity: Women's Humour and Group Identity." Sochen 57-81. Print.

Walker, Nancy, ed. *What's So Funny? Humor in American Culture*. American Visions. Readings in American Culture 1. Wilmington, DE: Scholarly Resources Inc., 1998. Print.

7. "If I Was a Woman as I Am a Man"

The Transgender Imagination in Newfoundland Ballads

PAULINE GREENHILL

STUDYING A TRANSGENDER IMAGINATION—the idea that a person, self or other, is or could be of a different sex or gender than they appear—in ballads collected in Newfoundland might to some readers look obscure at best. Traditional Atlantic Canadian narrative songs rarely make the Euro-North American academic mainstream, or the centres of social, political, or economic power and hegemony. And that is the point. Scholars such as Julia Epstein and Kristina Straub or Rudolf Dekker and Lotte van de Pol have identified transgender persons and concepts in elite European history and literature. But if a transgender imagination—shown, for example, in apparently female characters dressing, working, and acting as men, and apparently male characters wishing they were female—can be found in non-elite texts such as the Newfoundland ballads I discuss in this chapter, that notion may be more ordinary and less exceptional than many would suspect.

It remains difficult for those brought up with and within conventional Euro-North American sex/gender systems to imagine outside those structures' strictly regulated borders of understanding. Hence, the apparently rare texts from traditional and popular culture that do just that notional work offer precious examples not only of transgender and transsex, but also of those concepts' historicity, as Kay Turner and I have previously suggested. I argue here that these traditional ballads, most originating as broadsides from approximately the seventeenth to the nineteenth centuries, provide possibilities for individuals—performers and audiences—to think about themselves, or others, being translated into another sex. I am not claiming that those who first composed or sang these songs consciously intended to introduce a transgender imagination. I am suggesting instead that a "perverse reading" (to use Bonnie Zimmerman's formulation), against the grain of the heterocentric imagination, makes such an understanding possible. This perspective brings my topic squarely into the propositions and terrain of *Changing Places*, with a particular concentration on the possibilities for sex/gender transformations.

Undoubtedly, these songs are fictional representations. No one takes them as historical narratives of actual experience. But fiction can offer truths and present analyses of society and culture that speak to its performers' and audience's knowledge and feelings. Patricia Hill Collins, referencing Black feminist thought, argues for the importance of "the 'inside' ideas that allow Black women to cope with and, in most cases, transcend the confines of race, class, and gender oppression" (92-93). Transgender imagination, as the ability to think oneself or another beyond sociocultural confines of sex and gender, then becomes valuable for similar reasons. A free consciousness for transgender persons often depends on thinking about possibilities other than current experiences of marginalization and oppression—even if other material and social conditions make a more literal enactment or a personal embodiment of transgender impossible. Further, as Judith Butler argues:

> Fantasy is not simply a cognitive exercise, an internal film that we project inside an interior theater of the mind. Fantasy structures relationality, and it comes into play in the stylization of embodiment itself.... The thought of a possible life is only an indulgence for those who already know themselves to be possible. For those who are still looking to become possible, possibility is a necessity. (*Undoing* 217, 219)

Far from being epiphenomenal or even inessential, imagination is the necessary precursor to empathy, and becomes an integral part of practices that make transgender literally possible. Exploring its specific manifestations, contours, and trajectories in traditional and popular culture simultaneously plumbs the possible sources and the potential configurations of transgender itself.

I bring to this analysis feminist, queer, and particularly transgender perspectives, read via discourse analysis. As a feminist, I note a profound disjuncture between the social and cultural expectations for the sexes and their actual capabilities and desires that partly explains the motivations of the songs' characters. Queer theory emerges in my focus on the texts' apparent refusal to confine sexuality to heterosexual norms. As Annamarie Jagose comments, "queer" is useful for "its definitional indeterminacy, its elasticity.... Part of queer's semantic clout, part of its political efficacy, depends on its resistance to definition"

(1). These songs' characters similarly resist definition—as homosexual or heterosexual, as male or female, as masculine or feminine. They instantiate, in fact

> those gestures or analytical models which dramatize in-coherencies in the allegedly stable relations between chromosomal sex, gender and sexual desire. Resisting that model of stability—which claims heterosexuality as its origin when it is more properly its effect—queer focuses on mismatches between sex, gender, and desire.... Demonstrating the impossibility of any "natural" sexuality, it calls into question even such apparently unproblematic terms as "man" or "woman." (3)

The term "transgender" is contested. As I use it here, it indicates a lack of fit between gender identity (social, cultural, psychological) and sex identity (biological, physiological). As an encompassing term, it covers transsexuals (who identify as another sex than that into which they were born and may or may not have medical interventions to match their sex identity to their gender identity); intersexuals (whose biological identity includes markers of both male and female); cross-dressers or transvestites (who dress as another sex); and genderqueers or gender fuckers (who feel their sex/gender identity to be between, beyond, or in addition to the binaries of male and female).[2] Susan Stryker comments:

> If queer theory was born of the union of sexuality studies and feminism, transgender studies can be considered queer theory's evil twin: it has the same parentage but willfully disrupts the privileged family narratives that favor sexual identity labels (like *gay, lesbian, bisexual,* and *heterosexual*) over the gender categories (like man and woman) that enable desire to take shape and find its aim. (212)

Another benefit of these particular texts, then, is their apparent resistance to just those sorts of constrictions on sex, gender, and sexuality. They particularize the sex(es) and sexuality(ies) of individual characters, while not restricting them to a single or binarised category. For example, in the ballad "Short Jacket," a male character may sexually proposition a female character he takes as male because s/he is thus dressed, but he continues to do so when s/he reveals her/himself in female attire. In "The Soldier Maid," a female character dressed as a male may talk about not having sex with men, and be an object of desire for a woman, and choose an eventual fate that does not involve any sexual relationship.

I find compelling Jay Prosser's concern that transsexuality, particularly, can be theorised out of existence by an insistence on the performativity (in Butler's terms) of gender. However, at the time these songs were first created and performed (from the seventeenth to the nineteenth century), but also when the majority of them were collected and published (between the late 1920s and the middle 1980s), both medical technologies and legal options for dealing with a sense of being within the wrong body were non-existent or at best extremely limited in availability. Thus, transsex would have been confined, in fact, to performance—and to imagination, as Judith Halberstam suggests in "Telling Tales: Brandon Teena, Billy Tipton, and Transgender Biography."

It is an extensive leap for most people well socialized in Euro-North American culture to understand that sex, gender, sexual presentation/performance, and sexual orientation could be disconnected from one another—or that there could be more than two choices in each area. Euro-North American kinship systems binarise all four. These pairs are almost always presented in an order that gives priority to the most powerful and normative group, as in: sex equals men and women only; gender equals male and female only; sexual presentation/performance equals masculine and feminine only; and sexual orientation equals heterosexual (opposite sex) and homosexual (same sex) only.

These systems also simultaneously link normalcy with the production of the appropriate connections: people with men's biology should behave as masculine males and should partner sexually with feminine women, and so on. Sexual orientation cannot dislodge those patterned associations. More and more, a woman partnering sexually with another woman or a man with another man is understandable simply in terms of the binary of *same* sex attraction, rather than *opposite* sex attraction. The contrary of the normal re-establishes, even fixes more firmly, the binary itself; the standard is apprehended most clearly when contrasted with its inverse.[3] Such linkages do not threaten the status quo, as evidenced by the Canadian government's decision to legalise same sex marriage. No longer a revolutionary concept, same sex marriage is not only characterised in terms of basic human rights, but also as the presumed wish of lesbians and gays to have families just like those of heterosexuals. In fact, many queer folks, like many heterosexual people, do not seek conventional marriage. Stryker argues for a more politically charged understanding of both queer and trans:

> While queer studies remains the most hospitable place to undertake transgender work, all too often *queer* remains a code word for "gay" or "lesbian," and all too often transgender phenomena are misapprehended through a lens that privileges sexual orientation and sexual identity as the primary means of differing from heteronormativity. Most disturbingly, "transgender" increasingly functions as a site in which to contain all gender trouble, thereby helping to secure both homosexuality and heterosexuality as stable and normative categories of personhood. (214)

Yet bisexuality, transsex and transgender can disturb binary cultural categories as critics such as Holly Devor, Vivian Namaste or Jean Bobby Noble variously demonstrate. The reaction to such disruptions can include such errors as biphobia—the notion that bisexuals are really undecided, exploitative or experimenting—or transdenial. An example of the latter comes from a feminist colleague who told me in her very best authoritative voice that Brandon Teena was not a transsexual, she (*sic*) was a lesbian but because she lived in the rural midwestern United States, she was not aware of lesbianism, and thus could not self-identify as such. The explanation remains unlikely. A first step in avoiding such mistakes can come in recognising the paradoxes of culture where sex is concerned. For example, Euro-North American scientific mythology enjoins that incest is bad because reproductive incest produces monster-children, yet incest between adoptive relatives remains taboo outside any greater-than-usual genetic risk. In this sex/gender system, sexual divergence is analytically paramount, to the extent that a person who is (mistakenly?) sexually attracted to a trans*gender* person of the same *sex* raises concerns that they are homosexual; because homosexuality is about *same-sex* attraction. In this puzzle, *different-gender* attraction does not fit. Mainstream culture finds it practically incomprehensible that a male-born human might want gender-reassignment surgery to become a woman yet throughout be sexually attracted primarily or exclusively to women. Clearly, binary thinking does not encompass all the possibilities of human sex, gender, and sexuality, and emotional intelligence opens up other possibilities not constrained within binary oppositions.

Of course, I am not the first to have noticed the disconnect between sex, gender, and sexuality across historical time and geographical space. Numerous analyses from queer cultural studies show the many different ways that both normative and polymorphously perverse sex can unfold as cultural overlays upon biological diversity. A variety of discourses illustrate these processes. Randolph Trumbach, discussing the period from which the texts I will discuss here originate, indicates that "the paradigm of two genders founded on two biological sexes began to predominate in Western culture only in the early eighteenth century. It was a product of the modern Western gender system, which makes it peculiarly difficult for Westerners to see that this paradigm is not inherent in the empirical observation of the world." He shows that even within that system, "there was a third illegitimate gender, namely, the adult passive, transvestite, and effeminate male, or 'molly,' who was supposed to desire men exclusively" (111). He points out, as others have, the difficulty of imagining what would now be understood as lesbianism within this system, even in the face of manifest contemporary examples of women dressing as men, and having sexual relations with women. The eventual emergence of a four gender system, "men and women, and sodomites and sapphists ... has been obscured ... by the tendency to imagine a linked system of two sexes, two genders and two sexual orientations" (136).

But transgender can help to ontologically dismantle such systems, whether it imagines a third (or more) sex(es), or whether it simply asks for a recognition of locations between and beyond the binaries. Much work on transgender, such as Butler's *Bodies that Matter* (1993) or Prosser's *Second Skins* (1998), has very helpfully incorporated a focus on the body as well as upon discourse. The texts I consider, however, are less about *having* sex—*neither* a biologically/somatically specific bodily form *nor* sexual congress—than they are about *imagining or visualizing* sex outside binary systems—*either* a biologically/somatically specific bodily form *or* sexual congress. Given the lack of contemporary availability of medical interventions to transform the body, this perspective is hardly surprising.

Ballads exemplifying this transgender imagination were collected by folklorists in Canada, particularly in the Atlantic provinces, during the middle decades of the twentieth century. Versions have also been collected internationally and at other times, but I draw for this paper on those from Newfoundland because they represent a geographically and historically circumscribed series. My previous work on Newfoundland ballads and transgender issues focused on the largest of the area's collections, the three-volume *Songs of the Newfoundland Outports*

(1965), collected by Kenneth Peacock between 1951 and 1961. My analysis spoke in terms of "cross-dressing" rather than transgender, and concerned the songs' implications for understanding the social history of sexual orientation. Rather than reprising that study, I focus on texts from Peacock not detailed in my previous work, as well as those published in other Newfoundland song anthologies, collected by Elizabeth Bristol Greenleaf in 1929; by Maud Karpeles in 1929 and 1930; and by Genevieve Lehr and Anita Best from 1975 to 1983.

These songs' authors' names may be lost, but the texts have a relatively long history. They were originally composed and circulated as cheaply printed broadsides in Britain in the seventeenth, eighteenth, and nineteenth centuries, but when they were collected in twentieth century Newfoundland, they had spread in oral as well as written forms. The fact that these songs have been remembered and passed down in family and community repertoire for generations clearly indicates that what they have to say remains relevant for their singers and audiences. People do not learn or perform songs to which they are indifferent. Listeners always have latitude in interpreting songs, as singers do in presenting them. Thus, even if their original or current singers did not, or do not, see these songs as pertaining to transgender issues, it is not necessary absolutely to preclude that possibility. Audiences, especially now, may so interpret them. But it is not unreasonable to speculate that throughout their history, these songs' singers and audiences included folks who empathised with the characters because they shared their marginalised position. Again, this is not the only genre in which transgendering symbolic and ideological moves appear. Other fictional accounts of women dressing as men abound, as does recent historical work exploring cases of actual pre-twentieth century transgender Euro-American women.[4] Scholars' denials of all non-straight, non-vanilla readings of songs amount to silencing, ignoring, and suppressing their implications. Both storied and real-life transgender people's motivations—including getting access to contexts from which they are excluded—are similar to those of the ballad protagonists.

I argue here for an interpretation of songs' meanings based on current as well as possible historic understandings. However they may have been understood in 1700s London, in 1950s Newfoundland, or in my location in twenty-first-century Winnipeg, the messages they contain about the action and behaviour they depict cannot now be seen as exclusively heterosexual, straight, and mainstream. This reading is perverse—perhaps even polymorphously perverse—or undisciplined, in that it deliberately and willfully goes against the grain of conventional interpretations.

Taking transgender as a general term for those who actively practice messing up the rigid and stable binaries in the sex/gender system, the characters in these ballads live and thus personally instantiate what Marjorie Garber calls "category crisis"—a conceptual paradox coming from an inability to contain or fix their sex, gender, and sexuality. Whether their characters are explicitly "neither a man nor a maid" (Peacock 281) themselves, or whether they envisage themselves or another person switching sex/gender locations, these songs conceptualize sex/gender mutability. The crisis, of course, is the system's; the protagonists themselves are perfectly comfortable with their shifting positions.

Folklorists used to call many of these songs "female sailor," "female warrior," "female highwayman" songs. The sexist presumption that a woman cannot or should not be included in the designations sailor, warrior, or robber keeps the sex/gender categories nice and neat, while it allows a few individual rebels to be the exceptions that prove the rule. These songs have also been called "transvestite" or "cross-dressing" ballads, presuming that clothing choices are their intellectual centre. Yet a less restrictive notion of gender roles allows the same texts to be understood as points of disjuncture on a variety of levels. The protagonists are clearly working as well as playing gender. They both attract and are attracted to women and men alike. And they help deconstruct the fiction that masculinity (unlike femininity) is non-performative—that it is only sex and not gender.

The songs I work with here are not only about women dressing as men. I will also consider what appears to be the only song in the repertoire about a man dressing as a woman, as well as the two in which characters imagine themselves, or another, to be a sex/gender other than they appear to be. In sum, in this textual universe, clothes make the man, but clothes don't make the woman. Male characters exemplify the transgender imagination in two modes: imagining the other's transformation—"I wish you were a woman"—and imagining his own—"If I were a woman."

CLOTHES MAKE THE MAN/BOY

In previous work ("Neither"; "Handsome"), I have already discussed extensively "The Handsome Cabin Boy" and "The Soldier Maid" as they appear in Peacock's collection demonstrating the notion that "clothes make the man"—that women can dress and for the most part successfully pass as men. The characters' transgender position is usually positive, even enviable. The protagonists succeed in their work as well as in continuing to choose their sexual partners, often against strong family opposition. Compellingly, these cross-dressed women are always referred to as "boys" rather than as "men." Similarly, in early twentieth century vaudeville, "male impersonators...were judged on the degree to which 'real men' could *differentiate* themselves from them. That differentiation helped mark critical signs of masculinity in an increasingly public war over the ownership of male political and social privileges.... The most important attribute of a successful male impersonator, in fact, was that she not be *too* realistic" (Ullman 197). And yet the song characters had to be convincing as boys, and in the example of "William Taylor" (Laws N11),[5] one certainly demonstrates what could be seen as a form of phallic mastery. Willy Taylor is "a brisk young sailor/ Full of love and full of glee," who is "marched ... off to sea." "His true love" follows under a male pseudonym. During work "on the yardarm reefing ... her waistcoat did blow open,/And she showed her lily-white breast." The captain inquires as to "what wonders brought you here?" When she tells him she's following Taylor, the captain explains that her love has been untrue. The woman "called for two bright pistols,.../And she shot young Willy Taylor,/Standing at his bride's right hand." The captain promotes her to "a first leftenant (*sic*)." With her "[l]ong bright sword into her hand ... she gives orders,/ Makes men tremble at her command" (sung by Daniel Endacott, Sally's Cove, 1929; Greenleaf 49-50).

This text clearly shows that "wardrobe malfunctions," like transgender, are no new phenomenon. As in the Janet Jackson incident, the question inevitably arises: was this staged?[6] And in both situations, the answer is by no means self-evident. In another version, sung by Mrs. James Day (*sic*), Fortune Harbour, Notre Dame Bay, 1929, "As soon as her waistcoat did blow open/The captain saw her lily-white breast" (Karpeles 171). Both versions' phrasings avoid identifying responsibility, suggesting that the revelation is accidental, particularly given the heroine's forceful and determining actions in the rest of the song. And yet, though she goes "by the name of Richard Kerr," the pronoun reference is always female—she or her.

This text relies less on a transgender imagination on the part of a character than on a visual revelation. Yet it is one of the most explicit examples of gender role transgression of all the texts. The nameless (except as Richard Kerr) main character not only dresses as a man and "embraces" (Greenleaf) or "endures" (Karpeles) "the pitch and tar";

she brandishes "a case of pistols" and "a broadsword" (Karpeles) or a "long bright sword" (Greenleaf) with great success, gets away with assault with a deadly weapon if not murder, and makes "men" (Greenleaf) or "sailors" (Karpeles) "tremble at her command."

Neither version clarifies whether Taylor is fatally shot. In any case, the result of this extreme action is positive. Not only does the lady discover her "true lovyer's" infidelity, but she escapes the consequences of shooting him by once again cross-dressing—with the captain's collusion—this time in a position of power over men as a lieutenant, rather than "doing her work amongst the rest." She is further marked by the phallic "long bright sword" apparently always ready to ensure that her orders are followed. Presumably in this officer's position, wardrobe malfunctions might be less likely. Yet, "Willy Taylor" is exceptional in the genre. Usually it is unequivocally and explicitly the woman's own choice to reveal that her sex does not match her gender. The heroine's revelation in "William Taylor" may be inadvertent; in "The Soldier Maid" (below), it is inevitable in the circumstances of her pregnancy.

In "Polly Oliver" (Laws N14), in contrast, the title character changes dress at will. "[P]retty Polly … dresses like a man," and "[w]ith a pair of bright pistols and a broadsword by her side;/On her father's great stallion like a great man did ride." In London, s/he meets her/his "true love," a captain, and tells him that Polly, his "friend," has instructed that he and his "ship's company drink Polly's health all around." The captain offers the "young man" a bed, including a sexual innuendo, which s/he accepts, saying "since you are the captain I will be at your command." When s/he gets up the next morning s/he dresses "in her own suit of clothes." The captain appreciates Polly's joke but says "'If I didn't please you last night, love, the fault it was not mine;/I'm in hopes to please you better so now is the time.'" The couple marries (Gordon Willis, Fogo, 1929; Greenleaf 51-52).

In another Newfoundland version from Tom White and Will White of Sandy Cove, 1929, Polly's personal and emotional independence at the song's end explicitly matches the captain's: "O now she is married, *she* lives at her ease,/Goes out when *she's* minded, comes back when *she's* pleased" (Greenleaf 54, my emphases). The same version is not explicit about Polly's original dress, but uses an analogy: "Like a jolly young trouper all along Polly did ride" (53). Gordon Willis' later version (1952), sung for Peacock, describes Polly thus: "In every degree like a man she dressed so well" (344).

When dressed in men's clothing, this song's protagonist is called

"Jack" and referred to using male pronouns; when dressed or planning to dress as a woman, s/he is "Polly" and female pronouns are used. This character, then, actually seems to switch identity with her dress—a fairly literal performative gender. Her/his sexuality also seems quite malleable. Current Euro-North American readers may find it remarkable that Polly and the captain both treat his sexual dalliance with Jack as nothing more than a joke. Not only is his infidelity seemingly unproblematic, so is his apparent bisexuality. Despite the superficial likenesses between this song and "Willy Taylor," then, the sex/gender identities referenced in the two are quite dissimilar.

In "The Press Gang" (Laws N6), as in "Polly Oliver," family opposition to the match the heroine chooses does not dissuade her. A rich merchant's daughter spurns those of her class but "fancied her sailor, he was proper and tall." Her father persuades her to court the sailor in private, but arranges to have him press-ganged. The "lady... dressed herself up in men's clothes," and signs as a sailor with the same captain, bunking with her sailor. S/he asks why he sighs in his sleep and he responds that his "true love's father sent him away. S/he claims to be an astrologer, and predicts "[y]ou were born for right joy and mirth;/You shall gain this fair one in spite of them all," and identifies herself. They marry and conclude "here's a fig for her old father she'll never see more" (William Malloy, St. Shotts, St. Mary's Bay 1930, Karpeles 167-168).

Many traditional ballads, like this example, rely on the device that at least one of the erstwhile lovers does not know the other. Sometimes, the explanation is that he has been away at sea or at war and implicitly that time has changed one or both so completely that they are unrecognisable. In this case, perhaps her disguise and the act of passing are so complete that detection cannot take place. However, this is not always the case. In "The Simple Ploughboy" (Laws M24), the "handsome comely maid" finds out that her father has press-ganged her ploughboy:

> With jacket and trousers this damsel she put on,
> Two pockets were lined with gold.
> She walked down the street and the pumps were on her feet
> And she passed for a jolly sailor bold. (Karpeles 165)

Her passing is extremely short-lived, though. When she asks another "jolly sailor bold" if he knows the ploughboy, he answers "he's going to join the fleet,/And he said: My comely maid will you and I?" (165) Again, there is considerable variation on how similar situations may unfold, how the narrative will progress, and what will become the denouement. The outcomes can include marriage, a continued search for the lost lover, and a continued prosecution of the new occupation—soldiering, sailing, robbing.

In "The Wearing of the Blue" (unclassified), as in "Willy Taylor," sometimes true loves are not as true as they should be, even going as far as to attempt murder. But there are alternatives to grievous bodily harm. A "gallant lady all in her tender youth" loves a sailor and longs to go to sea with him to Canada. She bargains with a sailor to take her aboard and dress her in sailor's clothes. Her "true love" "flew into a rage" and wants to throw her overboard, but the captain refuses, saying he will dress her in sailor's clothes and take her with them. "[T]he captain married her and called her his dear./She's dressed in silks and satin and she calls a gallant show,/She's the finest captain's lady in Canada i-ho" (Clarence Coffin, Fortune Bay, 1930, Karpeles 169-170)

The male lover, in this song, is easily replaceable. Men take the roles of helpers—not only the sailor lad who takes the protagonist to the ship and dresses her "in sailor's clothes," but also the captain who saves her from her "true love" who wants to murder her, and again dresses her as a sailor. The male characters show considerably different features; they may be loyal or fickle, helpful or vengeful, loving or full of rage.

In a twist on a by-now familiar story of fatherly disapproval followed by disguise to follow the lover, a merchant's daughter falls in love with "[h]er father's prentice boy" in "The Rose of Britain's Isle" (Laws N16). The father sends the lad "[w]ith great disdain across the main." The daughter dresses "in man's attire" and follows on the same ship. Jane is wounded, and her love Edwin recognizes her. She recovers, and they return home. Her father "being dead and gone," and having willed Jane "a handsome fortune/Likewise a large estate" she marries Edwin (Lizzie Mahoney, Stock Cove, Bonavista Bay, 1929, Karpeles 173-175). As in previous examples, it seems that the lover Edwin fails to identify Jane in her sailor disguise; indeed it appears that the other sailors discover her first, but only because she is wounded in the "arm."

In some songs, women offer to dress in men's clothing and follow, but their lovers reject this option, saying things like:

Your dear little fingers cold cables can't handle,
Your dear little toes to the maintop can't go,
Your delicate body cold winds can't endure,

But advise, lovely Nancy, to the sea, do not go.
("Farewell Nancy," Bridget Hall, North River, Conception Bay,
1929, Karpeles 177)

The infantilizing language of "dear," "little," "delicate," and "lovely"
is all too familiar, but the argument from biological weakness is
throughout the genre belied by the many women characters who clearly
can "handle," "go," and "endure" with great success.

A similar explanation comes from "Jimmy and Nancy or Lisbon"
(unclassified). When the woman offers to put on men's clothing and go
as her lover's waiting man, he first answers:

Your waist it is too slender, love, your fingers they are too small,
To wait upon you in battle upon you I will call,
Where big guns do rattle and a musket will do fly.
The silver trumpet shall sound, my love, to drown all dismal
     cry.
(Bridget Hall, North River, Conception Bay, 1929, Karpeles
178)

The argument that women in battle would be a distraction to men is
evidently not new. Indeed, the notion that women invariably perturb
men has been an excuse to keep them from the professions, from non-
traditional work, and from all kinds of leadership positions. But one
suspects the true reason for Jimmy's refusal comes in the following verse:

If I should meet some other girl, so bonny, brisk, and gay,
If I should fall in love with her, what would my Nancy say?
What would your Nancy say, Jimmy, sure she would like her
     too,
She'd gently step on one side when she'd be kissing you. (178-
179)

Jimmy immediately suggests they marry and go to war together. The
option provided would not meet with approval from contemporary
social conservatives. By agreeing to ethical non-monogamy as well
as possibly to bisexuality, Nancy earns her place as a soldier maid.
Her agreement to the situation appears textually unforced, and both
partners seem happy with the outcome.

Almost without exception, the above songs present sex/gender identity
as being readily alterable by changing clothes. As Halberstam discusses

at length, many drag kings similarly embrace the "bastardized" or "bad" ("Mackdaddy" 108) reading of Butler's notion of performativity, that suggests that gender is quite literally a series of costumes that can be donned or doffed at will: "waking in the morning and picking clothes and genders out of closets and hanging them up at the end of the day" (109). Indeed, with the possible exception of "The Handsome Cabin Boy," that process seems to exactly describe what the ballad characters do. Their movement from one gender location to another is unhindered and easy, and thus fundamentally queer.

But I would also suggest that these songs retain a concern with passing (and failing) at male and female roles. The protagonists succeed, eventually, often in both personae. Failures are due to betrayal,, whether at the hands of another woman ("The Soldier Maid"), or by the woman's own body becoming pregnant ("The Handsome Cabin Boy"), or by a sometimes inadvertent inability of the clothing to disguise identity, providing a visual revelation. Linda Schlossberg's comments about passing are helpful in exploring these issues:

> Theories and practices of identity and subject formation in Western culture are largely structured around a logic of visibility.... We are subjects constituted by our visions of ourselves and others, and we trust that our ability to see and read carries with it a certain degree of epistemological uncertainty....Because of this seemingly intimate relationship between the visual and the known, passing becomes a highly charged site for anxieties regarding visibility, invisibility, classification, and social demarcation....If passing wreaks havoc with accepted systems of social recognition and cultural intelligibility, it also blurs the carefully marked lines of race, gender, and class, calling attention to the ways in which identity categories intersect, overlap, construct, and deconstruct one another. (1-2)

Schlossberg also notes that, "passing can be experienced as a source of radical pleasure or intense danger" (3). Clearly it is both for the transgender characters in these ballads, as it may be for those members of their audience who empathise with their position. When the characters are with men, they pass with little difficulty in the absence of a wardrobe malfunction; clothes truly make the man. "To be 'unmarked' is to occupy a position of privilege, in which the subject hides behind an apparent transparency" (5). Their cross-dressing is not intended to be read as such, and their masculinity no hyperbole. It is figurative and successful, not only because they usually pass, but also because they are so adept at the male roles they play. Further, in a social context in which, as Halberstam suggests, "eccentric, double, duplicitous, deceptive, odd, self-hating: all these judgments swirl around the cross-dresser, the non-operative transsexual, the self-defined transgender person, as if other lives—gender normative lives—were not odd, not duplicitous, not doubled and contradictory at every turn" ("Telling" 24), it is worth pointing out in this particular genre the fundamental straightforwardness (bad pun) of these (wo) men. Singers and audiences are textually invited to turn against the false "true lovers" and the bad fathers, not the main characters. It is difficult to imagine a better undermining of the sex/gender system's boundaries, that simultaneously points out their arbitrariness and their superficiality.

CLOTHES DON'T MAKE THE WOMAN

Schlossberg also talks about passing functioning "as a badge of shame or a source of pride" (5). Where pride overwhelmingly dominates the experiences of women dressing as men in Newfoundland ballads, the one example in the Newfoundland ballad oeuvre involving a male cross-dresser has considerably less happy results than the inevitably positive outcomes in the latter examples.

In "The Shirt and Apron" (Laws K42), a sailor who has returned from the sea with fifty pounds plans to head home but meets "a fair one," who invites him to a dance. He says his parents are expecting him in Wigginstown, but goes with her anyway. They visit a bar, and when she invites him to "'repair to a chamber all alone'" he goes. He wakes the next morning to find his "watch and clothes and fifty pound" gone, the "ducksie with it fled," leaving him "alone, stark naked on the bed." He is forced to wear the only clothes available, "a woman's shirt and apron." Having no money, he returns to the ship where the sailors taunt him: "'Is this the new spring fashion, Jack, the ladies got on shore?/ Where is the shop that's selling it, or is there any more?'" The song concludes with a warning to "[b]e sure and choose good company when you gets on a spree" (Abraham White, Sandy Cove, 1929, Greenleaf and Mansfield 222-223)

Insofar as Jack is not mistaken for a woman, but taken as himself dressed inappropriately, this text does not offer an example of passing. However, note that the comments of the sailors—"Is this the new spring fashion … the ladies got?"—presumes that it was Jack's intention to dress as a woman. That of the captain—"I know you could buy a better suit"—also presumes his clothing is his own choice, but a bad one. Indeed, heading back to the ship to return to work (instead of going home with money as he had planned), he does not want to pass as a woman since he would not be allowed to pursue his occupation as such. Thus, the question of (not) passing is crucial in this text; Jack does not choose women's clothing, nor is the outcome he faces one that he *would* choose. Cross-dressing is for Jack a humiliation and a failure, marking his inability to master his own fate. Thus, though a transgender imagination is at work in this ballad, it imagines a nightmare rather than the dream of personal fulfillment in those about women cross-dressing.[7]

I WISH YOU WERE A WOMAN

One cross-dressing ballad, "Short Jacket" (Laws N12), includes a passage in which the captain imaginatively transsexes into female a person he thinks is actually male. A "fair one" puts on "[s]hort jacket and blue trousers" and bargains her passage with a captain "to go and seek her own true-love." One night the captain propositions her, saying: "'I wish you were a maid./Your cherry cheeks and ruby lips/Have all enticed me." She discourages him, saying that the sailors "would make sport and game," if they knew, and that they can find "handsome girls" on shore. When they reach the Irish shore, s/he says "'Here's adieu forevermore./A sailor once I been on board,/A maid I reach the shore.'" He asks her to come back, saying "'A lady you might be,'" but she simply repeats her "adieu" (Mrs. Tom White, Jr., Sandy Cove, 1929, Greenleaf and Mansfield 100-101). Clearly, when a man is attracted to the transperson, this does not usually lead immediately to sexual activity. In another version of the same song, called "Blue Jacket and White Trousers," for example, the captain says: "'Your rosy cheeks and ruby lips they do entice me,/And I do wish with all my heart that you was a maid for me." The protagonist supports the captain's impression that she is male. So her reply is:

"Oh leave off talking captain, your talk it's all in vain,
For if the sailors they do know on us they will make game;
And when we reach the southern shores some pretty girls we'll find;
They'll roll us in their arms, to us they will prove kind."
(Charlotte Decker, Parson's Pond, 1958, Peacock 327-328)

The presumed male sailor does not dismiss sexual activity with the male captain as potentially eliciting violence or danger, nor, for that matter, as personally repugnant. S/he instead presents it as a lesser alternative to the heterosex that will be readily available on the southern shores—as unnecessary. Again, fully independent, this woman seeks her lover, is offered an apparently attractive alternative, but decides to continue searching.

The transgender imagination in this text is transferred to the object of sexual interest. But since sexuality is determined in Euro-North American sex/gender systems in terms of that object, it is difficult to contain within a simple homosexual/heterosexual binary a man who wants to have sex with a person he thinks is a man, but not with her as a man, with her as a woman. But it is not only folksong texts that instantiate such an imagination. Attributing his own idea to others, folksong scholar A. L. Lloyd exemplifies the transgender imagination in a response to the cross-dressing ballads in general: "The dream that one of their companions might be a girl dressed as a boy is an inevitable fantasy for lonely men in barrack bunk or fo'c'sle hammock" (225). Lloyd characterises this transgender imagination not as *possible*, but as *inevitable*. Such a move closes in on Butler's meaning when she comments that in some definitions "'transgender' is a not exactly a third gender, but a mode of passage between genders, an interstitial and transitional figure of gender that is not reducible to the normative insistence on one or two" (*Undoing* 43).

IF I WAS A WOMAN

In "Willy O' Winsbury," alternatively known as "John Barbour" (Child 100), a father asks his daughter why she seems sick; she replies that she is thinking of her "own true love./Who sails upon the sea." The father inquires "is he a lord or a duke,.../ "Or a man of note and fame?/Or is he one of our sailor lads?" She replies that he is a sailor, named John Barbour. The father threatens to hang him. But when he meets the sailor, "clothed all in white;/His cheeks were like the roses red,/And his teeth like ivory bright," the father says, "'If I was a woman as I am a man,/My bed-fellow you should be." He offers Barbour his daughter's hand and to "'go head over all my land?'" Barbour accepts the daughter but not the land, saying that he is three times wealthier than the father (Elsie Best, St. John's, 1977, Lehr and Best 109-110). Another version questions:

"Oh what is the matter with my daughter?" he said,

"She looks so pale and wan,
I think she has got some sore sickness.
Or have laid with some young man."
(Charlotte Decker, Parson's Pond, 1959, Peacock 534)

The daughter denies the sexual aspect: "I have not a-got any sore sickness/Or have laid with some young man" (534). Here the father directly addresses the lover, rather than speaking to her:

"No wonder for my daughter, John Barbour," he said,
"That she might fall in love with you,
For if I was a woman instead of a man
I would surely fall in love with you." (535)

In another version:

"I will make no wonder," the old man said,
"That my daughter is in love with you,
For if I were a maid instead of a man,
I would die for the love of you."
(Peter Abbott, Twillingate, 1929, Greenleaf 33)

A version collected by Karpeles also implicates a sexual involvement between the daughter and her lover:

Dear daughter, dear daughter, the father did say,
What makes you look so pale and wan?
You look like you've had a fit of sickness
Or been lying with some young man.
(Janie Augot, Rencontre, Fortune Bay, 1930, Karpeles 73)

The daughter's response does not deny a sexual relationship: "'It's no wonder for me to look pale and wan,/For all the troubles of my poor heart,/My true love is long at sea" (73). The father's reaction is also slightly different: "if I was a woman instead of a man/I would die for the love of he" (74). The lines in the version sung by Maude Roberts, Sally's Cove, 1930, are almost identical (Greenleaf 29). A second example, sung by Florrie Snow, North River, Conception Bay, 1929 is less sexually explicit. The father asks "'Have you had some heavy sickness,/Or are you in love with some young man?'" (Karpeles 75). Again, the Maude Roberts version is extremely close to the Augot, as is that by Abbott, which makes the same diagnosis—sickness or love (32). The father's attraction, however, remains clear:

> O daughter, O daughter, the father cries,
> I'll lay no blame to thee,
> For if I was a woman instead of a man,
> I'd die today for he. (Karpeles 75)

In the Abbott version there is no apparent commentary on John Barbour's mode of walking downstairs, and his physical appearance is male-identified: "his suit were all in green,/His teeth were of the ivory white,/He was fair as any king" (Peacock 33). But in several texts, the lover's arrival is queered. His gait, if marked, is hardly a manly one, and his physical appearance is decidedly femme, allowing for a possible transgender imagination of the other, as in "Short Jacket." Note, indeed, the similarity to the descriptions of the "fair one" in "Short Jacket": he comes "tripping down,/He was clothed all in silk,/His cheeks was of the roses red,/ His skin was white as milk" (Augot, Karpeles 74). Or he descends "step by step,/All dressed in a suit of silk,/With his two rosy cheeks and his curly bright hair/And his skin as white as milk" (Snow, Karpeles 76). Or alternatively, he is "Dressed in his suit of green,/With his two rolling eyes like diamonds bright,/And he was neat and clean" (Peacock 535). He can even come "a-trembling down,/He was clothed all in silk,/With his cherry cheeks like the roses red,/And his skin so white as milk" (Roberts, Greenleaf 29).

All but one of these versions are sung by women. The one performed by Dennis Walsh, Fleur de Lys, 1929 is tellingly different. It has a de-sexualised questioning by the father: "'What makes you look so pale?/ And what is the trouble on your poor heart's mind?/Have your true love been long at sea?'" (Greenleaf 30). This version also sports a more butch-moving and butch-looking Young Barbour:

> O downstairs, downstairs tumbled Young Barbour,
> And he was clothed in silk,
> With his dark-brown eyes and his coal-black hair,
> And his skin faded white as milk. (Greenleaf 31)

The text skips straight from this verse to the question "O, will you marry my daughter" (31) with no intervening reflection by the father on what would happen were he a woman. But that reflection is not absent; it actually closes the song, addressed to the daughter: "If I was a woman instead of a man,/I would die for the love of he" (32).

There are seven full texts published in the collections, of which only two come from men. A further four are mentioned, two from women and two from men. This ballad, then, although by no means ignored by men, seems popular with women. It is not entirely surprising that women would appreciate a song in which a patriarchal figure imaginatively puts himself in his daughter's place; some women apparently understand this transformation as his identification with her. Yet it is difficult to imagine a more gender-troubled scenario than one in which a patriarch not only imagines himself as female, but also sexually subjected to another arguably female-identified figure. The "if I was a woman" locution, then, is less about an imagined change of sexual orientation (which could be, but apparently never is, expressed as "if *you* were a woman"—as happens in the cross-dressing ballads) but an imagined re-gendering from a position of power to a position of subjection as well as from male to female.

Never underestimate the extent to which such readings, if apparently obvious, can be explained away by scholars. When Martin Lovelace presented his paper on "Willy O' Winsbury" at the American Folklore Society (2005), in which he referred to the father's "apparent change of sexual orientation," I commented in the discussion that this looked a lot more like a transgendering move than one related to sexual orientation. A female participant approached me afterwards and explained that this text had nothing to do with either sexual orientation or transgender; it simply indicated the father was identifying with his daughter. Given the actual text's contents, which seem very clearly about a transgender imagination, and given that a reader or hearer cannot know audience or singer intentions if the individuals involved have not explicitly detailed them (and perhaps not even then!), my interlocutor's explanation, while by no means entirely implausible, seems to go out of its way to avoid a textually reasonable explanation. It unnecessarily precludes empathic possibilities. Again, in the absence of certainty about what the singers and their audiences thought, her reading requires a strong presumption of heterosexuality and a strong denial of any other possibility, which especially now that texts can be read transgressively or perversely, seems forced at best.

THE TRANSGENDER IMAGINATION

Many songs in many versions describe women dressing as men and passing, but they comprise only a tiny minority of the entire *oeuvre* of songs in Newfoundland or elsewhere. And there appears to be only one text concerning a man dressed as a woman (and not passing), and similarly only one in which a man expresses a desire for another person to change sex, and only one in which a man expresses a desire to change his own sex. Were I arguing quantitatively, the numbers speak against my presumption of a transgender imagination. Yet I am not contending that such a concept is extensive and encompassing, any more than I think that transgender persons form a majority of the population. But I suspect that if ritualised forms of cross-dressing (like Hallowe'en, mock weddings, or costume parties)[8] and psychological valences of binary sex identity, for example, were taken into consideration, transgender folks would form a larger minority than many might think:

> "Transgender" proves to be an important term not to people who want to reside outside of categories altogether, but to people who want to place themselves in the way of particular forms of recognition. "Transgender" may, indeed, be considered a term of relationality; it describes not simply an identity but a relation between people, within a community, or within intimate bonds. (Halberstam "Telling" 15)

The value of this analysis attaches to the general value of the deconstructive concept of iterability. Reiterate these song texts in a context that draws attention to their possible interpretation in terms of transgender identities and practices, and their meanings may open different symbolic systems.[9] They may shed light, for example, on how texts instantiate and construct heterosexuality. However, they also draw attention to one another as indications of at least the germ of an idea that the world need not be constructed in simplistic binaries. That is, in this case, changing places can be literal, wherein female and male do not need to be fixed and immovable categories, and one can become the other. They show the instability of interpretations, including those that support the status quo.

Empathy also figures in this understanding. I am sure I am not the only woman who has identified strongly with the female protagonists of these transgender ballads. Apart from the lure of their romantic and active stories, I was attracted by the characters' heroic actions and escape from the constraints of kinship. Thus, in the 1980s, my discussion of these songs concluded that women—singers and audiences—in traditional communities might, as I did, perceive these female protagonists as heroic. Further, I surmised, women's interest in such songs could stem from the texts' unusual representation of women's role in the libidinal political economy—(male) society's obsession with the exchange of women and control over their reproductive power. That is, the songs portrayed women's command over their own reproductive use value; the protagonists choose to marry the man they want, or to continue searching, in a society in which that power was/is often limited.

That interpretation presumes a heterosexual personal identification or empathy by female audience or singer. But Women's Studies students and other feminists with whom I discussed this work were disappointed with my interpretation in which a marriage plot appeared as the primary and focal choice. Following their ideas, in the 1990s I explored interpretations of these ballads as expressions of same-sex attraction. I looked at how "The Handsome Cabin Boy" and "The Soldier Maid" showed women gaining sexual access to each other, and pointed out that "Blue Jacket and White Trousers" allows a woman to at least discuss such access. I examined the use of paradoxical and impossible tropes such as the pregnant man in "The Handsome Cabin Boy," and the woman who sleeps with men but remains a virgin in "The Soldier Maid," as a mode for imagining non-straight sexual possibilities ("Neither"; "Handsome").

But I can now add yet another possibility. Maybe these texts are explorations of phenomena of female masculinity and other trans identities. It is not, I think, an entirely implausible explanation. Halberstam argues for "greater taxonomical complexity in our queer histories ... and embrace[s] categorization as a way of creating places for acts, identities and modes of being which otherwise remain unnameable" ("Masculinity"). And Gilbert Herdt's suggestion opens possibility:

> Third-sex/third-gender desires are more than matters of erotic arousal and more than the commitment to the social functions of gendered roles or sexual hierarchies, although they may include these matters. Desire represents a mode of being, a way of linking personal reality to cultural ontology; it represents the creation of an ontological space, situated halfway between the private and the public, between the individual and the secret side of the social person...; and it represents a publicly defined cultural standard or institutional norm, with its symbolic expressions time honoured as tradition and presented to the person and self as immutable cultural reality. (77)

Of course, though these ontologies are *presented* as immutable cultural realities, they are in fact relatively malleable. The transgender imagination is itself an example of the potentially yielding nature of interpretations, which might further assist in extending the understandings of personhood, community, and indeed humanity for transgender and non-transgender folks alike.

[1]The line "If I was a woman as I am a man" comes from the classic ballad "Willie O' Winsbury." Martin Lovelace's 2005 paper, presented at the American Folklore Society meetings in Atlanta, Georgia, first brought the transgendering possibilities of this text to my attention. Ironically, I heard Martin's paper while Michelle Owen was presenting the current work's earlier iteration (Greenhill 2005) at the Drag King Extravaganza in Winnipeg, October 2005. With a focus upon the cross-dressing ballads as expressions of a drag king sensibility, it led directly to this broader consideration. My thanks to Martin and Michelle. I am also extremely grateful to RM Kennedy, who read and commented on a draft, for warm appreciation and excellent suggestions. Finally, I must thank the Social Sciences and Humanities Research Council of Canada for funding my Standard Research Grant, Transgender Imagination and Enactment in Traditional and Popular Culture in Canada, 2008-2012.

[2]Jacqueline N. Zita defines the general understanding of genderfuck as "tampering with the codes of sex identity by mixing male and female, masculine and feminine, man and woman signifiers on one body" (120), to which I add the imagination and/or representation of such acts.

[3]This process makes homosexuality more clearly a sexuality than heterosexuality, which is too often seen simply as existentially normal. The same process applies in other locations. In conventional understandings of ethnicity, for example, the mainstream—the allegedly non-ethnic—is rarely defined; it is only understood in terms of its difference from the qualities of the allegedly ethnic. English Canadians, mainstream Canadians, White Euro-North Americans are difficult to see as ethnics; only those with marked differences from a purported norm—language, rituals, dress, skin colour, and so on—are understood as ethnically marked (see Greenhill, *Ethnicity*).

[4]As well as more recent examples, such as Brandon Teena or Billy Tipton, discussed by Halberstam or the male impersonators of the vaudeville stage discussed by Sharon Ullman.

[5]Standard practice in folkloristics identifies specific songs by their

inclusion in indices by G. Malcolm Laws of native (north) American (1964) and British broadside ballads (1957) and by Francis James Child (1882-1894) of classic ballads. Those who wish to find versions of those discussed from other locations in North America may consult either Laws's index or, for versions of classic or "Child" ballads, Coffin and Renwick. Various electronic databases and indices are also available, including <http://www.ibiblio.org/folkindex/>.

[6]At a Superbowl half-time show 2004, singer Justin Timberlake ripped off Janet Jackson's top to reveal her breast. Several parties explained this event as a "wardrobe malfunction."

[7]Margaret Mills discusses a not-dissimilar pattern in Afghan storytelling about transgender—women who acquire men's clothes or characteristics and men who acquire women's clothes or characteristics. Again, the result is increased power for the women and humiliation—often sexualised humiliation such as rape—for the men.

[8]These are included in my SSHRC Standard Research Grant, Transgender Imagination and Enactment in Traditional and Popular Culture in Canada, 2008-2012.

[9]In a different context, Jack Balkin's discussion of deconstruction usefully delineates its forms.

WORKS CITED

Balkin, Jack. "Deconstruction's Legal Career." *Cardozo Law Review* 27 (2005): 719-40.

Butler, Judith. *Bodies That Matter: On the Discursive Limits of "Sex."* New York: Routledge, 1993. Print.Butler, Judith. *Undoing Gender.* New York: Routledge, 2004. Print.

Child, Francis James. *The English and Scottish Popular Ballads.* 5 volumes. 1882-1898. New York: Dover Publications, 1965. Print.

Coffin, Tristram Potter and Roger de V. Renwick. *The British Traditional Ballad in North America.* Rev. ed. Austin: University of Texas Press, 1977. Print.

Collins, Patricia Hill. *Black Feminist Thought: Knowledge, Consciousness, and the Politics of Empowerment.* New York: Routledge, 1991. Print.

Dekker, Rudolf M. and Lotte C. van de Pol. *The Tradition of Female Transvestism in Early Modern Europe.* New York: St. Martin's Press, 1997. Print.

Devor, Holly. *Gender Blending: Confronting the Limits of Duality.* Bloomington: Indiana University Press. 1989. Print.

Doty, Alexander. *Flaming Classics: Queering the Film Canon*. New York: Routledge, 2000. Print.

Epstein, Julia and Kristina Straub, eds. *Body Guards: The Cultural Politics of Gender Ambiguity*. New York: Routledge, 1992. Print.

Garber, Marjorie. *Vested Interests: Cross-Dressing and Cultural Anxiety*. New York: Routledge, 1991. Print.

Gierman, Naughty(ly). "Scandalous Secrets Revealed: Performing Queer on *The Jerry Springer Show*." *Canadian Woman Studies/les cahiers de la femme* 20/21.4,1 (2001): 120-23. Print.

Greenhill, Pauline. *Ethnicity in the Mainstream: Three Studies of English Canadian Culture in Ontario*. Montreal: McGill-Queen's University Press, 1994. Print.

Greenhill, Pauline. "'Neither a Man nor a Maid': Sexualities and Gendered Meanings in Cross-Dressing Ballads." *Journal of American Folklore* 108 (1995): 156-77. Print.

Greenhill, Pauline. "'The Handsome Cabin Boy': Cross-Dressing Ballads, Sexualities, and Gendered Meanings." *Undisciplined Women: Tradition and Culture in Canada,* Ed. Pauline Greenhill and Diane Tye. Montreal: McGill-Queen's University Press, 1997. 113-130. Print.

Greenhill, Pauline. "'The Handsome Cabin Boy': Cross-Dressing Ballads, Sexualities, and Meanings Revisited." 7th Annual International Drag King Extravaganza. Winnipeg, MB. 20 Oct. 2005. Print.

Greenhill, Pauline. "'Who's Gonna Kiss Your Ruby Red Lips?' Sexual Scripts in Floating Verses." *Ballads Into Books: The Legacies of Francis James Child*. Ed. Tom Cheesman and Sigrid Rieuwerts. Berne: Peter Lang, 1997. 225-36. Print.

Greenleaf, Elisabeth Bristol. *Ballads and Sea Songs of Newfoundland*. St. John's: Memorial University of Newfoundland, 1993. Facsimile Reprint 2004. Print.

Halberstam, Judith. "Mackdaddy, Superfly, Rapper: Gender, Race, and Masculinity in the Drag Scene." *Social Text* 52/53 (1997): 104-31. Print.

Halberstam, Judith. *Female Masculinity*. Durham: Duke University Press, 1998. Print.

Halberstam, Judith. "Masculinity Without Men: Annamarie Jagose interviews Judith Halberstam About Her Latest Book, *Female Masculinity*." *Genders* 29 (1999). Web. May 6, 2008.

Halberstam, Judith. "Telling Tales: Brandon Teena, Billy Tipton, and Transgender Biography." *Passing: Identity and Interpretation in Sexuality, Race, and Religion* Ed. Maria Carla Sanchez and Linda

Schlossberg, New York: New York University Press, 2001. 13-37. Print.

Herdt, Gilbert. "Introduction: Third Sexes and Third Genders." *Third Sex, Third Gender: Beyond Sexual Dimorphism in Culture and History,* Ed. Gilbert Herdt. New York: Zone Books, 1994. 21-81. Print.

Heyes, Cressida J. "Reading Transgender, Rethinking Women's Studies." *NWSA Journal* 12.2 (2000): 170-180. Print.

Jagose, Annamarie. 1996. *Queer Theory: An Introduction.* New York: New York University Press, 1996. Print.

Karpeles, Maud. *Folk Songs from Newfoundland.* London: Faber, 1971. Print.

Laws, G. Malcolm Jr. *American Balladry from British Broadsides.* Philadelphia: American Folklore Society, 1957. Print.

Laws, G. Malcolm Jr. *Native American Balladry.* Philadelphia: American Folklore Society, 1964. Print.

Lehr, Genevieve and Anita Best. *Come and I Will Sing You: A Newfoundland Songbook.* Toronto: University of Toronto Press, 1985. Print.

Lloyd, A. L. *Folk Song in England.* New York: International, 1967. Print.

Lovelace, Martin. "Interpreting Social Meaning in Newfoundland Ballads: Problems and Possibilities." American Folklore Society, Atlanta, GA. 21 Oct. 2005. Print.

Mills, Margaret. "Sex Role Reversals, Sex Changes, and Transvestite Disguise in the Oral Tradition of a Conservative Muslim Community in Afghanistan." *Women's Folklore, Women's Culture.* Ed. Rosan A. Jordan and Susan J. Kalcik. Philadelphia: University of Pennsylvania Press, 1985. 187-213. Print.

Namaste, Viviane. *Sex Change, Social Change: Reflections on Identity, Institutions, and Imperialism.* Toronto: Women's Press, 2005. Print.

Noble, Jean Bobby. *Sons of the Movement: FtMs Risking Incoherence on a Post-Queer Cultural Landscape.* Toronto: Women's Press, 2006. Print.

Peacock, Kenneth. *Songs of* Print.*the Newfoundland Outports.* 3 volumes. Ottawa: Queen's Printer, 1965. Print.

Prosser, Jay. *Second Skins: Body Narratives of Transsexuality.* New York: Columbia University Press, 1998. Print.

Rubin, Gayle. "The Traffic of Women: Notes on the Political Economy of Sex." *Toward an Anthropology of Women.* Ed. Rayna R. Reiter. New York: Monthly Review, 1975. 157-210. Print.

Rubin, Gayle. "Thinking Sex: Notes for a Radical Theory of the Politics of Sexuality." *Pleasure and Danger: Exploring Female Sexuality.* Ed. Carole Vance. Boston: Routledge, 1984. 267-319. Print.

Schlossberg, Linda. 2001. "Introduction: Rites of Passing." *Passing: Identity and Interpretation in Sexuality, Race, and Religion.* Ed. Maria Carla Sanchez and Linda Schlossberg. New York: New York University Press. 1-12. Print.

Stone, Sandy. "The *Empire* Strikes Back: A Posttranssexual Manifesto." *Body Guards: The Cultural Politics of Gender Ambiguity.* Eds. Julia Epstein and Kristina Straub. New York: Routledge, 1992. 280-304. Print.

Straub, Kristina. "The Guilty Pleasures of Female Theatrical Cross-Dressing and the Autobiography of Charlotte Charke." *Body Guards: The Cultural Politics of Gender Ambiguity.* Eds. Julia Epstein and Kristina Straub. New York: Routledge, 1992. 142-66. Print.

Stryker, Susan. "Transgender Studies: Queer Theory's Evil Twin." *GLQ: A Journal of Lesbian and Gay Studies* 11 (2004): 212-15. Print.

Stryker, Susan and Stephen Whittle. 2006. *The Transgender Studies Reader.* New York: Routledge, 2006. Print.

Trumbach, Randolph. "London's Sapphists: From Three Sexes to Four Genders in the Making of Modern Culture." *Third Sex, Third Gender: Beyond Sexual Dimorphism in Culture and History.* Ed. Gilbert Herdt. New York: Zone Books, 1994. 111-36. Print.

Turner, Kay and Pauline Greenhill. *Transgressive Tales: Queering the Grimms.* Detroit, MI: Wayne State University Press. 2012. Print.

Ullman, Sharon. "The "Self-Made Man": Male Impersonation and the New Woman." *Passing: Identity and Interpretation in Sexuality, Race, and Religion.* Ed. Maria Carla Sanchez and Linda Schlossberg. New York: New York University Press, 2001. 187-207. Print.

Zimmerman, Bonnie. "Perverse Reading: The Lesbian Appropriate of Literature." *Sexual Practice, Textual Theory: Lesbian Cultural Criticism.* Ed. Susan J. Wolfe and Julia Penelope. Cambridge: Blackwell, 1993. 135-49. Print.

Zita, Jacquelyn N. "Male Lesbians and the Postmodernist Body." *Hypatia* 7. 4 (1992): 106-27. Print.

8. "Two Brothers Came Out from Ireland..."

Relocating Irish-Newfoundland Women
from the Periphery to the Centre of the Migration
and Settlement Narrative

WILLEEN KEOUGH

WHAT FOLLOWS IS A HISTORIAN'S REFLECTION on an Irish-Newfoundland migration myth. Many historians have banished myths to the realm of story-telling—treating them as narratives created by unsophisticated peoples about their pasts without the benefit of empirical evidence and scientific inquiry. Yet concerns about "objective truth" overlook the significance of myths in creating knowledge about human experiences. Historians who engage with language and the creation of meaning have realized that history and myth are not mutually exclusive means of accessing the past. Rather, these narratives can enrich our understanding of history by revealing patterns of cultural memory—provoking questions about why the past is remembered by groups in particular ways, and how and why this collective remembering and disremembering changes over time.

The narrative thread of escape from oppression and travel to a promised land is common to many migration myths. Some of these narratives—from the Exodus story of the Judeo-Christian tradition and the migration canoe stories of the Maori to the legend of the great migration of the Colhua Mexica to Anáhuac—are interpretations of long-ago transitions; but not all migration myths hail from antiquity. More recent migrants from Europe to North America created their own relocation narratives that incorporated similar themes of exile and ultimate success in a land where silver grew on trees and the streets were paved with gold. These motifs appear consistently, for example, in Irish migration stories of the seventeenth, eighteenth, and nineteenth centuries. In the process of changing places, then, cultures often develop an historical understanding of the relocation that must be read not just literally but also more empathically for the symbolic markers that have been embedded in the narrative. We might reasonably assume, for example, that we can learn much about power relations, including gender dynamics, within migrant groups by examining the protagonists in these migration stories—those who are portrayed as the active shapers of experiences in new lands. And yet, the "truth," if it is to be found, is more likely to lie in the complex interplay between the rhetoric and the reality.

What has struck me particularly about relocation narratives among the Newfoundland Irish has been the male-centeredness of the odyssey, despite the presence of women in migration streams. When I began my research on the lives of Irish women on the southern Avalon Peninsula of Newfoundland in the eighteenth and early nineteenth centuries, an oral informant warned me: "Every family history here begins with, 'Two brothers came out from Ireland...'" (HE). There were variations in this formula: an older brother remained behind while the younger came out to Newfoundland; a father and his sons crossed the Atlantic to seek their livelihood in the fishery (Oral Tradition [OT]).[1] On the paternal side of my own family, or so I have heard, "three Keough (Kehoe) brothers came out from Ireland: one stayed in St. John's; one went to the Southern Shore; and one went on to the 'Boston States' [New England]." In an alternative version, the three brothers settled in King's Cove, Placentia, and Ferryland (Seary 284). All these family chronicles share a plot and focus: men carving a living out of the merciless sea and infertile soil of Newfoundland and bringing forth more sons through a process from which women are curiously absent. Only men, it would seem, change places in a culturally significant way.

My interview narrator was referring to a skewed focus in the oral tradition, but the problem was amplified in the historiography of Newfoundland, which ignored women settlers altogether until the latter 1980s.[2] Written records of the period of early settlement also rarely mentioned women unless they ran afoul of the law, with official discourse constructing an image of the Irish immigrant woman as a drain on the community and a threat to moral order in the fishing station and, later, the colony. Yet a far different understanding of Irish-Newfoundland womanhood developed within the plebeian fishing community of the southern Avalon—one that challenges the central image of the "two brothers" in retellings of family histories. In this chapter, I would like to explore two significant tensions: the gap between hegemonic discourse and the lived experiences of these Irish-Newfoundland women in the period of migration and early settlement; and the disjuncture between the male-centered narrative trope employed in Irish-Newfoundland migration stories and the way that women have otherwise been remembered in the collective historical memory of the southern Avalon. What I am suggesting is that we attend more carefully to a counter-narrative that has actually (if sometimes subtly) been articulated and has persisted in the local culture—one that positions women centrally in the story of transition from the south of Ireland to Newfoundland.

This area, like the rest of the Avalon Peninsula, was originally the site of an extensive migratory fishery from the West of England. By the late seventeenth century, English planter (resident, as opposed to migratory, fishing proprietor) families were living there, but the Irish were also arriving on board English fishing ships that regularly stopped at southern Irish ports for cheap salted provisions and labour for the Newfoundland fishery (Berry "A list"; "Berry Census"; "List of Inhabitants"). A small number of Irish traders also made the voyage in the late 1600s, bringing out "a great many women passengers wch they sell for serv^s & alittle after theire coming they marry among the fisherman that live with the Planters…" (Story). Irish numbers swelled in the eighteenth century with the development of an extensive Irish-Newfoundland trade in passengers and provisions.

British authorities at Newfoundland watched the growing numbers of Irish migrants with increasing concern. British naval officers worried that tensions from the old world had been carried to the new and frequently warned that the local Irish would take up arms with Britain's enemies in the area, such as the French and the rebellious Americans.[3] Official discourse also equated Irishness with vagrancy, drunkenness, and misrule. In 1765, Governor Hugh Palliser described over-wintering fishing servants as "perfectly idle, abandon'd to every sort of debauching and wickedness … perfect savages … [who] always did and always will join an Invading Enemy and full 3/4 of them are Roman Catholics Therein lay the rub for British authorities, because the Irish who came to Newfoundland were almost entirely Catholic, and they were by now predominant in the fishery's labour force as the numbers of English fishing servants dwindled due to increasing English press gang activity. So there was a tension in official attitudes towards the Irish at Newfoundland. They knew that Irish servants were essential to the fishery, but authorities still perceived them as outsiders and undesirables. Governors and naval officers therefore made efforts—ultimately unsuccessful—to ensure that Irish Catholics did not settle on the island. Throughout the eighteenth century and into the nineteenth, a battery of orders and regulations required fishing servants to return home after the fishing season. These regulations targeted the Irish in particular and constructed "Irishness" as inherently intemperate, unruly, and treacherous; the Irish were a "problem" group that required constant regulation and surveillance. Within this context, a gendered element emerges in the image of the Irish woman immigrant as vagrant and whore. British authorities had been discouraging the presence of all women in Newfoundland in order to limit settlement and maintain the migratory nature of the fishery with its hub in the West of England. But the construction of the undesirable woman took on ethnic undertones as Irish immigration increased. Local authorities linked Irish women with poverty, improvidence, and disorder. Vessel masters transporting Irish women to the island were required to give security for their employment and good behaviour before landing. In particular, the single Irish female servant was targeted because her sexual autonomy and social and economic independence from father or husband transgressed growing middle-class feminine ideals of passivity and dependence. In the eyes of colonial authorities, this Irish female migrant—doubly dislocated from homeland and from a properly gendered sphere of influence—was deviant and dangerous to the social and moral order.

Typical was the 1777 proclamation by Governor John Montagu, which fashioned an image of the Irish woman servant as promiscuous and conniving. Lacking economic options, he warned, many would become pregnant outside of wedlock and hire themselves to unwary employers without revealing their condition, ultimately becoming a charge on the "respectable" community. Montagu's solution was to prohibit the transportation of female Irish servants to Newfoundland altogether. And these orders had a subtext: if Irish women were permitted to remain, there would be nothing to stop the reproduction of this undesirable ethnic group on the island.

Nonetheless, Irish women (and men) came to the southern Avalon in increasing numbers in the late eighteenth and early nineteenth centuries. Given that the Newfoundland passenger trade was largely unregulated, the passage for most was difficult: the provisions ranged from very basic to dangerously inadequate; the accommodations, from rudimentary to appalling.[4] Still, the majority survived the Atlantic crossing and either landed on the southern Avalon or disembarked at St. John's and found their way southward. Some women crossed the Atlantic "on order" from local employers; others "shipped" themselves when they arrived. Some came alone, while others arrived in family groups, accompanying husbands or fathers who had already had some experience as servants in the fishery and were hoping to strike out on their own.

As a resident fishery gained ground on the migratory fishery, Irish servants stayed and married, having weighed declining conditions due to overpopulation and economic recession in the old world against opportunity in the Newfoundland fishery, a potential that was always tempered with risk and uncertainty. Some became fishing employers themselves; others headed family production units. Along the southern Avalon, an Irish planter society was taking root and would be reinforced through further Irish migration up to the 1830s. Irish women were a vital part of this process of changing places, not just in the moments of relocation, but in terms of community formation and economic survival. Thus perceptions of Irish womanhood in these fishing communities evolved rather differently from those constructed by authorities in St. John's and, ultimately, by the "two brothers" migration narrative form.

Women played an integral role in early settlement, for it was their presence that stabilized community populations. While male fishing servants moved in and out of the southern Avalon and from harbour to harbour within the area in response to labour demand, women were a more permanent element in local populations. Migrant fishermen found wives or cohabiting partners among a growing population of Irish women and first- and second-generation Irish-Newfoundland daughters, and couples settled on land occupied by the wife or apportioned from or adjoining the family property of the wife.

Irish women were also instrumental in the processes of intermarriage, conversion, and assimilation that saw the older English-Protestant planter society of the area almost completely subsumed by the Irish-Catholic ethno-religious group. Numerous English patrilines—families with surnames such as Glynn, Martin, Williams, and Maddox—were incorporated into the Catholic population through marriage with Irish-Newfoundland women and soon considered themselves as fully Irish as their neighbours. According to parish records, by 1845, what had once been an English Protestant planter shore had become 97 percent Catholic. So Irish women were agents of stability and cultural transmission.

But even more fundamental to Irish community formation was women's contribution within the work cycle. Absolutely key to the success of the relocation process was these women's ability to adapt to fishing production—no mean feat for women with backgrounds in farming and the woollen industry of southeast Ireland. Some, primarily widows, operated independent fishing premises (*Clements v. Rouse*; *Dunn and Whealon v Thomas*; Jones; Goodridge Collection 1839, 413; Goodridge Collection 1841, 266 and 292; Goodridge Limited, 363-381; Sweetman). More managed fishing plantations with husbands or cohabiting partners, boarding fishing servants in addition to their other responsibilities. Increasingly, women processed fish in family production units, replacing the hired, transient, primarily male shore crews of the traditional planter fishery. This transition was underway in the later eighteenth century, but it escalated in the severe depression and massive bankruptcies that followed the Napoleonic Wars to such an extent that household production had become widespread in the area by the mid-nineteenth century (Governor; *Newfoundland Population Returns* 1836, 1845, 1857). When the migratory fishery was nearing collapse and the traditional planter fishery based on hired labour was in crisis, women took the place of male fishing servants in producing saltfish for market. Their intervention was critical. Without women's capacity to adapt their routines to include this additional work, the beleaguered resident fishery would have been hard-pressed to survive, and the denouement of the migration narrative would likely have been set elsewhere.

Women processed fish on shore—splitting, washing, and salting it, carrying it in "barras" over rocky shores and steep cliff faces, spreading and re-spreading the fish on flakes, carefully monitoring the drying process. The substantial wages that had been paid in the traditional fishery to hired shore crew—wages that were consistently higher than those for boat crews other than the boatmaster—signify the importance of this work to the industry. And while family members received no wages in household production, this fact does not diminish the intrinsic value of the shore work that women did. Indeed, many women performed the same duties as a "master of the voyage"—the supervisor of the shore crew, whose work had been of equivalent value to that of the boatmaster in the older planter fishery. Women's skill and judgment were critical throughout the curing process, for if the fish was damaged or did not contain the right amount of salt or moisture for its intended market, the quality was ruined. It was difficult, physical work that had to be juggled with childcare, housework, and other outdoor work. Yet the processing of fish took absolute priority. As one elderly Cape Broyle woman observed, "If the fish wasn't spread when the men came in [from the water], there'd be some racket" (QSF).

Still, these women did not view shore work as drudgery. According to the oral tradition, many fishing families hired female servants not just to help their mistresses with household routines, but to "free" them from childcare and housework so that they could process fish. Nor was the "respectability" of this outdoor work at issue. Women saw themselves as full participants in a family enterprise in which they held an equal stake, and they took pride in their capacity to contribute to the process. Furthermore, the value and dignity of their work was acknowledged by the larger community. The perception of these women as essential, skilled workers in the fishery was an integral part of their own self-image and of the construction of womanhood within the fishing community.

The collective historical memory of the area also recalls women's vital contribution to the subsistence agriculture that was crucial to the survival of the family work unit. Women performed numerous labour-intensive tasks—clearing land, planting, fertilizing, weeding, trenching, haymaking, and harvesting. Men and women worked together in the spring and fall; but in the summer, when men spent most of the day fishing, women assumed the greater responsibility for the gardens. Women also shared in the care of a variety of livestock. In fact, the fattening of the family pig and the care of fowl, with their potential for earning cash or credit, were primarily carried out by women. Women also performed physically arduous outdoor work in relation to housewifery—shouldering windfall branches home from the woods on wooden frames or in brin (burlap) bags; or carrying five or six gallons of water from wells perhaps a half mile away from the house. Those who were "too sickly" or "too grand" to go down to the flake (platform for drying cod) or into the fields or woods were objects of pity or scorn (QSF; OT). Only local middle-class women, a very small, predominantly English group, followed the pattern of withdrawing into domesticity during the period.

Women also salvaged and recycled items from wrecked vessels, according to oral interview subjects. Of course, salvage of derelict vessels was legal, but there were numerous complaints against local inhabitants for removing items from vessels that had not been fully abandoned or for hoarding more than their share. There was considerable discrepancy between formal legal definitions and local interpretations of entitlement to salvage. While women generally did not take to boats to reach foundering vessels, they did scavenge wrecks that came ashore and combed the beaches for items washed in by the tide. They were quite pragmatic about using salvaged foodstuffs, furnishings, and building materials; these items were the bounty of the sea, a gift that it would be a "sin" to waste. There was no perception within the community that women should distance themselves from such activities; their work as both salvors and recyclers of wrecked property was simply one more component of a comprehensive package of survival skills that helped economic ends meet for their households and made year-round settlement of families in the area more viable.

Women also contributed to community growth through paid work, and as tavern-keepers, shopkeepers, nurses, midwives, doctors, and teachers. The most common form of paid work for women was domestic service; most worked in fishing and mercantile households, but a significant number were hired as fishing servants to do shore work for wages. Many women in the area washed and sewed for single men in the population and a small middle-class clientele. Some sold their agricultural labour for wages or payment in kind. More sold hay, eggs, fowl, pigs, cream, and butter to local customers or their merchant for cash, credit, or exchange. These activities brought additional purchasing power to families living on the margin, and were sometimes the only source of cash for families mired in the truck system. Additionally, their services provided an essential support network for the fishery and helped to drive the local exchange economy, as most of their customers "paid" them through adjusting entries that were made in merchants' account books: the woman's account was assigned a credit value for the work, while a corresponding debit entry was made in the account of each of her customers. The ledgers of the Goodridges in Renews, extant for 1839 to 1841, indicate that 68 women held separate accounts with the firm. Given that the census returns for 1836 and 1845 (*Newfoundland Population Returns*) reported, respectively, only 146 and 153 women over the age of 14 in Renews (or 247 and 272, adding those in nearby Fermeuse), this was a very vigorous participation by women in the local exchange economy.

Indeed, merchants' ledgers indicate that many women combined household production with various types of paid work in a broad package of economic coping strategies. Julia McCarthy's account with Goodridge's of Renews, for example, indicates that she sewed and washed for the Goodridge family and local fishermen, worked as shore crew on Goodridge's flakes, and sold hay to the firm (see Table 1). There are numerous similar examples of women's accounts for selling their services or produce. Some even had their profits applied towards their husbands' debts. Most had their debts carried over from year to year, but so did most men in the area—a chronic symptom of the truck system that underwrote the local fishery.

So we can see the vital and multi-faceted role that Irish-Newfoundland women played in community development and family economies. And while some work routines were delegated along sex lines, those mutually exclusive gender dichotomies that are often used to differentiate men's and women's work—skilled/unskilled, primary/secondary, outdoor/indoor, paid/unpaid, all those binary opposites that we see in the literature on the encroachment of capitalist agriculture and industrialization in other areas in the late eighteenth and nineteenth centuries—are too rigid for examining the sexual division of labour along the southern Avalon. Rather, tasks were delegated more on the basis of availability and expedience than on gendered notions of ability or strength. According to the collective historical memory, there was much blurring of the boundaries in the division of labour: the sharing of some tasks, for example, and variations in participation depending upon the season of the year. Work roles were fluid, as men and women crossed over boundaries on an "as needs" basis. When women did "men's work" or men did "women's work" on a temporary basis, they were perceived to be "helping." But the blanket designation of women as mere "helpmates" to their husbands did not develop on the southern Avalon as it did in many mainland colonies. This Irish-Newfoundland community simply assigned the status of "helper" to either sex within specific work contexts, based on a sexual division of labour that assigned essential work to both men and women.

Nor was a woman who performed men's tasks seen as anomalous. Rather, a woman who could manage her own routines and also do a man's work when necessary was highly regarded. Versatility and capacity for hard work were central to the way that womanhood was defined by the women themselves and by the larger community. Marriages were seen as partnerships in which both spouses held equal shares and carried equal risks. This perception of women's centrality in the relocation experience does not mesh with the "two brothers" protagonists of the local migration myth.

Furthermore, this understanding of Irish womanhood had repercussions not just within their families, but in the broader social and economic life of their communities, where they enjoyed considerable status, power, and decision-making autonomy. On the southern Avalon, women were primary household managers, balancing requirements and contributions and overseeing any small amounts of cash the family may have accumulated. This responsibility had nothing to do with male absence, for most men fished inshore and returned from the water every day during the season. The oral tradition acknowledges that a woman's management could "make or break" a fishing household. Her ability to make very little stretch in hard times and put a bit aside in good, and especially to budget resources to see the family through the "long and hungry month of March,"[5] was crucial to the survival of the family (OT).

Most women also had considerable influence over how the family was represented in the larger community because their opinions were consulted and respected by husbands and sons. As one elderly male informant told me: "Well, the man was *supposed* to be in charge [laughs]. That was the way it was given down. But a woman had to have a voice too, you know" (AG). Men sought their wives' advice, for example, before attending public meetings or settling up with the merchant in the fall. In fact, many women actually kept track of the account with the merchant and were known to go to the merchant's store themselves to argue about the bottom line. So while a veneer of patriarchal authority was maintained in the male spokesperson, there was often a gap between the rhetoric of male authority and the reality of plebeian family power relations.

Irish-Newfoundland women also exercised informal power in the spiritual realm, as spiritual guides and symbolic figures in both formal and informal religious practice. With the scarcity of priests in the area, women played a vital custodial role in Catholicism, performing religious rites such as baptisms and marriages, and generally keeping the faith alive (OT; Fleming, *The State* 90). Female figures—St. Brigid, Mary, and "good St. Anne"—were central in the Irish-Catholic hagiolatry of the area. Women were also important mediators and symbolic figures in the non-Christian beliefs and practices that ran in tandem with formal Catholicism. They were prominent in death rituals—cleansing and preparation of the body, waking the corpse, and keening[6] to articulate the community's grief. They were central in fairy lore and primarily responsible for the rituals that would protect their families from these menacing creatures that could steal children from their cradles and make children and adults lose their way in woods and meadows. Women read tea leaves and told fortunes. Certain women had special healing powers. A widow's curse, by contrast, had the power to do great harm to person and property if it was invoked against a legitimate threat to herself or her family. A number of powerful supernatural creatures within the non-Christian system were female figures: the bibe, or banshee, whose wailing cry warned of a household death; the "old hag," who rendered many a poor soul insensible in the night; and Sheelagh, who brought the fierce winter storms that battered the island in March and covered the trees and landscape in a blanket of ice, still known today as "Sheelagh's Brush." So women and female figures played important roles in the spiritual life of the Irish-Newfoundland community and in reinforcing the identity of the ethno-religious group.

Another indicator of women's informal power within the Irish community was their engagement in individual interventions and collective actions, fighting for personal and group interests in the public sphere. Women participated in mixed communal actions emanating from an alternative sense of plebeian justice—pillaging items from wrecked vessels, sheltering deserters, destroying mercantile premises as a form of protest, or raiding merchants' stores in times of high distress. And the court records provide ample evidence of smaller-scale actions in which these women used verbal confrontation and physical violence to sort out their daily affairs. These were common methods of conflict resolution in the days of early settlement, and women were not reluctant to use them. In assault cases brought before the local courts, women were aggressors almost as often as they were victims (by a proportion of 86:100). Furthermore, women assailants were not particular about the sex of their victims: roughly half were women and half were men. Motivations varied—defence of personal or family reputation, employment disputes over wages or ill-treatment, defence of family business or property, enforcement of community standards. The physical assertiveness of these women and the court's routine handling of these cases suggest that women's violence was no more shocking to the community than men's. Within this context of migration and early settlement, Irish-Newfoundland women felt they had the right to carve out territory for themselves and their families in the public sphere, and their presence there was accepted by their community.

When informal methods of conflict resolution failed, these women staked out their claims within the formal court system, appearing before the magistrates in a variety of matters ranging from matrimonial and bastardy actions to civil and criminal matters (Court Records). Quite striking is the pragmatism of local magistrates in dealing with female complainants and defendants. Men and women before the southern Avalon courts tended to receive fairly equitable treatment, and the magistrates appeared relatively unconcerned with using the court room to dictate standards of respectable behaviour for plebeian women or to relegate them to more "feminine" spheres of activity. This practice contrasts with other British jurisdictions, even in Newfoundland, where middle-class magistrates encouraged a modified form of respectability among the lower orders—one that included female domesticity, passivity, and economic dependence. However, southern Avalon magistrates were predominantly mercantile men who made their money by supplying local fishing families in return for their fish and oil. And the resident fishery had become overwhelmingly dependent on household production in which the labour of plebeian women—work that took place in public spaces on stage head and flake—was essential. Also, these women were an important part of the service network and exchange economy that underwrote the local fishery. It was, therefore, not in the interests of local magistrates and merchants to encourage the withdrawal of plebeian women into the respectability of the private sphere.

By contrast, the Catholic Church suffered no such conflict of interest when it brought its civilizing mission to the area in the late eighteenth century. Early priests and bishops were appalled at local family arrangements in which many couples cohabited in long- and short-term relationships. Father Thomas Ewer, for example, complained in 1789 "that there are women living here with their 4th husband each man alive & form[ing] different familys in repute"—echoing a concern that had already been expressed by Prefect Apostolic James O Donel four years earlier. The church tried to introduce middle-class standards of behaviour to the congregation by focusing on the ideal Catholic mother, freed from outdoor productive work and situated firmly within the home, the moral compass of her family. It was essential to "fix the character of the female portion of our community in virtue and innocence," wrote Bishop Michael Fleming, to promote "that delicacy of feeling and refinement of sentiment which form the ornament and grace of their sex" so that they might instill in their own children the values of virtuous citizenship at "the domestic fireside" (18). Still, church constructions of femininity met with resistance from the Irish-Catholic community on the southern Avalon because they clashed with the realities of women's lives.

Along the southern Avalon, the economy continued to rely on family production in its main industry, supported by a multi-faceted package of economic survival strategies in which women still played a prominent role. Because Irish-Newfoundland women continued to be seen as essential contributors to the collective enterprises of both productive and reproductive work, they were neither pressured by their community, nor did they seek themselves, to withdraw into domesticity and economic dependence. Nor could the local mercantile elite afford to pressure them into domesticity. Only the Catholic Church attempted to curtail women's behaviour, but the power of its rhetoric was defused by women's vital economic role and their informal power within the plebeian community.

This chapter has thus far proposed an alternative narrative of relocation that moves Irish-Newfoundland women to the centre of the frame, situating them as co-founders of their communities in the period of early settlement. It is an interpretation that is drawn as much from the oral tradition as from other historical sources. So why has the myth of the "two brothers" insinuated itself into family histories of the area? Was this merely the unreflective adoption of a narrative trope from a broader corpus of Irish migration stories that speak of male-centered movements? Or was it more fundamental to organizing knowledge about relocation? How long has this framework been part of family migration stories on the southern Avalon? Here, my comments turn to informed speculation. Variations on the "two brothers" theme seem particularly prominent in Irish-American family histories.[7] It is possible that the motif was picked up in New England by Irish-Newfoundlanders who moved there either temporarily or permanently in the late nineteenth and early twentieth centuries. In that highly industrialized corner of the world—where many Newfoundland men found employment in ironwork, helping to build the bridges and skyscrapers of New York, Boston, and Philadelphia, while wives and single women worked at home or in "women's" occupations such as domestic service and retail—perceptions of male breadwinners and female domesticity could have altered understandings of family gender relations. Could the "two brothers" interpretation have been fed back to Newfoundland through the expatriate community? Certainly, a more male-centered interpretation of relocation would have been reinforced during this period of increasing formal education and literacy by Newfoundland history books that virtually left women out of the story of European settlement on the island. Framing the narrative in terms of hardy fishermen pitted against greedy West Country merchants, historians made little reference to the stabilizing presence of women, other than cursory comments about fishermen's marrying "native" or "local" women—terms that generally referred to women of English or Irish, not aboriginal, descent, as if their presence on the other side of the North Atlantic required no further explanation. And ultimately, the marginalization of women from the fishery after the mid-twentieth century, as it shifted from family saltfish production to fresh-frozen technology (as explored by both Ellen Antler and Miriam Wright), might help to explain the adoption of a male-centered migration narrative. Of course, this is merely educated guesswork, and it is possible that the form was older and helped to maintain a veneer of male centrality in a context in which it was constantly challenged by lived experience.

But the surviving writings of James Joseph ("Jim Joe") O'Brien of the southern Avalon further problematize the "two brothers" form and suggest a more recent vintage. Jim Joe was a repository of the oral tradition and the acknowledged community historian and genealogist of Cape Broyle during his long lifetime (1888-1985). In his later years, he began to transcribe much of the information he had accumulated about the community and individual families who had settled there (O'Brien "Cape Broyle, 1959–60."). These writings, steeped in local understandings of community formation from the late nineteenth and early twentieth centuries, are amazingly accurate when compared with more traditional historical sources, such as nominal census material and newspaper notices of births, marriages, and deaths. Significantly, they are far more gender inclusive, tracing the movements of men and women, sons and daughters, as the following excerpts reveal:

Richard Furlong and his wife Johannah (nee Doran) came to Cape Broyle in the year 1815. Richard and Johannah Furlong were married at the church in County Galway Ireland and walked from the church to the ship that was to bring them to Newfoundland not a nice passage in them days. There were a certificate of their marriage in Cape Broyle at one time. It was in the possession of their daughter Sarah known as Sally. She was married in the year 1841 to James Aylward, one of the first [of the] Aylward family that came to Cape Broyle in the early 1780 years....

When Michael and Mary Ryan were coming from County Wexford Ireland to Nfld. their first child was Born at sea. It was the year 1826. [T]he boy was named Thomas Ryan.... Michael Ryan ... was drowned near Petty Harbour Motion, in the year 1830 on a sealing voyage. His wife Mary Ryan was left with 3 three young children, Thomas who was born at sea. Michael and Thimothy Ryan. After some years Mary Ryan Married again. Edward Coady also a native of County Wexford. They had a family of 2 sons and 1 daughter.... They have many decendents at Cape Broyle, many places in Canada and also in the United States....

Michael O'Brien married Bridget Aylward in the year 1873 and Michael and Bridget O'Brien's son James O'Brien born 1876 married Julia Ann Ryan in the year 1908. January 1908. Julia Ann Ryans mother was Bridget Leahey, grand daughter of William and Mary Ann Leahey family who came to Cape Broyle. They were the first family to live at Fairy pond in the year 1812. William and Mary Ann Leahey came to Nfld. in what they called or named Kehoes gang [fishing servants for George and Thomas Kough, Irish Protestant merchants who had fishing premises in Cape Broyle].... (O'Brien "Cape Broyle," 1971)

Certainly, when I conducted oral fieldwork in the area, I immediately noted a disjuncture between narrative motif and the collective historical memory of immigrant women's lives. When I asked specifically about these women, interview subjects were very forthcoming and almost hagiographic in their comments about women's contribution to early community formation. "Women did it all," one subject told me. "They'd be dead without the women" (EO). This perception resounded throughout the interviews I conducted, and was articulated in the sense that women pulled extra weight because of their combined productive and reproductive responsibilities. Men and women also readily acknowledged the significance of women's decision-making behind the scenes. "If she [the wife/mother] wanted something done, it was done," one male respondent offered (ESF). Historian L. A. Clarkson described similar family power relations in eighteenth-century Carrick-on-Suir, a source area for migrants to the Newfoundland fishery, as a "matriarchal management behind a patriarchal exterior" (30). The oral tradition on the southern Avalon offers a more homespun equivalent: "She made the cannonballs, and he fired them" (EW). One elderly man framed his discussion of this older form of marriage partnership in contrast to more contemporary gender relations: "There was none of this 'men against the women' stuff back then," he observed. "Everybody was equal. Everyone was the same. Everyone had their work to do and they did it. That was all there was to it" (VF).

It appears, then, that the myth of the "two brothers" has not yet been successful in subverting the collective historical memory of Irish migration and settlement in Newfoundland, but it may be warning us that cultural memory has been moving in a dangerous direction—a shift that, I suspect, tells us more about twentieth-century gender relations than those of an earlier period. Still, when specifically pressed, my interview subjects on the southern Avalon moved beyond the convenience of form and readily acknowledged women's essential contributions to household production and the settlement process. These women were still remembered as pivotal characters in migration experiences, not just (to borrow from another myth) helpmates fashioned in the "paradise" of the new world from the ribs of the "two brothers."

The author gratefully acknowledges the financial support of the

Social Sciences and Humanities Research Council of Canada and the Institute for Social and Economic Research, Memorial University of Newfoundland. Much of the empirical research that substantiates the observations in this paper appears in the author's 2006 e-monograph, The Slender Thread.

[1]Oral Tradition (OT). 1999-2003. Information from the oral tradition comes from interviews that I conducted with twenty-one male and female informants from seven communities on the southern Avalon: Brigus South, Cape Broyle, Calvert, Ferryland, Renews, Trepassey, and St. Mary's.

[2]Older writings that overlook women's contributions to settlement include: Head; Innis; Matthews; McLintock; Prowse; and Reeves. Among the more inclusive writings of the 1980s and 1990s are: Cadigan; Cullum and Baird; Handcock; Johnson; Porter; and Pope.

[3]Such warnings can be found in the archival records of Naval Officer Cummins (1705), Governor John Montagu (1778), Captain Michael Richards (1702), and Governor Philip van Brugh (1728).

[4]Although a series of British *Passenger Acts* were passed in the first half of the nineteenth century to improve conditions on board passenger vessels bound to the new world, the legislation was rescinded in 1804 in relation to vessels bringing "shipped" (hired) servants to the Newfoundland fishery. At the urging of authorities at Newfoundland, regulations were tightened in 1816, but enforcement remained difficult, and by 1825, the regulations for the Newfoundland passenger trade had again been relaxed (Duckworth; Governor 1803-1833; Keats; Hogsett).

[5]March was a critical period in Newfoundland fishing households, when the winter's "diet" (store of provisions) was virtually gone and the spring supplies had not yet been advanced by merchants.

[6]Keening was a ritualistic crying and eulogizing to mourn the departed, placate his or her spirit, and mark his or her transition to the afterlife.

[7]A quick browse of the Internet on any given day will reveal any number of such family migration narratives. See, for example: the saga of Seven Alexander brothers who came from Ulster to Maryland, Virginia, Delaware, and Pennsylvania (Thornton); an excerpt about four brothers Armstrong who emigrated from County Tyrone to Falmouth (now Portsmouth), Maine (Bolton); and the story of four Shannon brothers who came from Ulster to Pennsylvania in the early eighteenth century (Freels). Also see the family history of three O'Connor brothers who emigrated to Mississippi (O'Connor).

WORKS CITED

Antler, Ellen. "Women's Work in Newfoundland Fishing Families." *Atlantis* 2.2 (1977): 106-13. Print.

Berry, Sir John. "A list of ye Planters Names with an acct. of their Concerns from Cape de Race to Cape Bonavista." 12 September 1675. (from CO 1, vol. 35 [17ii], fols. 149v-156). Keith Matthews Collection, 16-C-2-035, Maritime History Archives, Memorial University (MHA). Print.

Berry, Sir John. "Berry Census." 1675 and 1677. GN 2/39/A, Provincial Archives of Newfoundland and Labrador (PANL). Print.

Bolton, Charles Knowles. *Scotch Irish Pioneers in Ulster and America.* 1910. Web. 3 Feb. 2008.

Cadigan, Sean. *Hope and Deception in Conception Bay: Merchant–Settler Relations in Newfoundland, 1785-1855.* Toronto: University of Toronto Press, 1995. Print.

Campbell, John, Governor, to Capt. Lane of *HMS St. Johns*. 14 October 1782. GN 2/1/A, vol. 9, 363-64, PANL. Print.

Carter-Benger-Nason Papers. MG 247, PANL. Print.

Carter Family Papers. MG 31, PANL. Print.

Carter, Robert. Diary. MG 920, PANL. Print.

Clarkson, L. A. "Love, Labour and Life: Women in Carrick-on Suir in the Late Eighteenth Century." *Irish Economic and Social History* 20 (1993): 18-34. Print.

Clements, Catharine, v. James Rouse. 31 August 1785. 340.9 N45, Ferryland, Provincial Reference Library, St. John's, Newfoundland (PRL). Print.

Court Records of Newfoundland. 1755-1860. GN 5/1/C/1, GN 5/1/C/6, GN 5/1/C/9, GN 5/2/C/1, GN 5/2/C/3, GN 5/2/C/4, GN 5/2/C/8, and GN 5/4/C/1, PANL; 340.9 N45, Ferryland and St. Mary's–Trepassey, PRL. Print.

Cullum, Linda, and Maeve Baird. "'A Woman's Lot': Women and Law in Newfoundland from Early Settlement to the Twentieth Century." *Pursuing Equality: Historical Perspectives on Women in Newfoundland and Labrador.* Ed. Linda Kealey. Social and Economic Papers no. 20. St. John's: Institute for Social and Economic Research. Memorial University. 1993. 66-162. Print.

Cummins, Naval Officer. "Remarks of Naval Officer Cummins in relation to Newfoundland." CO 194, vol. 3, fols. 424-25, 1705? (received at the Colonial Office via the House of Commons 25 February 1706). Centre for Newfoundland Studies, Memorial University (CNS). Print.

Duckworth, John T., Governor, to Colonial Office. November 1811. CO 194, vol. 51, fols. 17-23, CNS. Print.

Dunn, Lawrence, and J. Whealon v. Alice Thomas. 5 October 1775. 340.9 N45, Ferryland, PRL. Print.

EO of Calvert, NL. Personal interview. 26 August 1999

ESF of Cape Broyle, NL. Personal interview. 25 August1999.

EW of Calvert (formerly of Trepassey), NL. Personal interview. 21 July 1999.

Ewer, Father Thomas, to Archbishop Troy, Dublin. 30 November 1789. *Gentlemen-Bishops and Faction Fighters: The Letters of Bishops O Donel, Lambert, Scallan, and Other Irish Missionaries.* Ed. Cyril J. Byrne. St. John's: Jesperson Press, 1984. 77-79. Print.

Fleming, Michael Anthony, Bishop. *The State of the Catholic Religion in Newfoundland Reviewed in Two Letters by Monsignor Fleming to Rev. P. John Spratt.* Rome. 1836. Print.

Fleming, Michael Anthony, Bishop. "Letter on the State of Religion in Newfoundland," 11 January 1844, addressed to the Very Rev. Dr. A. O'Connell, Dublin. Dublin: James Duffy. 1844. Print.

Freels, Melinda Shannon. "The Legend of Four Brothers." *The Shannon Family of East TN: A Story of the Scots-Irish.* Web. 3 Feb. 2008.

Goodridge, Alan and Sons. Collection. 1839 and 1841 ledgers. MG 473, PANL. Print.

Goodridge, Alan, and Sons Limited fonds. 1840 ledger. MHA. Print.

Governor of Newfoundland. *Annual Returns of the Fisheries and Inhabitants of Newfoundland. 1735-1825.* CO 194, CNS. Print.

Governor of Newfoundland. Incoming correspondence. 1759, 1777. GN 2/1/A: vol. 3, 57-59 and 80-86, September-October 1759; vol. 6-reverse end, 134-38, and vol. 7-reverse end, 3-4, May 1777, PANL. Print.

Governor of Newfoundland. Incoming correspondence. 1818. GN 2/1/A, vol. 28, 309-15, and vol. 29, 297-300. Correspondence and case summary. April and ca. December 1818, PANL. Print.

Governor of Newfoundland. Incoming correspondence. 1803-1833. GN 2/1/A: vol. 27, 408-11; vol. 28, 362-64, 409-15, 433-34, 446, and 482; vol. 30, 139-40, 166-67, and 192; and vol. 31, 423-25, 473, and 490-92, PANL. Print.

Green, Donald Henry, Master of the *Matilda* of Halifax. 5 January 1850. Complaint. GN 5/4/C/1, box 2, 1848-66 file, PANL. Print.

Handcock, W. Gordon. *Soe longe as there comes noe women: Origins of English Settlement in Newfoundland.* St. John's: Breakwater Books, 1989. Print.

HE of Ferryland, NL. Personal interview. 20 Jul. 1999.

Head, C. Grant. *Eighteenth Century Newfoundland*. Toronto: McClelland and Stewart, in association with the Institute of Canadian Studies, Carleton University, 1976. Print.

Hogsett, Capt. Aaron. 1 May 1825. Report of Naval Officer at St. John's. CO 194, vol. 71, fols. 313-15, CNS. Print.

Howard, Mildred. Collection. Nineteenth-century Newfoundland Newspaper Index. Vol. 1, transcriptions from *Royal Gazette*, 26 November 1816, 11 March 1817, 17 December 1831, and 9 July 1844, PANL. Print.

Innis, Harold A. *The Cod Fisheries: The Study of an International Economy*. Rev. ed. Toronto: University of Toronto Press, 1954. Print.

Johnson, Trudi D. *Matrimonial Property Law in Newfoundland to the End of the Nineteenth Century*. Diss. Memorial University of Newfoundland, 1998. Print.

Jones, James Howell, Surrogate. Grant of a Fishing Room to Mary Shea, Ferryland. 15 September 1773. 340.9 N45, Ferryland, PRL. Print.

Keats, Richard, Governor, to Colonial Office. 1 October 1814. CO 194, vol. 56, fols. 63-70, esp. fol. 66, "A List of Vessels that have arrived at St. Johns Newfoundland from Ireland with Passengers," CNS. Print.

Keough, Willeen. "'Now You Vagabond [W]hore I Have You': Plebeian Women, Assault Cases, and Gender and Class Relations on the Southern Avalon." *Two Islands: Newfoundland and Prince Edward Island*. Ed. Christopher English. Toronto: Osgoode Society for Essays in Canadian Legal History/ University of Toronto Press. 2005. 238-71. Print.

Keough, Willeen. "The 'Old Hag' Revisits St. Brigid: Irish-Newfoundland Women and the Spiritual Life of Southern Avalon Communities." *Weather's Edge: A Compendium of Women's Lives in Newfoundland and Labrador*. Ed. Linda Cullum, Carmelita McGrath, and Marilyn Porter. St. John's: Killick Press, 2006. 11-22. Print.

Keough, Willeen. *The Slender Thread: The Slender Thread: Irish Women on the Southern Avalon, 1750-1860*. New York: Columbia University Press, 2006, Web. Print edition, 2008.

King v. John Hayes. 8 November 1817. GN 5/1/C/1, 13-14, PANL. Print.

"List of Inhabitants' Names, the No. of Their Families, 1708" (from CO 194, vol. 4, fols. 253-56). 1708. R 95/20, MHA. Print.

Magistrates, Trepassey. 16 November 1816. Notice. GN 2/1/A, vol. 27, 308, PANL. Print.

Matthews, Keith. *A History of the West of England–Newfoundland Fishery*. Diss. Oxford University, 1968. Print.

McLintock, A. H. *The Establishment of Constitutional Government in Newfoundland, 1783-1832.* London: Longmans, 1941. Print.

Montagu, John, Governor. 20 October 1777. Order. GN 2/1/A, vol. 7, 35-36, PANL. Print.

Montagu, John, Governor. To Robert Carter, Magistrate, October 1778. GN 2/1/A, vol. 7-reverse end, 159-60, PANL. Print.

Newfoundland Population Returns. St. John's: n.p, 1836. Print.

Newfoundland Population Returns. 1845. St. John's: Ryan and Withers. Print.

Newfoundland Population Returns. 1857. St. John's: Queen's Printer, 1858. Extract from the Journal of the House of Assembly (Sessional Papers). 1858. Print.

O'Brien, James Joseph. "Cape Broyle, 1959-60." 1960. TS. Collection of Willeen Keough, Vancouver.

O'Brien, James Joseph. "Cape Broyle." Unpublished chronicle of the old families of Cape Broyle. 1971. TS. Collection of Willeen Keough, Vancouver.

O'Brien, James Joseph. "Leahy Family." Unpublished and untitled notes on the Leahy family at Cape Broyle. 1971. TS. Collection of Willeen Keough, Vancouver.

O'Brien, James Joseph. "The Oldridge Family." Unpublished notes on the Oldridge family at Cape Broyle. TS. Collection of Willeen Keough, Vancouver.

O'Connor, Maureen. "Fearful Symmetry: An Emigrant's Return to Celtic Tiger Ireland." *New Hibernia Review* 10.1 (2006): 9-16. Print.

O Donel, James, Prefect Apostolic of Newfoundland, to Leonardo Antonelli, Cardinal Prefect of Propaganda Fide. [December] 1785. *Gentlemen-Bishops and Faction Fighters: The Letters of Bishops O Donel, Lambert, Scallan, and Other Irish Missionaries.* Ed. Cyril J. Byrne. St. John's: Jesperson Press, 1984. 55. Print.

Oral Tradition (OT). Personal interviews. 1999-2003.

Palliser, Hugh, Governor. "Annual Return on the Fisheries and Inhabitants, etc., at Newfoundland for the year 1765." CO 194, vol.16, fol. 188, CNS. Print.

Parish Records. Church of England, Petty Harbour–Ferryland parish; Roman Catholic Church, Bay Bulls, Witless Bay, Brigus South, Renews, Trepassey, and St. Mary's parishes, PANL. Print.

Pope, Peter. *The South Avalon Planters, 1630-1700.* Diss. Memorial University of Newfoundland, 1992. Print.

Porter, Marilyn. "She was Skipper of the Shore Crew: Notes on the History of the Sexual Division of Labour in Newfoundland." *Labour/*

Le Travail 15 (Spring 1985): 104-25. Print.

Prowse, Daniel W. *A History of Newfoundland from the English, Colonial and Foreign Records.* London: Macmillan, 1895. Belleville: Mika Studio, 1972. Print.

QSF of Cape Broyle, NL. Personal interview. 22 Jul. 1999.

Reeves, John. *History of the Government of the Island of Newfoundland.* London, 1793. Yorkshire: S. R. Publishers, 1967. Print.

Regina v. William Neal, Francis Gearin, and Martain McCarthy. 3 December 1853. GN 5/4/C/1, box 2, PANL. Print.

Regina v. William Williams, John Dullanty, and John Reed. 1, 2, and 10 June 1845. GN 5/4/C/1, box 2, PANL. Print.

Richards, Capt. Michael. 1702. "Hearings at Fort William, 9-12 March 1702." Letterbook, 1700-1703, MF-105, MHA. Print.

Seary, E. R. *Family Names of the Island of Newfoundland.* Corrected edition. Ed. William Kirwin. Kingston: McGill-Queen's University Press, 1998. Print.

Story, Capt. James. 1 September 1681. "An account of what fishing ships, Sack Ships, Planters & boat keepers from Trepasse to Bonavist & from thence to faire Island the Northward part of Newfoundland" (from CO 1, vol. 47 [52i], fols. 113-121v). Matthews Collection, 16-D-1-006, MHA. Print.

Sweetman Collection. 1756-1848. Boxes 2 and 3, MG 49, PANL. Print.

Thornton, F. W. 1996-2007. "Seven Brothers from Ireland." Thornton. *They Came from Ireland.* The Hartslog Society. Web. 3 Feb. 2008.

VF of St. John's (formerly of Calvert/Caplin Bay), NL. Personal interview. 26 Mar. 2001.

Van Brugh, Philip, Governor, to Commissioners for Trade. 6 November 1738. Matthews Collection, 04/058, coll. 24, box 9, sub-series 04-056/01, file 25-B-2-1 (from CO 194, vol. 10, fol. 93), MHA. Print.

Wright, Miriam. "Women, Men and the Modern Fishery: Images of Gender in Government Plans for the Canadian Atlantic Fisheries." *Their Lives and Times: Women in Newfoundland and Labrador: A Collage.* Ed. Carmelita McGrath, Barbara Neis, and Marilyn Porter. St. John's: Killick Press, 1995. Print.

9. Women in the Ivory Tower

Graduate Students Speak Out

SONIA CORBIN DWYER

> Women will starve in silence until new stories are created which confer on them the power of naming themselves. (Gilbert and Gubar 627)[1]

L ISTENING TO THE VOICES of graduate women is a critical strategy in examining how the educational system influences their academic decisions (Corbin Dwyer, Sabatini, and Mohr 5). Surprisingly few studies have investigated women's own perspectives on their learning experiences. However, women's subjective experiences are an important source of information in the study of something as complex and personal as learning (Hayes and Flannery 29). As social psychologist Sandra Pyke states, it was not just from archives, or official academic performance indicators comparing men and women that the chilly climate for women in academe was identified: that required an examination of the lived experience of graduate students as well (154). The research presented here indicates that there continue to be large parts of universities that are untouched by the arguments for considering affect as an important influence on learning.

The difficulty women experience in trying to fit into traditional educational settings is often blamed on women. The social context and social structures are not considered. Socialization, sex roles, and sex stereotyping encourage patterns of interpersonal relationships that disadvantage women (Acker 6) and the negative effects of these patterns are particularly evident in graduate school. For example, many women experience "double duty"—being the primary caregivers and the ones responsible for housework while trying to complete their degrees and work outside the home.

On relocating to the Ivory Tower, many women have experienced difficulty in feeling they belong. Some women find themselves so ignored, even invisible, that they feel they are in the Ivory Basement instead (Eveline 4). But by changing places and becoming students, many women have claimed the power to define themselves and to speak themselves, as Carol Schick suggests (52), in the world of post-secondary education.

How do women manage their lives while they are pursuing a graduate education, and how might similarities in the lives they lead as students generate the understanding we know as empathy? As Stanley and Wise maintain, "the analytic use of feeling and experience in an examination of 'the personal' should be the main principle on which feminist research is based" (174). With this in mind, I developed with a colleague the following script, a collection of women's voices, presented in a format which can be adapted for a reader's theatre (Corbin Dwyer and O'Reilly-Scanlon). Over a three-year period, I surveyed and interviewed women who had been enrolled in master's programs at two Canadian universities. Of those surveyed and interviewed, fifty-eight women volunteered to participate in a follow-up interview. Forty individual (telephone) interviews and two face-to-face focus groups of eight and ten women were conducted. The interviews and focus groups were audio-recorded and transcribed. The script was developed from the transcripts in response to the thematic concerns the women raised.

As this is a performance script, it is envisioned that a class could have students stage their own reading, respond to what the various voices say, themselves theorize about the problems, and connect the critiques implied to theories they have studied. While feminist theory can be considered as a road map for understanding feminism (Calixte, Johnson and Motapanyane 1), the term "theory" is disputed within feminism. There is no singular version of feminism; this non-singularity is not necessarily a problem, but is rather an opportunity to critically interrogate the ways in which our world is organized (Rosenberg 40).

The research findings presented in a non-traditional form here focus on the comments of women students. The intention is to challenge established expectations, just as the women students who speak the words challenge the university's expectations that they should "fit" its established practices. Formal practices of producing and representing knowledge are usually taken for granted and considered as "the right way" (Rosenberg 44). The intent of presenting students' statements, questions, or exclamations in sequences is to draw the reader's or listener's attention to expectations of standard practices, and their comfort with them. While the numbering used here indicates that five performers speak the women's words, the numbers do not represent particular women. The quotations were selected from the observations of the 58 participants. While third-wave feminism and anti-racist feminism recognize the intersectionality of race, class, gender, dis/ ability and sexuality (Reece 92), the women were not asked about their inclusion in these socially constructed categories. As the women's lives are heterogeneous and multi-vocal, they speak from various social locations (Reece 104), which are often implied or identified in their speech. Theories of multiple identities as possible ways of negotiating multiple oppressions have been proposed (Jones and McEwen 405). Amy Reynolds and Raechele Pope have suggested four possibilities for identity resolution for individuals belonging to more than one oppressed group: identifying with only one aspect of the self in a passive way; identifying with only one aspect of the self in an active way; identifying with multiple aspects of the self in a segmented fashion; and identifying with multiple aspects of the self in an integrated fashion (174). There is no right way to be a woman graduate student as it is a product of multiple influences—it is not explained by one single role (Paludi 198-199). Indeed, women graduate students are a diverse group with interests, attitudes, and identities that do not always conform to those considered to be traditional for graduate students (Golden 33), as many of the women in this study pointed out. It is beyond the scope of this study to address the participants' identities. Therefore, future studies need to explore ways women experience graduate school as differentiated by social class, processes of racialization, sexuality and physical abilities (Webber 263).

Almost all of the women had completed their programs[2] and, as participants in this research, they were asked to reflect on their experiences. This is what they had to say.

> Voice 1: I have a family, I'm a wife, I'm a mother, a community member. I worked full-time, and I was a student. Juggling multiple roles was just *damn difficult*.

> Voice 2: I certainly juggled multiple roles during my program. I probably was not able to do the best work that I could have done. I was holding down a full-time job and was a participating member of a household—a fairly traditional household—so I was doing all of the cleaning, shopping for groceries, cooking—I was doing a lot of that.

Voice 3: And being a spouse, a mother, a volunteer in the community, looking after an elderly parent. I think that affected my decision about whether or not to pursue a doctorate. I find that I just don't have the time to really do it justice. I think I probably could do it, but I just can't juggle the competing demands of so many roles in my life.

Voice 4: I worked as a teaching assistant and I really like doing that.... I would have to say it was such a positive experience for me. I would have really liked to pursue a Ph.D. but I haven't done that yet. With two children, I sort of burned out—writing until 2 o'clock in the morning. I also worked, sometimes part-time, sometimes full-time. Because I was running off—home or to work—my time was very tight and very divided. I was pretty tired by the end.

Voice 5: I juggled. I was a mom, I had kids—one in university and one in high school. By the time I finished I had two in university. I was working. Now I'm raising my granddaughter and there are several women who have raised families who are raising second families, who are in this situation like myself. I know I'm not alone. I'm not an exceptional case.

Voice 1: I was a caregiver for my father—I started my graduate degree because my father was very ill and I couldn't leave the city to do anything else.

Voice 2: At the start of my master's, it was fine. I didn't find that juggle too much. But then I had a child when I turned forty and that required a lot of juggling to complete my thesis. That's when it got a little tricky.

Voice 1: In another life I might do a doctorate. But two kids and a husband and you know, the whole nine yards...

Voice 2: I juggled a lot of things because I worked and I had my first child and the husband saying "You spend too much time doing these other things." My child came when I was doing my thesis work so I was on maternity leave and writing. Good timing. If I was a full-time student, would I have enjoyed it more? Or if I was a full-time single person?

Going back to school was a difficult choice. I had been working part time since the twins were nine months old, but my work schedule was stable. Now as a student, my schedule changes every ... four months: it's inconsistent—two hours one morning, three hours the next afternoon, all day the day after that—and then homework outside of classes. We juggle care-giving options to cover the costs. Ian and Sarah spend two full days in their regular daycare ... on another day a friend comes in to watch them without charge and ... they go to a babysitter who offers part-day rates. Financially, the juggling helps, but it's difficult for Ian and Sarah ... and they don't understand why mommy can't play with them as much as she used to.

While working, I was good at keeping my lives separate. When I left the office, I rarely thought about work issues until I returned the next day or after the weekend. My home time was focussed on the kids and other activities. Schoolwork, on the other hand, is insidious. It creeps into every activity and haunts me at all hours, sometimes even while I sleep. At times, I've even resorted to leaving the kids in front of the TV—something I'd sworn I'd never do—so I can work on an assignment. I try to make up. I schedule time to take them to a playground, or to a park, or ... I let them sneak into bed with me at night so we can cuddle. (Russell 26-27)

Voice 3: The main challenge associated with my graduate experience was just the time factor—juggling, working full-time, life and—well, you had no life. And this went on for a lot of years.

Voice 1: The main challenge associated with my graduate experience wasn't academic—it was the time crunch. That was probably the greatest thing. It wasn't when I was taking my classes—it was the time crunch at the end when I was really scrambling. But you get through it.

Voice 2: Trying to keep up with the reading and the workload and the time to do all of that is difficult....But, pursuing a doctorate is in the back of my mind. Every now and then I think, "Well, when I am retired and my kids are grown up and I have nothing to do, then I'll go back to university."

Voice 3: On a personal level, I had a lot of changes in my life at that time. I was recently married, I was starting a family, and I was facing all of those things and also trying to grow professionally, and learning to balance all those things or trying to balance all those things ... what a challenge! Previously I had been one of those people who could stay up all night and burn the midnight oil. But doing everything was getting a bit much....

Voice 4: During my program, my husband was also experiencing a lot of changes in his career and becoming really involved with that. And so, as time progressed it was that "competing careers" thing. So you know, something's gotta give.... It added a negative tone and certainly added to the stress. It also made me question the difference between men's and women's lives. Something that I noticed was that many of my male colleagues and male fellow graduate students would be going home and their dinner would be on the table and I would be going home to make it. And many, many people included in their papers and theses thanks to their wives for word processing and editing and being there at every moment. And really, I was doing it all myself.

Voice 5: I was doing it all myself.

Voice 1: I was doing it all myself.

Voice 2: I was doing it all myself.

Voice 3: I was doing it all myself.

Voice 4: So I felt a bit alone. My female colleagues would laugh when they came to pick me up when we had to go off site for a few days and I would have my stuff at the door and be finishing the diapers in the dryer and making sure everything was teed up. They were laughing, saying "Does your husband do that for you when he leaves?"

Chorus: No.

Voice 5: My child was born in September so going back to school that semester was just not an option. I had hoped to go back the following January. When you have children, remember what I say—a month after you have a baby you're just not chompin' at the bit to go back to school. You're still trying to get out of your pyjamas.

> *I wonder to what extent I have internalized this idea that I will not be perceived as a committed academic if I become pregnant. Where did it come from and is it real or imagined or both? ...I don't know of any other women doing what I have done (borne two children while completing their Ph.D.), and it's easy to think that if I'm having trouble coping it's my own stupid fault.... The phrase "postpartum depression" hovers about. I decide to rename this condition for what it is: chronic patriarchy.* (Kelly and Strivastava 59; 71)

Voice 1: I lived so far away from the university that that was the key thing. Being a mom, having 18 horses and trying to run a little farm at the same time—and I was two and a half hours away from the university.

Voice 2: I think in some situations I was quite different than a lot of people in the program because I wasn't married. I was single and I had no children. So I could focus just on my education and my work. I didn't have to worry about children and a partner. Or the money issues.

Voice 3: Because of the support that I had, I was able to juggle. It wasn't like I was facing a lot of pressure from my advisors or from the department to be completing within a certain time frame. [pause] Having said that, they were "You know you've only got X number of years and you have to get this finished."

Voice 4: I really had to learn how to try and balance that and not to be too hard on myself if things didn't work or if I were having an incredibly frustrating time. Trying to keep grounded was very challenging.

I am Tammy and the women in the circle are very much
like me or
like me looking for connection
uniting the disjointed

bits

of our/the
lives
we create to
live in community our voices, our beauty, our pain, our spirit.
we are here—affirming self/other into existence—
have you
heard us yet?

I am Tammy and the women in the circle are very much

not
like me
at all.

I am
not wife, not mother, not juggler, not…
—not woman?

I cheat with luxury—guilt—of time

and space.

I can have a bath whenever I want. There's no one else to think
about…

Tammy Dewar

Voice 5: I think it was, from everybody's point of view, just
a chore. I got married, I had children, I just did everything at
once. It was just too much.

Chorus: Too much.

> Balance
>
> Balance is the most difficult of all academic illusions to maintain but essential. If at all possible, practice at home (if you fall on your face, no one will see you), using a high wire and a balance bar. You can set up such a contraption in the back yard. As a cheaper alternative, try walking up and down stairs with a minimum of three books piled on your head. (van Herk 155)

Voice 1: My personal life was put on hold. For me, in my first free summer for seven or eight years, my daughter said, "This seems so weird having you at home during the summer. What are we doing to do?"

Juggling multiple roles was a major theme in the women's responses. Feeling isolated was another:

Voice 2: I do have *one* thing to say. Having a support group of other students who are doing the same courses would have helped me. It would have been nice to have had a few social get-togethers so that we could have created some connections with other people. I would have liked to have connected with other students, perhaps even some students who had finished the master's program and who could offer some advice.

Voice 3: During my studies there were only three Aboriginal students and I was one. All three were women and all three women were parents of younger children. I felt like I was constantly teaching [other people] about First Nations people. I would have liked to have had some focus on Aboriginal issues. In this particular area I did not learn any more than I already knew.

Voice 4: I feel that Aboriginal issues need to be addressed in the course work. I found myself "educating" many faculty members about the issues, culture, etc. It would be beneficial for *everyone* to be aware of these issues. I didn't see this as discrimination or racism but merely ignorance.

Voice 5: Doing it part-time, I was only on campus maybe an evening a week, and it was a rush to get there.

Step 7: Develop or join a supportive community that understands and shares your addiction (or a similar version of it). (Keahey 51)

Voice 1: After I taught a summer class I did go on to create a little group of women and they really enjoyed the interaction and they asked me to meet with them in the future so we did meet for about three years—pretty sporadically—but they really found it useful to have someone who had gone through the program to offer advice and read papers, give feedback and help support them. We started out with five and then a couple of months later added one more and we felt that because we had created such a close knit little group we really didn't want to have anyone else join. It's not that we meant to be exclusionary—it just took us such a long time to get to know one another and be comfortable with one another and to create a safe place. I think that was the biggest thing, to create a safe kind of forum where we could speak our feelings and not worry.

Voice 2: I didn't get very much support during my program... from anyone, really. The university didn't have a women's support group and I didn't have that much support at home

Voice 3: I found the support of other female faculty members extremely important. I did some writing and papers and conference presentations with other people who were not even on my committee. And that mentoring—the sharing of experiences they had had working through their graduate degrees was extremely valuable to me. Also, their life experiences as women who had raised families and had faced the challenges of working and raising a family and being involved in academic life was *really* important.

Voice 4: My husband said, "You know, you're so fortunate because you have this small student ratio in your program, it's almost like Oxford." And in a sense it was. There was a lot of personal attention and mentorship available. Also, my academic interests expanded quite a bit too. My experience influenced my decision about pursuing a doctorate and I decided I would. It was through that experience of confidence building, the mentorship, the practice and success I had at publishing papers and participating in conferences. These other women encouraged me to do that.

Voice 5: I withdrew from my master's program because I wasn't being supported. Creating support for myself was really hard. I just had to organize myself really well and deny myself a lot. I wasn't participating in a lot of family things.

Voice 1: There was a group of grad students—we had been together through our bachelor's degree and about three or four of us stayed at the university for our graduate work, so we formed our own support group.

Voice 2: My family definitely supported me, my work supported me, but other than that, I did not have a cohort.

Voice 3: There were a couple of us that became friends. But there wasn't a lot of support. And realize, of course, that I was doing my program while I was working full-time.

Voice 4: I was married and I had a very supportive husband. And I had a network of other graduate students as well while I was doing my master's.

Chorus: Some of us are really lucky.

Voice 5: Most people were taking part-time studies and because there was only a handful of us that were taking it full-time, for that one year, we were more into it, more diehard into it. We had our own little group and were able to discuss a lot more. We didn't have the distractions of working full-time.

Voice 1: How did I create support for myself during my program? Well, actually, I don't think I did. I got to know a *few* people as I was taking courses....

Voice 2: I had an excellent advisor who was very understanding and very flexible because I did have two kids during the course of my master's program. And so, it did take me five years to do an M.A. but he never had a *problem* with that.

Voice 3: As a woman I was never led to believe that having a child was a "good" enough reason to be granted an extension!

Voice 4: I actually got a one-year extension. I wasn't done the thesis in five years. Because I had two babies in that time—it slowed me down. I live almost 4 hours away from the university so when I took evening courses during the year, I traveled. I would leave work early, go to the university, take the course and then get back home about 1:00 in the morning. So maybe I should actually give myself a pat on the back.

Chorus: Yes, a pat on the back!

Voice 5: There were times when I wondered if my advisor was helping his male students a little bit more. But at the same time I was getting support that a male wouldn't get from these other female faculty members so maybe he was looking at that and saying "Well, she's already got her support network, she doesn't need more." So I don't know.

Voice 1: I didn't feel that my supervisor thought I was quite the smartest person he had ever had, although I really had good marks. I felt he looked down on me a little bit. What's the word? Patronizing.

Voice 2: I do feel there was a lot of gender tension that I experienced as a sessional lecturer from male faculty members, because my field tends to be male dominated and right now there is a lot of competition for jobs and I think that this is seen as a mechanism to try to keep women out because then there will be less competition for those positions.

Voice 3: I experienced harassment during my program because I also taught. So it wasn't related to being a student, it was related to just being alive and being in the faculty. I felt embarrassed, angry, stressed—because of the feeling of the chilly climate kind of thing. You would be working really hard and then there's just always somebody who is going to come along and try to bring you down, one way or another.

Voice 4: I think I missed out on opportunities throughout my master's program due to being female because I think sometimes … that people focus more on men moving up and being successful, than women. Some of the men in the program got more special attention than women, even by female professors.

Voice 5: I would say I missed out on opportunities because I think what I saw was men were able to negotiate a different kind of support, family-wise, work-wise, and so on, than what the women, in my experience, were able to. Maybe it was where we were in our careers or whatever, but it seemed that there was a difference.

Voice 1: I experienced sexual harassment and sexism when dealing with more than one male professor.

Voice 2: It was not fair that because I wanted to use a feminist technique, it was also viewed as a political statement and more a war on men.

Woman's discontent increases in exact proportion to her development.
—Elizabeth Cady Stanton, qtd. in *The Quotable Woman* 13

Voice 3: I had very good marks and before my convocation I was nominated for a special award. The other nominee was a man. Even though our marks were equal, I was told he was chosen because he completed his program in less time. I had a baby during my program which slowed down my studies, so I felt this decision was unfair.
Chorus: Go figure.

Voice 4: I would have to say I experienced financial discrimination. The day that the scholarships were announced for our program, all the—there was three guys in our program, and 11 women. The guys all got scholarships and not one of the women knew about them. Not one. Funny how that worked out.

Voice 5: I feel I missed out on opportunities during my master's program due to my gender. My husband went through and did his master's at the same time. And had the same experience in his faculty—the guys were told about the scholarships and gosh, they kinda forgot to tell the women. What a shock.

Chorus: Funny how that worked out.

Voice 1: I believe this program was intended for young adults who live at home and are not responsible for doing their own laundry. There has been no consideration or acknowledgement of the fact that as a mature student with children I am carrying a heavy burden. Having a family is seen as evidence of a lack of commitment.

Voice 2: Because I was in a largely male field, it wasn't always as comfortable as it could have been. There were less supports or you felt less able to access even in-class support because not everyone understood the difficulty of multiple roles. And there were assumptions made—that many of the fellows in the class were full-time students with support, from family taking care of all the other things that women have to take care of.

Voice 3: I didn't feel like I missed out on opportunities due to my gender. My field in particular is an extremely male dominated field and my individual experience had been that they were trying hard to make opportunities available to females within the discipline, encouraging females to go through because they were unrepresented within the discipline. And I didn't ever feel disadvantaged but I also never had female advisors or female teachers. So when I started my Ph.D. and I had my first female instructor, that's when I started to go, "Hey, this is a little bit different, when you *do* have somebody who shares the same multiple roles as mother and as scholar." And although I have absolutely no complaints with the advisors I had, I recognize that having females, as a female, has its advantages. I guess it's like increasing a comfort level because they just understand more directly.

Voice 4: At the time I went, there was just one female in my department and it was sort of The Boys Club. No, I don't think I missed out on opportunities throughout my program due to my gender. I think it was likely just that I was too busy and doing it part-time to even think about it.

Chorus: Go figure.

Voice 5: Whether you're looking at an academic setting or you're looking at a workplace setting, The Old Boys' Club is still very much in place. And I suspect if I went back to graduate school tomorrow I would find the same thing. I remember confronting one of my professors about it and it was sort of like "wow, gosh" he's got a family and "blah blah blah blah." "Okay, yeah, me too." You can rationalize that any way you want; the fact is, I think men are more likely to get privileges and the road is smoothed out for them a little more than it is for women.

Voice 1: Maybe the master's program should be called a mistress's program these days?

Chorus: Go figure.

So, how do women's experiences in their master's programs influence their decision to pursue a Ph.D.?

Equity is defined as those mechanisms in place at a provincial level to ensure that all students, regardless of gender, place of origin, or socioeconomic status, can make
optimal use of higher education in whichever location and discipline they choose. ...It also refers to the facilitation of full participation in the higher education experience by all members of the post-secondary community. (Doherty-Delorme and Shaker 8)

A university education, in its methodology and values if not always in its subject matter, is an induction into masculine thought processes, a preparation for a male career pattern. Universities are hierarchical institutions.... As well as being a hierarchy built on exploitation, the university is a breeding ground for masculine values: of competitiveness, of status-seeking, of public accomplishment, of the supposed supremacy of so-called objectivity and scientific neutrality. (Oakley 203)

Voice 2: I'm too old to pursue a doctorate. I withdrew from my master's program at age forty-nine. And what would it do for me? The master's program was for me and not for getting a better job.

Voice 3: The structure of the program deterred me from future study. I'm going to reassess everything when I retire and see how I feel about finishing it then.

Voice 4: Although I did extremely well in grad school, the entire experience has soured me and I know that my self-esteem was damaged. I believe I'm still struggling to regain the confidence in myself I had prior to entering the graduate program.

Voice 5: I need time to forget the way I felt during my Master's experience.

Voice 1: I always took the blame for everything that went wrong. I see now that there were some factors beyond my control and that some help along the way would have made all the difference in my success in my first attempt.

Voice 2: The fact that I'm raising a granddaughter has more to do with my decision whether or not to pursue a doctorate. The reality is, if I can work it out, I will go on and I will do it and I'll take her with me. I'm forty-nine, coming fifty. But I think that I probably have a few good years left.

Voice 3: Juggling multiple roles played into my decision to not pursue a doctorate. But I know I could do it. I'm tough. I can be really tough. I know I can do it. It's just I'm putting it off. I had always kind of planned on doing it when I was about 55. I think I'm going to have to push that back. But the reality is, I don't think it's going to make any difference—all that juggling.

Voice 4: My multiple roles influenced the decision on post-graduate studies because I would never take on that amount of work again, working full-time and doing that type of program. And I couldn't financially see a way of doing it other than that.

Voice 5: My experience influenced my decision whether to pursue a doctorate because unless I can stop working and really concentrate full-time on it, I'm not pursuing it even though I would like to.

Voice 1: Night classes and summer school eat up all of your spare time, so to speak, and that's deterred me because I'm not doing that for the Ph.D.

Voice 2: I am not pursuing it until I am in a position to be able to pursue it as a full-time student or there is real recognition given to a different kind of support for someone who is trying to work or has a need to work while they are pursuing a Ph.D.

Voice 3: I think it's much easier as a man to get some kind of leave and come back to the position you left. It's supported. Whereas for a woman, it's like "Well, there she goes again." You know, it's like mat leave.

Voice 4: I received a lot of encouragement, first of all, to do my master's, and once in my master's, a lot of encouragement to continue to pursue a Ph.D. And the opportunity to teach— that really encouraged me to go on because I enjoyed doing that. And even though my field work was limited, it did provide networking and presentation opportunities that I hadn't had prior to that.

Voice 5: It just hasn't worked out for me. If I won the lottery, I would go back.

Voice 1: I've always had that goal, to do a doctorate, but the master's program discouraged me because when I did it, all of my instructors, except one, all the people, were male and they were a lot older than me and I didn't really get the feeling that I could fit in in *any* way.

Voice 2: I think the structure of my master's program deterred me from future study but I think also the multiple roles. I mean it wore me out.

Voice 3: I had hoped, at one time, that I would go on and do a doctorate, but that was before I had children. Now that's just not possible.

Voice 4: The thesis made me think I didn't want to go through this again. It wasn't the course work, it was the thesis and the isolation involved.

A woman must have money and a room of her own and "the courage to write exactly what we think." (Woolf 113)

Voice 5: The graduate experience could be improved with more mentorship in my area for women. That's hard because there are still relatively few faculty members who are female. Females understand and they can show you how to be balanced.

Voice 1: Or be sympathetic or empathic with the challenges and sometimes *that's* enough.

Voice 2: We have lives and our lives change as we go through our degrees. In a four or five year commitment, a lot happens in a person's life. We move around. It's a mobile society. If you get married and your husband or you have a job somewhere else and your degree's not finished, what are you going to do? Stay behind? Probably not. You move around and I think there should be resources built in so that people can, with a degree of success, take the resources and use them elsewhere and be supported. Many times people quit—they were people who had all the ability to do it but they ran into blocks.

Voice 3: I think there needs to be more cohesiveness between students, like a support group so people who are at varying stages can stay motivated.

Voice 4: I think there has to be more consideration for people who are working full-time and pursuing graduate work.

Voice 5: I had a very hard time completing the master's degree. I think Gloria Steinem talks about this—on one hand you feel that you don't measure up in so many ways, because of the experience of just trying to finish the thesis. You tell yourself you're getting better but yet, at the same time, you have so many questions asked of you and you don't feel like you're measuring up.

We have clear and consistent support for the operation and negative impact of at least some components of the chilly climate. This evidence was not to be found in the archives, in the official academic performance records of men and women students. Not until we examined the lived experience of graduate students was the full impact of the chilly climate revealed. What is particularly astonishing about this research however, is that in spite of the multitude of apparent inequities, women do not abandon their academic studies nor do they allow these barriers to retard their progress in terms of time taken to complete degree requirements. These women are not victims. They are, in fact, impressive survivors of an inequitable system. (Pyke 161)

Voice 1: Professionally, for me, it was a period of enormous growth as I became more self-confident. You just learn to, well, get ballsy and go for it. If you don't, you're just going to sit back and never get anywhere.

Voice 2: I discovered, on a personal level, that I had a lot of perseverance that I didn't know I had. I discovered I had creativity under pressure that I wasn't aware of.

Voice 3: I got a lot more vocal in my master's program. I never used to talk much in class in my undergrad program. But I saw the master's program as a place to be able to challenge ideas and to question. That's probably what got me into trouble with some of the male professors. I questioned a lot of their thinking.

Voice 4: Knowledge is power. I do believe it.

Voice 5: I'm hoping that what comes out of this research is some kind of recognition that women—oh, we're not so special, we're human beings like everybody else—but we do have that other dimension in our lives. Our families are tremendously demanding and it's very, very tough for women to do this.

> There are a number of ways we might warm the academic climate to make the university a more hospitable place for women faculty and students. Adequate childcare, flexible career paths, longer tenure tracks, and job-sharing need to be part of the institution's way of life. I can no longer try to fit into a predominately male culture. We need to redefine who the institution should serve. In order to humanize the system we need to feminize it. (Sulliman 29)

NOW WHAT?

These statements and their depiction here are important because they help interrogate situations which are of concern to feminists, such as why women do not pursue doctoral studies, why women tend to not study fields related to engineering and science, and why women do not seek promotion. The representation conveys the social realities they struggle with as women—realities which co-exist and overlap, and therefore can conflict and contradict—and as students who are, in many ways, excluded from the "reality" of the university system: they *live* these conflicts and contradictions (Stanley and Wise 169). Indeed, as Rosenberg points out, poststructural feminisms encourage writers and readers, and I would include researchers, to live with and hold contradictions and to learn from what we might not otherwise have thought (41).

As these statements demonstrate, an aspect of invisibility experienced by these women is the lack of recognition of the many roles they assume. These roles include student, parent, child, friend, colleague, professional, community member/citizen, and one-half of a primary relationship with a significant other. The women identified subtle influences which affect the nature and degree of responsibility in these roles, including an informal reward system, the labour market, familial expectations/responsibilities, academic tradition, role-models/mentors. Corroborating other work in the area (Hartsock 70), they expressed how having a family is generally seen as an indication of stability and responsibility for the male university student but is more often viewed as a hindrance or a demonstration of lack of commitment for the female university student. And instead of learning about critical self-awareness, collaborative and nurturing education, or even the social construction of knowledge, the women learned about the structures of the university to which they must conform in order to be acknowledged as educated people (Schick 80).

The women in this study expressed what the results of the Statistics Canada General Social Survey confirmed: that women are still largely responsible for looking after their homes and families. Indeed, women aged 25 to 54 averaged almost two hours more per day on unpaid work activities than their male counterparts. This commitment included an hour a day more on basic chores than men, cooking, cleaning, and keeping order for instance; and almost another hour per day more than men to responsibilities such as primary child care and shopping (Lindsay 2). In his meta-analysis of the literature, Coltrane concluded that most men still do much less housework than women do, with married men creating about as much demand for household labour as they perform (1226). He found that consistent predictors of sharing household labour include both women's and men's employment, earnings, gender ideology, and life-course issues. Further, when men perform more housework, employed women feel that the division of labour is fairer, they are less depressed, and they enjoy higher levels of marital satisfaction. The gendering of time demands was a major theme in my study as many women had the additional role of being a student while working outside of the home and caring for children. Women are often tasked with finding a "balance" between these roles while men are not.

Claire Etaugh and Judith Bridges give three reasons for women's disproportionate share of child care and household duties: time constraints, relative power, and gender attitudes (332-333). The phrase "time constraints" speaks to the allocation of housework, with full-time homemakers usually spending more time on household labour than employed women. However, this explanation does not address why mothers often spend more time than fathers caring for their children even if spouses' work hours are comparable. "Relative power" is ostensibly dependent on income. If household chores have little prestige, the person with the greater income may use his or her power to limit engagement in these duties, but again, wives' greater work responsibilities, even if better paid, may not counter expectations about males' higher status, value, and power. Gender attitudes involve the roles expected for each gender and how they guide behavior. According to Etaugh and Bridges, many couples have internalized the traditional gender beliefs that children and the home are primarily a wife's responsibility and that husbands should be the main financial providers. Men with traditional attitudes to family roles unsurprisingly spend less time doing household duties than their spouses.

The results of this study are comparable with those of Rachel Cinamon and Yisrael Rich, who identified three profiles of workers who differ in attributions of importance to work and family roles: persons who assigned high importance to both the work role and the family role ("Dual" profile); participants who ascribed high importance to the work role and low importance to the family role ("Work" profile); and participants who attributed high importance to the family role and low importance to the work role ("Family" profile) (531). They used these profiles to clarify the relationship between gender and work–family conflict in a study of male and female participants who were employed in computer or law firms. More women than men fit the Family profile, and more men than women fit the Work profile, while no gender differences were found for the Dual profile. Women reported higher parenting and work values than men did and between-gender differences in work–family conflict were apparent. The women in my study talked about the challenges of being a mother and a graduate student, particularly in an inflexible educational system.

Perhaps it is no wonder that women often feel out of place in the academy, since most institutions of "higher" learning were designed and developed by men for men (Solomon 2). When women began to enter universities in increasing numbers, it was up to them to fit within the confines of an already established context. As a result, research has focused on the problems that women graduate students present for higher education, rather than on the difficulties that higher education presents for women (Younes and Asay 451). Just as women are open to changing places, universities need to be open to change as well. Women students must be involved in helping to improve the emotional as well as intellectual environment for all.

While universities may conclude that they have made women welcome, recruitment is only part of the story. As Lynn Wiest attests, "It is not enough for higher-education institutions to recruit and admit female students. Universities also must examine issues of *retention*, investigating the influential factors that help or hinder female graduate students in their pursuit of advanced degrees" (33). Universities need to investigate whether their policies and practices meet the needs of their students by first finding out who makes up their student population—as well as the challenges the institution poses for them in their pursuit of a graduate education (Corbin Dwyer and Burnett 228).

As one woman participant in my research remarked, to truly understand something, one must experience it: "I think that is part of the learning in graduate school. We learn by doing it—not just by reading it and watching it." Therefore, listening to what graduate women have to say is a critical component in examining how our educational system and society influence their education. If universities are to respond to the needs of all students they must listen. The need to study part-time, lack of access to child care, financial difficulties, and issues of isolation, discrimination and sexism have to be examined as systemic, institutional issues. Many of the women did not anticipate having to contend with these issues when they decided to pursue a graduate degree. Further, these were not issues their male peers had to consider. As women reflect on what changing places means to them, universities also have to reflect on the same question. Finding space for emotional intelligence in the work that goes on in universities depends on it.

While the results of this study focused on the commonalities among the women's experiences, there were certainly differences as well. Some educators and students express concern that drawing attention to gender is unegalitarian and that the goal of equity is to treat everyone alike, so that gender (and race and class) are invisible. But, I would argue, we are not yet "beyond gender" (Overall this volume). We cannot act as if historic inequities do not exist; treating everyone "the same" when they are not the same can entrench inequities. Even if significant systemic changes occur in our education practice, women's experiences will still be impacted by sex-role socialization in the wider social context and the expectations women face at home. However, making "space" for women on campuses would help them to negotiate their place outside the Ivory Tower as well.

As the women's stories demonstrate, there is much left to be done to make universities responsive to their student population. Most of the issues raised by my participants are not new, but they demonstrate that changes are not happening fast enough for women. If the social context of universities does not change to make graduate programs more attractive for women, the lack of female mentors/faculty in many fields, and certainly in administration, will continue. The task of social transformation is not women's alone, it's everyone's.

Author's Notes: I gratefully acknowledge the funding for this study provided by the Social Sciences and Humanities Research Council, and the additional support from the Humanities Research Institute at the University of Regina and Memorial University of Newfoundland's Undergraduate Career Experience Program (MUCEP).

I am also appreciative of the invitation from Memorial University of Newfoundland's Women's Studies Speakers' Series committee and funding I received from the Inter-Campus Collaboration Fund, Memorial University of Newfoundland which enabled me to present the "monologues," which are at the heart of this chapter, at the series. Thanks to readers Kanta Chechi, Jacqui Walsh, Peggy Miller, Judith Hearn and Angela Morgan.

This chapter is adapted from my book, Surviving and Succeeding in the Ivory Tower: A Woman's Guide to Negotiating Graduate Studies *(Ottawa: Creative Bound, 2008).*

[1]Quotations in boxes are from published sources. When performed for Memorial University of Newfoundland's Women's Studies Speakers' Series, I presented the boxed text on PowerPoint slides to introduce a visual component. Therefore, different font styles were sometimes used. The slides and quotes helped to "interrupt" the participants' voices, to give listeners an opportunity to pause and consider what the women were saying. I also read an introduction and conclusion and five graduate or former graduate women students read the numbered parts.
[2]Of the 491 women who completed surveys, at the time of responding 8.6 percent had withdrawn from their graduate program, 14.3 percent still had to complete their program, and 13.8 percent had received an extension.

WORKS CITED

Acker, Sandra. *Gendered Education: Sociological Reflections on Women, Teaching, and Feminism.* Philadelphia: Open University Press, 1994. Print.

Calixte, Shana, Jennifer Johnson and Maki Motapanyane. "Liberal, Socialist, and Radical Feminism: An Introduction to Three Theories about Women's Oppression and Social Change." *Feminist Issues: Race, Class, and Sexuality.* 5th ed. Ed. Nancy Mandell. Toronto: Pearson, 2010. 1-39. Print.

Cinamon, Rachel G. and Yisrael Rich. "Gender Differences in the Importance of Work and Family Roles: Implications for Work-family Conflict." *Sex Roles* 46 (2002): 531-541. Print.

Coltrane, Scott. "Research on Household Labor: Modeling and Measuring the Social Embeddedness of Routine Family Work." *Journal of Marriage and Family,* 62 (2000): 1208-1233.

Corbin Dwyer, Sonya and Jody Burnett. "Listening to the Voices of Women Graduate Students: An Approach to Institutional Self-Assessment in Higher Education." *Proceedings of the First International Conference on Teaching and Learning in Higher Education* (2004): 224-229. CD.

Corbin Dwyer, Sonya and Kathleen O'Reilly-Scanlon. "The Regina Monologues: Experiences of Graduate Women." Humanities Research Institute Profiling Scholarship Series, University of Regina, 2005. Paper.

Corbin Dwyer, Sonya, Linda Sabatini and Alice Mohr. *"Who's That Girl?: Exploring a Profile of Women Graduate Students."* Canadian Society for the Study of Education Annual Meeting, St. John's, Newfoundland, 1997. Paper.

Dewar, Tammy. "Circling Women." *The Madwoman in the Academy: 43 Women Boldly Take on the Ivory Tower.* Ed. Deborah Keahey and Deborah D. Schnitzer. Calgary: University of Calgary Press, 2003. 54-57. Print.

Doherty-Delorme, Denise, and Erika Shaker. "Missing Pieces III: Introduction." *Missing Pieces III: An Alternative Guide to Canadian Post-secondary Education.* Ed. Denise Doherty-Delorme and Erika Shaker. CCPA *Monitor,* 2002. 1-6. Print.

Etaugh, Claire A. and Judith S. Bridges. *Women's Lives: A Psychological Exploration.* 2nd ed. Toronto: Allyn & Bacon, 2010. Print.

Eveline, Joan. *Ivory Basement Leadership: Power and Invisibility in the Changing University.* Perth: University of Westerna Australia Press, 2004. Print.

Gilbert, Sandra and Susan Gubar. *The Madwoman in the Attic: The Woman Writer and the Nineteenth-Century Literary Imagination.* New Haven: Yale University Press, 1979. Print.

Hartsock, Linda S. "The Woman Graduate Student: Roles, Relationships and Realities." *Graduate and Professional Education of Women: Proceedings of AAUW Conference.* Washington, DC: American Association of University Women, 1974. 62-74. Print.

Hayes, Elisabeth and Daniele Flannery. "Adult Women's Learning in Higher Education: A Critical Review of Scholarship." *Initiatives* 57.1 (1995): 29-37. Print.

Jones, Susan R. and Marylu K. McEwen. "A Conceptual Model of Multiple Dimensions of Identity." *Journal of College Student Development* 41.4 (2000): 405-414. Print.

Keahey, Deborah. "Nine Steps Towards a Twelve-step Program for Recovering Academics." *The Madwoman in the Academy: 43 Women Boldly Take on the Ivory Tower.* Ed. Deborah Keahey and Deborah D. Schnitzer. Calgary: University of Calgary Press, 2003. 49-52. Print.

Keahey, Deborah and Deborah D. Schnitzer, eds. *The Madwoman in the Academy: 43 Women Boldly Take on the Ivory Tower.* Calgary: University of Calgary Press, 2003. Print.

Kelly, Jennifer and Aruna Strivastava. "Dancing on the Lines: Mothering, Daughtering, Masking, and Mentoring in the Academy." *The Madwoman in the Academy: 43 Women Boldly Take on the Ivory Tower.* Ed. Deborah Keahey and Deborah D. Schnitzer. Calgary: University of Calgary Press, 2003. 58-76. Print.

Lindsay, Colin. "Are Women Spending More Time on Unpaid Domestic Work Than Men in Canada?" *Matter of Fact, No. 9 The General Social Survey Statistics Canada Catalogue No. 89-630-X.* 2008. Print.

Mandell, Nancy, ed. *Feminist Issues: Race, Class, and Sexuality.* 5th ed. Toronto: Pearson, 2010. Print.

Oakley, A. *Telling the Truth About Jerusalem.* London: Basil Blackwell, 1986. Print.

Paludi, Michelle A. *The Psychology of Women.* 2nd ed. Upper Saddle River, New Jersey: Prentice Hall, 2002. Print.

Pyke, Sandra. "Education and the 'Woman Question.'" *Canadian Psychology* 38.3 (1997): 154-163. Print.

The Quotable Woman. Philadelphia: Running P, 1991. Print.

Reece, Raimunda. "Feminist Theorizing on Race and Racism." *Feminist Issues: Race, Class, and Sexuality.* 5th ed. Ed. Nancy Mandell. Toronto: Pearson, 2010. 87-109. Print.

Reynolds, Amy and Raechele Pope. "The Complexities of Diversity: Exploring Multiple Oppressions." *Journal of Counselling & Development* 70 (1991): 174-180. Print.

Rosenberg, Sharon. "An Introduction to Feminist Poststructural Theorizing." *Feminist Issues: Race, Class, and Sexuality.* 5th ed. Ed.

Nancy Mandell. Toronto: Pearson, 2010. 40-62. Print.

Russell, Sharon. "Day Cares." *The Madwoman in the Academy: 43 Women Boldly Take on the Ivory Tower.* Ed. Deborah Keahey and Deborah D. Schnitzer. Calgary: University of Calgary Press, 2003. 25-27. Print.

Schick, Carol. *The University as Text: Women and the University Context.* Halifax: Fernwood Publishing, 1994. Print.

Solomon, Barbara. *In the Company of Educated Women: A History of Women and Higher Education in America.* New Haven: Yale University Press, 1985. Print.

Stanley, Liz and Sue Wise. *Breaking Out Again: Feminist Ontology and Epistemology.* New York: Routledge, 1993. Print.

Sulliman, Celeste. "(M)othering in the Academy." *The Madwoman in the Academy: 43 Women Boldly Take on the Ivory Tower.* Ed. Deborah Keahey and Deborah D. Schnitzer. Calgary: University of Calgart Press, 2003. 28-30. Print.

Van Herk, Aritha. "A Guide to Academic Sainthood." *The Madwoman in the Academy: 43 Women Boldly Take on the Ivory Tower.* Ed. Deborah Keahey and Deborah D. Schnitzer. Calgary: University of California Press, 2003. 155-163. Print.

Webber, Michelle. "Women and Education." *Feminist Issues: Race, Class, and Sexuality.* 5th ed.Ed. Nancy Mandell. Toronto: Pearson, 2010. 247-271. Print.

Wiest, Lynn. "Addressing the Needs of Graduate Women." *Contemporary Education* 70.2 (1999): 30–33. Print.

Woolf, Virginia. *A Room of One's Own.* New York: Harcourt Brace, 1929. Print.

Younes, Maha and Sylvia Asay. "Resilient Women: How Female Graduate Students Negotiate their Multiple Roles." *College Student Journal* 32.3 (1998): 451-462. Print.

York Stories: Women in Higher Education. Toronto: Tsar, 2000. Print.

10. Alternative Thinking for Engineers

GLORIA MONTANO

R ATHER THAN DISCUSS equity-balancing initiatives in this male-dominated field, I have chosen to concentrate on women who already work as engineers and computer scientists. Thus I can consider what the women who are creators of technology, and consumers of its products, think, do, and say about technology. I am interested in the culture of the industry's professionals and I ask: under what conditions could women change their profession's priorities and make life-improving technology an effective response to household and community needs? But might the word be *affective*? Effective modeling has efficiency as an important outcome. My point in this chapter is that, as illustrated by the case studies, much is overlooked in engineering when outcomes are modeled as efficient rather than affective.

This essay describes how the author was able to look beyond her engineering training and conditioning to see how much difference a gendered lens could make. The journal entries interspersed in what follows, and indicated by italics, capture lessons learned mostly in the Virtual Development Center (VDC), an innovative program of the Anita Borg Institute for Women and Technology. The VDC was designed to engage a broad spectrum of women in all aspects of technology. They started from various levels of technical expertise; they also differed in age, as well as cultural, socioeconomic, and educational background. As part of the planned process, they considered institutional improvements. This educational and community-based program was originally approached by the author as simply another engineering project management task like those common in business and industry, but it was to profoundly change her perspectives on the potential value and impact of engineering and computer science professionals. Of concern to the author was the question of how women in the engineering and computer science professions represent and address the needs of all women, not least because when female professionals are involved, the perception is that they automatically respond to these particular needs.

Journal Entry: *After more than 20 years as an engineer in the high tech sector, I never imagined that my profession would take me to a small room behind an old church in a rural, agriculture town. Even further from my mind was the prospect of conducting a technology brainstorming session with 41 adult farm workers, two babies, and a small black dog named Chico. To complicate matters even further, the regular facilitator was unable to attend, and the workshop required simultaneous translation from English to Spanish. Given the countries represented—Mexico, Lebanon, Korea, the United Kingdom, India, Peru, Colombia, Canada, and the United States—I would not have been surprised to find that Spanish was the most common language in the room. Despite my deep immersion in the Silicon Valley culture, this setting was strangely comfortable and perhaps the logical conclusion to a series of 31 brainstorming sessions. Called Innovation Workshops, these were specifically designed to provide a forum where women and others underserved by technology could identify and prioritize which of their needs would be addressed by university students studying engineering, computer science, and other related fields. What mattered most was to hear directly from individuals—especially those whose age, gender, race, and socioeconomic status were largely ignored by creators of technology—on what needs were most pressing. It was through these Innovation Workshops that my mental image of what engineers could and should do began to shift.*

Given the impact of technology, how can women engineers and computer scientists become part of a solution that fully engages women and not part of the problem that further isolates women? The significance of women engineering and computer science professionals perhaps seems slight if we are guided by the small percentage of women in the workforce: approximately 11 percent of engineers and 27 percent of computer scientists are female. But should we make inquiries into the actual number of women engineers and computer scientists employed in North America, we discover at least one million, a figure that is not unimpressive (see Statistics Canada; U.S. Department of Labor); and this figure might easily be doubled by including the women who have left the professions (Frehill *et al* 52-56; Hewlett *et al.* 50). The exact number of women engineers and computer scientists varies depending on the sources of data and which fields are included in the definition, but even so, one million is a conservative number. If properly engaged, a complement of this size could be a powerful advocate for women's needs as technology users. It could turn engineering in a more empathic direction.

CONTEXT AND BACKGROUND

Before going into detail, it is useful to sketch the economic and social environment in which the VDC program was created in 1999. It is important that the work of engineers and the engineering profession differs from the work of computer scientists and the computer science profession. But the general population experiences modern technology as a blend of the work of both professions. Hence, in the VDC and in this essay, the terms "engineer" and "engineering" include computer scientists and computer science.

During the latter half of the 1990s, web-based technologies and businesses, nicknamed "dot-com" companies by the popular press, captured the imagination of many investors. In particular, well-known technology venture capitalist John Doerr spurred widespread optimism after publicly declaring the Internet to be "the largest legal creation of wealth in the history of the planet" (O'Brien, "Mother"). Rhetoric such as this, combined with an increase in venture capital, unleashed a flow of funding to dot-com companies so plentiful that many executive teams suspended adherence to standard business practices in pursuit of market share. Engineers in the Silicon Valley in California, where many of the dot-com companies emerged, were puzzled as to how the new companies, who touted products that were perceived to be of little value, could attract significant investments. The reaction of the working engineers (often referring to the new product offerings as "vaporware") could be compared with Hans Christian Andersen's fairy tale, "The Emperor's New Clothes," exposing an elaborate deception in which many were complicit. But while the crowd only laughed at the emperor's foolishness, the consequences of vaporware were more severe. The burst of the dot-com bubble in 2000 led to a protracted recession, and John Doerr issued a public apology for failing to disclose that there were two sides to the potential of the Internet. He corrected his original statement by saying that the Internet was "the largest legal creation (and evaporation) of wealth in the history of the planet" (O'Brien, "Investor"). Significantly, he went on to caution that "there is a battle going on for the soul of the entrepreneur," explaining that the real contest was between "missionaries," who sought to develop Internet technology to its greatest potential, and "mercenaries," who were intent on rapid return on investment (O'Brien, "Investor").

As speculation on the economic benefits of the Internet and the World Wide Web stimulated the thinking of business people, others were growing concerned about the dangers of such rapid proliferation of technology, and especially the inequities that were implicated in differential access to information and communications technology (ICT). Wary that the result would be to widen and deepen digital divides, many sought to moderate its effects. Discussions at the United Nations Fourth World Conference on Women, held in Beijing, China in 1995, led to agreement on two objectives that were significant to women and set the stage for further world discussion on ICT rights. Two aims were documented in the "Women and the Media" report of the Beijing "Declaration and Platform for Action": to increase women's participation in decision-making by bettering women's access to the media and new technologies of communication, and a commitment to promoting a balanced and non-stereotyped portrayal of women in the media (Zorn 35).

WOMEN AND TECHNOLOGY

One individual in the United States who was very interested in both the technological and social consequences of change was the feminist, computer scientist, and researcher Anita Borg. Increasingly concerned about the possible negative consequences of technology for the world's women, she questioned whether the technological applications currently being designed would improve women's lives. In 1997, in a speech at a technical women's conference, Borg addressed an audience of women in computing, describing the current environment, and posing a fundamental question.

> We are all surfing the tidal wave of change that you hear about in all the trade rags and popular press, and it is a very, very exciting time. We are all riding that wave with all of our colleagues, but this is a potentially dangerous tidal wave. This is not necessarily something that is going to do the world tremendous amounts of good. The promise of computing is really tremendous for everybody, but the question that we have to ask ourselves is: If we aren't able to make (technology) work for everybody, is it really worth it at all? Is it really worth all this change? (Keynote)

During the heady times of the dot-com explosion, ideas ran wild about what was coming in the future—networks of computers on our bodies, umbrellas that would jump out of the stand saying "take me with you" when weather reports indicated rain, and the ability to send loved ones virtual snuggles while away at a conference. Borg, however, sounded a note of caution: society was too stratified and the benefits of this revolution were likely to affect only a small portion of the world's population. Focusing on access, Borg proposed that the only way to realize the full potential of the knowledge economy was to expand its reach. She emphasized the empathic over the purely commercial application of technology, knowing that the enabling nature of technology renders profit an inadequate measure of its full value. By embracing the perspectives of a broader diversity of people, it becomes possible to understand actual human needs more fully and thereby develop more appropriate technology while still providing profit.

> Access without the knowledge to use what is behind it, is no access at all. Access to things that were designed without you in mind, that are not relevant to your life, is no access at all.... The knowledge economy has a huge potential, but who is going to participate in that economy? Is it really going to be everyone out there beyond this room, everybody represented by the mixed ability, mixed genders, mixed races all around the world? It seems to me that until everyone is involved in the design process, in the decision process, until everyone is represented in the lab and in the boardrooms ... we will not really fulfill this tremendous potential. (Keynote)

Borg's desire was to "simply change the world" and, against the backdrop of a tidal wave of change and concern for the impact of technology on the world's women in 1997, she announced the creation of the Institute for Women and Technology. Although Borg had previously founded two other venues—Systers and the Grace Hopper Celebration for Women in Computing—the Institute was a move from virtual into physical. The Institute's mission was to give women a larger say in all aspects of technology, to increase the positive impact of technology on the lives of the world's women, and to bring benefits to communities, industry, education and government from these changes (Emerson 1). Borg's original idea was to develop the Institute into a world-class, interdisciplinary research facility dedicated to examining the intersecting worlds of women and technology. To encourage the proliferation of ideas, half of the researchers were to be resident and half were to be visiting scholars. Anita Borg died prematurely of brain cancer in 2003 and the Institute was then renamed in her honour. Fortunately, she left us with a vision of the challenges still ahead.

> In this century, we have the responsibility to learn, be involved in, and have an opinion about technology, and to ensure that women and girls are actively involved in creating the future. We hope to catalyze the active participation of women throughout the world in the new technical democracy. We will cast our votes by deciding what we want, by becoming technically literate, and by applying our genius to build the technology for a positive future. (Borg, "Technology" 1)

Journal Entry: *While Borg was busy breaking new ground in areas related to computing, I was deeply involved in efforts to increase the number of women engineers. I found my career choice when my father, an immigrant from the Philippines who became a draftsman in the US Army Corp of Engineers, suggested that I study engineering. A practical man, he felt that engineering was a good career and would be a step up the economic ladder for any of his children. Two factors influenced my career decision. First, I received a scholarship. Second, in reading the university catalogue I came across a description of the student section of the Society of Women Engineers. I figured that if there were enough women engineers to form a society, then it must be okay for women to be engineers. In retrospect, I came to realize that in my father's eyes, raising my economic status was reason enough to ignore the limitations of prevailing gender roles. He also believed that given a chance, women would exceed expectations, and as evidence, he would call attention to three Filipina women, the people he admired most, who had managed to achieve a high level of success despite conventional narrow thinking on what women could or could not do.*

In reflection, my path crossed Borg's path several times; however, it was not until 1999 that our paths drew closer. That year, an article entitled "Mother of Invention" appeared in the San Jose Mercury News describing one of the early brainstorming sessions she coordinated. For me, the article was pivotal. Throughout my own career, I represented my employers at numerous engineering recruitment activities to promote engineering and to promote the company as the best place for engineers to work. The percentage of women studying and working in engineering rose quickly in the 1980s, but despite everyone's effort, it has since remained relatively flat. As my own experience expanded, I began to doubt whether engineering really deserved so much promotion, especially among women. Borg's article renewed my enthusiasm because it helped me to reconceptualize the purpose of engineering and see a way to recapture the attention of young women whose eyes would so often glaze over at the mere sound of the word "engineering." The concept was simple: get women and girls to talk about what they need technology to do, and they would begin to value technology in a personal way and eventually become interested in what it took to create technology. Voila! More women studying engineering and computer science meant more women working in technical roles. The simplicity of the idea was enough to move me out of the security and comfort of the high-tech business world to the uncertainty of the non-profit, public-benefit world of the Institute. I changed places enthusiastically.

PUTTING WOMEN'S IDEAS INTO PRACTICE

A fascination with what technology can do is not typical of most women, so Borg needed a way to engage the minds of the women and girls who were used to being ignored by technology creators. She sought to kindle the imaginations of women and girls about what really mattered at a personal level and to inspire them by what technology could make possible. Soon after establishing the Institute, Borg and her colleagues developed ways for women from all walks of life to overcome traditional obstacles and willingly offer their thoughts regarding technology by means of a structured discussion process. The VDC was created at this time to bring these ideas to fruition.

Established in 1999, the VDC began as a partnership between the Institute, its corporate sponsors, and three universities; by 2005 it had grown to a diverse network of ten colleges and universities in the United States. The specific objectives of the VDC were to develop a strong cognitive association between technology and its social relevance among VDC participants, who included engineering students and community clients; to develop the technical solutions through student projects that addressed needs in appropriate ways; and to identify and promote best practices for addressing and coping with systemic change in academia and industry. The idea was to amplify the voice and elevate the priorities of women, and to drive the development of technology to benefit a much broader range of people.

VDC sites were located at Purdue University, Santa Clara University (a Jesuit university with emphasis on education and social justice, which had the highest percentage of female engineering faculty in U.S. institutions accredited by the Accreditation Board for Engineering and Technology), Smith College (the only women's college with an engineering program), Texas A&M University, the University of Arizona at Tucson, the University of California at Berkeley, the University of Colorado at Boulder, the University of Texas at El Paso (the university with the largest national Hispanic enrollment), the University of Washington at Seattle, and Notre Dame de Namur University (the first college in California authorized to grant the baccalaureate degree to women). Each of these institutions had the essential ingredients: dedicated faculty and administrators who understood the potential and limitations of technology and technological education; willing community partners; and students eager for direct connections between their studies and benefits to the community. Each VDC Site was managed independently by a Leadership Team composed of faculty, administrators, and community representatives.

The VDC program enhanced project-based undergraduate courses at each partnering university through VDC Courses that included a structured brainstorming session (Innovation Workshop) at the beginning of traditional design course syllabi. In those courses, community-based customers determined project requirements and students were challenged to develop solutions by methods which ensured that learning benefits were realized by all participants. The students worked for one or more semesters with community participants and professionals and the resulting solutions were often, but not always, technology-based. Students presented the results of their work at an annual VDC conference attended by Institute staff and advisors, VDC sponsors, and community partners (see Fig. 1).

The essential difference between VDC courses and traditional project-based courses was that the ideas for the projects had to originate in a need raised by community participants in an Innovation Workshop, rather than in recycled project lists or faculty research interests. The Innovation Workshops brought together women who differed in educational background, age, socioeconomic status, and ethnicity, as well as in the levels of comfort each felt with technology. Early workshops focused on the needs of women and girls, and consciously excluded male participation. Later workshops were expanded to organizations that made serving the needs of women a priority. This measure gave men the opportunity to participate and enhanced the program in two important ways. First, most technology was and is conceived and developed by men, so to exclude male engineers was to reinforce separateness, paradoxically confirming their dominant position. Second, there are men who are also marginalized by a profession that is dominated

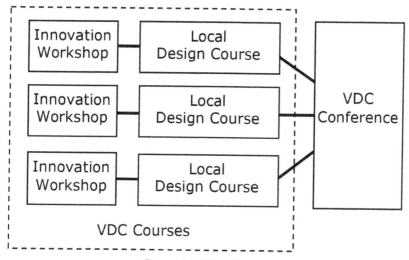

Figure 1: VDC Block Diagram

by mostly white, North American males of a specific socioeconomic level. The inclusion of men who had previously been excluded from influencing technology allowed for the shared perspectives of women and men to surface.

Between 1999 and 2004, over 800 students, faculty, and community representatives participated in 31 Innovation Workshops. Over 370 students completed VDC courses. More than 1500 ideas were generated, and over 120 projects were undertaken by students to serve the needs of 30 or more community groups (Emerson 6). Some of the student projects are described in Sidebar 1.

Journal Entry: *By 2001, I had taken responsibility for the* VDC *as its director. Despite the news of Borg's illness and the prospect of her prolonged absence, I brashly believed, in keeping with the confidence commonly associated with the engineering culture, that my engineering project management skill was enough to bring about change.* VDC *sites existed at four major universities in the U.S., so clearly Borg and her colleagues already had a successful prototype. It was now up to me to find ways to streamline procedures and standardize products or, as I may have conceived it then, to "scale up" the* VDC, *an industry expression for the expansion and proliferation of a valued product or process. The intent was to mass-produce and distribute the* VDC *process as education modules so that universities all across the country could establish their own* VDC *sites. But as I became more familiar with the inner workings of universities through the* VDC, *I began to see that different institutional cultures might work against transferability of the program and I started to seriously question the wisdom of replicating the VDC system as educational modules. Many times before, I had seen what happens when a system or process is automated without reflection. Streamlining can become an end in itself while the real problem takes on invisibility as participants derive gratification from the elegance of an approach, thus creating a bureaucratic nightmare that numbs the minds of all those involved and confounds any external attempts to bring thinking back to the original problem. The last thing I wanted was to replicate yet another program that in the end simply meant more work for already busy people, especially for women. I also felt that the VDC had much more value than we could quantify at the time. Answers would not come without a dramatic shift in direction, and this realization created a very personal dilemma for me. My first step in relocation was not enough.*

WHAT WOMEN SAY ABOUT TECHNOLOGY

The processes and outcomes of the VDC have not been rigorously examined; however, several general observations can be made regarding the types of ideas generated, ideas not generated, and individual perspectives on technology. It should be noted that as part of the structured brainstorming process, participants were taken on their own terms, with the result that inexperience with technology was not a barrier to contributing. Imaginations could run free without preconceptions or expectations.

First, and contrary to popular notions, the women who participated in the Innovation Workshops generally were not afraid of technology; rather, they were uninterested in technology that did not serve them. Women said their lives were complicated enough, and that if technology was to make sense for them, it should do what they expected and nothing more. Listed below are some examples from the workshops.

> •*One not enough.* Unlike personal digital assistant devices such as the Palm Pilot, women in the workshops wanted a calendar that could handle an entire family's schedule, a task familiar to most mothers. To underscore the point, Borg would add that perhaps if women had created the Palm Pilot, it would have been designed to fit elsewhere than the breast pocket.
> •*Listen first.* During the height of the dot-com boom, companies were looking for new markets for their technologies, even citing the kitchen as the last frontier to benefit from intelligent

Sidebar 1: Representative community-based projects from the Virtual Development Center

TOYTech is an elementary and middle school collaboration that designs fun, marketable, gender-neutral toys that teach technology principles. As a result of their innovative project, Smith has partnered with the Sally Ride Science Club, toy manufacturer Hasbro and Sigma XI, the Scientific Research Society, to launch the outreach activity, TOYChallenge (Smith 2004).

The GO Boulder (Giving Online in Boulder County) project is an Internet database hosted by the Boulder Community Network to aid residents in making targeted in-kind donations to non-profits. The site also gives non-profits a way to coordinate activities and share furniture and other resources (University of Colorado, Boulder 2001).

The Tucson Community Food Bank expressed the need for an ergonomic assembly-line system for volunteers who pack thousands of boxes of food every month for distribution to needy families. The system that the team designed and implemented with the input of their client includes components such as ergonomic mats, a lifter, and assembly-line rollers (University of Arizona, Tucson 2004).

The Smart House PowerAid is an in-house real-time system to inform domestic shelter residents of power utilization for better financial management decision-making (Santa Clara 2004).

A Fingerprint Identification System for blood donors was developed to support United Blood Services to track donations more efficiently and accurately (University of Texas at El Paso 2004).

Remark is a visually-based communicator designed for hearing-impaired individuals to assist in their day-to-day interactions with non-hearing-impaired individuals (University of California, Berkeley 2004).

A suite of Internet products has been designed in a continuing partnership with community middle-school girls. They include an interactive collaborative paint e-Art Program and an education-based Trivia Board Game (Purdue 2004).

A newly redesigned website is used by CASA Latina, a community organization that empowers Latino immigrants. The site is now more attractive to donors and volunteers, and effectively highlights services to ensure a smoother transitional experience for immigrants (University of Washington 2006).

Source: Virtual Development Center: Changing the World for Women and for Technology, Anita Borg Institute for Women and Technology (Emerson 9-10).

appliances. One popular idea was a refrigerator that would recite recipes that matched the refrigerator's contents. Echoing the sentiments of many workshop participants, one woman proclaimed that she wanted a kitchen that would listen to her, not talk at her.

•*No frills.* Both women and men favored software that was not so overloaded with features that it compromised basic tasks.

Second, only one idea promoting a violent or aggressive solution was expressed in the course of 31 workshops. The fact that no such ideas surfaced during at least the first 28 workshops became evident only after a person who had recently heard about the workshops facetiously requested a device that would blow away cars that got in his way during his commute to and from work. In contrast, participants in all workshops produced a number of ideas that fell into the category of improving safety for their families and themselves. The following needs identified by workshop participants illustrate the range of concerns.

•Women who had escaped domestic violence were always concerned with knowing where their children were. During group sessions at their shelter, their children gathered together in a central play area; however, some women were concerned that their children could leave the area undetected by the supervisors. They suggested an identification bracelet that would sound an alarm if a child moved out of range.

•In one city, a child had died in a swimming pool full of children because the lifeguards could not see the child at the bottom of the pool. In order to prevent a recurrence of the tragedy, women asked for a device that could detect when a child was under the water too long and notify the parent as well as lifeguards.

•During a winter workshop, one woman noted that she would like a heated bus shelter, which prompted another woman to request that a display in the shelter show where the next bus was located so she could tell how long she needed to wait. Mindful of recent rapes in the area, others added the need for a panic button that would immediately establish a bidirectional communication link with police.

•One woman requested a simple device like a brooch that she could touch and instantly signal her child or other loved one that she was thinking of them. A cell phone was considered excessive, too complicated, and too expensive for this basic human expression.

Third, the majority of people attending the Innovation Workshop changed their perception of their relationship to technology in positive ways. Workshop survey results from community participants for 2003–2004 revealed the following: 53 percent agreed that their understanding of what technology "is" had been broadened; 88 percent affirmed that after the sessions, they felt they could demand more of technology; and while 68 percent were now convinced that their views on technology were important, 80 percent said their general interest in technology had increased; 74 percent reported an increased interest in being involved in creating technology. Of the students in technical fields who had participated in workshops during the 2003–2004 academic year, 41 percent reported broadened personal understanding of what technology "is," 79 percent realized that they could demand more of technology, and 67 percent revealed increased interest in creating technology (Emerson 8). The reasons that a population generally assumed to be fearful or apathetic towards technology can experience such a significant shift in perception so quickly during a six-hour workshop demand further examination.

Journal Entry: *Discussion at most of the meetings at the Institute inevitably turned toward women's discomfort with and fear of technology. I was annoyed because the women in my life were not uncomfortable with technology. Eventually it dawned on me that while most of the women in my life were engineers and quite at ease with all forms of technology, Institute staff and the general public were not. When I finally understood the rare profile of my circle of friends, I realized that I needed to include a broader range of women in my perspective and to readjust what I considered the technological capability of women. Even in this enlightened state, my own often-presumed disconnection between women and technology was still disturbing. On further reflection, I came to understand that the homogeneous profile of my women friends had begun to develop at university and continued throughout my life. As I mentioned this to other women engineers, they would also acknowledge similar homogeneity in their own circle of friends. While it is not unusual to associate with people primarily in the same profession, there was something about engineering that felt different. Perhaps this homogeneity, coupled with the need to blend into the dominant engineering culture for survival, helped to establish a*

narrow field of vision that has the effect of creating widespread gender
blindness among women engineers. I suggest this but expect that it will
be fiercely resisted by my female colleagues.

ENSURING THAT WOMEN SPEAK

Women's perspectives on technology emerge from many sources. For example, a ninety-four-year-old, wheelchair-bound grandmother found the conventional method of reaching back to grab and rotate the wheels of her chair was too painful. After watching other seniors at her residence she conceived the idea of a "rod that went through a gizmo that hugged the big wheel" in a way that would allow her to propel her chair by pushing on a lever (O'Brien, "Mother" 1991; "Mother" 2004). In this case, her grandson heard her request, built a prototype, and, in 2005, Madeline T. Facer was named as a co-inventor on the patent (Patent Storm). As another example, a team of men was brainstorming for ways to help the disabled. They wanted to make use of breathing power but had trouble imagining clothing that could harness the energy from chest expansions and contractions. Any woman who has worn a bra would have had an instant answer for the team; however, in this case, no woman had the opportunity to contribute from her experience. Lastly, in an innovators' and inventors' conference separate from the Institute, one male speaker elicited chuckles from the mostly male audience when he said that his wife wanted a bathroom scale with no numbers: "What good is a scale without numbers?" Perhaps buoyed by the presence of each other, several women in the back of the room almost simultaneously voiced disagreement that surprised the speaker and the other men in the audience. The women agreed that knowledge of one's weight down to a pound is pointless detail and that weight within a reasonable range is good enough. One woman argued that numbers cause unhealthy emphasis on ideal weight and questioned whether most home bathroom scales are even capable of a fine degree of accuracy. Views such as these are important to address, but visibility raised in this way is uncertain and ephemeral. This is why Innovation Workshops succeed: they provide a structured environment that allows a consistent prompt from needs and gives free flow to ideas.

As indicated earlier, the Innovation Workshop was designed to establish the tone of the pedagogical methods for the rest of the program, and to facilitate a sustainable relationship between the community and the academic institution. It was also a place to realize the value of interdisciplinary involvement from fields such as education and the social sciences. One of the biggest challenges was to create an environment in which each person in a very diverse mix of technical and non-technical participants would feel that their presence was valuable and necessary. Borg tried several group communication processes and eventually settled on the Thinking Environment™, which promotes the idea that the quality of decisions is influenced most by the quality of the context where the thinking occurs. This approach suggests that the most valuable thing we can offer each other is the framework in which to think for ourselves. With expert assistance from Dr. Sara B. Hart, the Innovation Workshop was created based on four of ten Thinking Environment™ concepts: attention, appreciation, equality, and ease (Kline 24). Hart would point out, "Casual listening produces casual thinking. Profound listening produces profound thinking" (personal communication). In the workshop space, the participants were responsible for shaping the environment so that all those present could do their best possible thinking, especially with respect to their own relationship with technology. Great care was taken to infuse equality and ease into the process. As a result, the workshop participants created an ideal space for thinking that unlocked minds and produced a wealth of ideas for the group to consider (see Sidebar 2).

Journal Entry: *Of all the* VDC *processes, the environment in the Innovation Workshops was the most promising because it established a safe space for empowering individuals and effecting positive institutional change. I recalled several occasions in my own past where individuals created, probably unconsciously, an ideal space for my best thinking. It was only in Anita Borg's institute, however, that so calm and yet so stimulating an environment provided the foundation for quality thinking and a simple request for a "thinking partner" would instantly invoke supportive behaviour from colleagues. Borg's commitment to the Thinking Environment™ meant that we also "walked the talk" by conducting meetings in accordance with the principles of the Thinking Environment™. Deceptively simple in concept, the principles were easy to pick up, much harder to perfect, and even harder to abandon. On two separate occasions, several of us, Borg included, would declare how intolerable other meetings were, where the concepts of attention, appreciation, equality, and ease were absent.*

As an engineering project manager, I learned to value the tabulating of activities, participation, and products as a convenient way to quantify progress against predefined requirements. That type of measurement process in the grand scheme of putting women's ideas into practice, however, is simply inadequate to capture the full value of benefits emanating from the VDC work. As we conducted more workshops, I began to recognize how quickly participants' perceptions of their relationship to technology changed during the six-hour sessions. This was especially true of community participants who would often enter the sessions timid and unsure, and by the second half of the workshop confidently state their needs, often demanding appropriate solutions, and sometimes lobbying other participants to vote for their ideas.

As another example, one female middle-school student was constantly distracted by her male companions at the beginning of the workshop. Eventually, the structured process allowed her to suggest an issue, but it was not selected for discussion by her group. Quick thinking by one of the teacher participants prevented the girl from retreating in disappointment. The teacher pointed out that so many other participants liked the idea that two new groups were to be formed and she suggested that the student join one of them. By the end of the workshop that same girl presented her new group's solution to all 90 participants. The outcome for her could have been very different had the teacher, who was trained in emotive factors that affect learning, not been in the room to intervene. It was in these workshops that I came to appreciate that the greatest value came not from the technological artifact or the retention of engineering and computer science students, but from the emancipation of the individual from technological subjugation, whether the subjugation was real or imagined.

To tell the story and to effect change required different knowledge than what I had gained from an engineering education and from my experience in corporate environments. By 2006, I had left the Institute and begun a master's in education in an attempt to gain knowledge that would help me to understand what I felt was happening in the VDC and to find the language to explain it to others. As I would discover in my first-semester formal research methods class, what we were trying to do was in the realm of participatory action research and the first thing that kind of research requires is a reflexive approach. No wonder my previous efforts had been so difficult; how different my work at the Borg Institute might have been had I come to it knowing about these methods.

UNDER WHAT CONDITIONS WILL WOMEN EFFECT CHANGE?

In light of the results from the ten colleges and universities in the VDC,

Sidebar 2 - Participant comments from the Virtual Development Center

Direct connections to social benefit and community

This project has helped me see that engineering is not just about sitting in the classroom all day but is instead about having interactions with community and having relationships with people. There were so many cultural subtleties we couldn't have even seen, let alone understood, unless we had spent time with these women. (Student)

...when you can hear the ideas of the workers or clients, you see they are at least as good if not better than yours. If you're not open to hearing those ideas, you miss opportunities. (Student)

The VDC experience brings the benefits of increased motivation, confidence, enhanced communication skills, and leadership development in the students ... as a CS major I have always felt I would end up programming boring software, but now feel more that I can end up doing work that interests me. (Student)

More than anything, the VDC program is empowering. At my first Innovation Workshop, I realized how many things women have invented, how much we contribute to society. I felt inspired to be creative and dedicated, to be organized and meticulous and carry out a new idea to the finish. (Student)

The expectations are high. But at the end of the day, what I see in the students who participate in the VDC program is a jump in confidence. (Faculty member)

The experience that the team members get by developing their projects is unlike any other experience in undergraduate engineering classes. And the exposure they get at the conference is wonderful. It helps them learn to value what they know and what they're doing. (Team advisor, former student)

Increased gender awareness

[This was] my first time to be involved in open discussion. (fourth year male EECS student)

The day was not about competition and the ideas just flowed. (fourth year male EECS student)

Community empowerment

I have always felt passive about my relationship to invention and technology, whereas I now feel that I can choose to impact development. (Community participant)

I saw that I am more "technical" than I realized. (eighty-two-year-old female, retired professor of literature)

Faculty enrichment

It's been really rewarding to be part of the VDC; I've met such interesting people and seen a different side of computer science. I've grown as a professor and a person through this work. I've learned more than I ever imagined.

[The] students' dedication to the projects was something I'd never seen before in the math-based computer science classes I usually teach.... [I've] seen a different side of computer science ...

It's thrilling for me as an instructor, too—I don't get the chance to teach an interdisciplinary class like "Designing Technology for Girls and Women" very often.

It's so easy to get so focused on my work. I forget to look at different aspects of technology.... [It's] helped me refresh my perspective.

Source: Virtual Development Center: Changing the World for Women and for Technology, Anita Borg Institute for Women and Technology. (Emerson 8,11)

one could ask why similar programs are uncommon. The practical and logistical requirements for service-learning project-based courses can be challenging; however, in this author's opinion, the most significant obstacles lie in the culture of engineering. Despite the popular association with innovation, engineering culture is generally conservative and resistant to change (for pertinent discussions, see NAE "The Engineer"; "Educating"), aggressive, competitive, and technically oriented (Robinson and McIlwee 406). In order to survive, women adopt and defend the values of engineering culture and are eventually assimilated into the engineering profession (Tonso 29). Under these conditions, it is not unusual to find women engineers who label sexism in engineering as an exception. By doing so, women engineers convey the assumption that their male counterparts do not discriminate by gender, because to suggest otherwise would break solidarity in the profession (Dryburgh 674-676).

An important question to ask is what conditions are conducive to women making the kind of changes that will allow women to benefit more fully from all that technology has to offer. Women engineers and computer scientists potentially hold tremendous power to effect changes that can result in the full participation of a wider spectrum of women in technology-related issues relevant to all of their sex. This is especially true for designers and design team managers who sit at the top of the engineering hierarchy; the women who achieve that level have an added influence. But in order to realize the potential for change, some areas need to be addressed.

First, women engineers must recognize that their ability to see gender issues has been compromised through day-to-day exposure to an engineering environment. A common premise of the calls to diversify engineering and computer science through the recruitment and retention of women is that women think and act differently than men and will bring something different to the discussion. For women and men in the general population this may be true; however, as previously noted, the situation is different for women in engineering. Environmental influences are not always so benign; indeed when the climate is hostile, significant personal energies have to be directed towards creating and maintaining defensive survival zones. More often, though, it is the subtle pressures that wear down the commitment to change. Project priorities that consistently focus attention towards ever-deeper design details, for example, slowly direct the minds of women and men alike away from larger contextual issues wherein gendered perspectives can be seen to matter. Before women engineers can truly make a difference to the profession and to the products of the profession, women engineers must recognize that they are more like their male counterparts than they are like women in the general population. Women engineers must consciously make use of their gender lens.

Second, women engineers should become better informed about feminist theories and methodologies. Women engineers must recognize that it is irresponsible to disengage simply because the word "feminist" is used, and that to do so is akin to rendering an engineering judgment that does not consider all available and relevant information. Most women engineers are uninitiated in formal gender studies since little room has been made in conventional engineering programs for anything other than engineering. It is the author's guess that most women engineers draw without reflection from the liberal tradition primarily because this is the most prevalent approach communicated among policy-makers in government and industry. In this tradition, numbers count most, and remedying the deficit of women in engineering becomes an end in itself rather than a means toward a solution. Taken to its logical end, the liberal tradition means that once all barriers are removed, women engineers are involved in the same proportions as men and in the same way as men. But, as Watson and Froyd state, "Engineering is not something we *do*, we *become* engineers" (21, my emphasis). Assimilation into the profession begins at the undergraduate level where conditions favour survival of those who subscribe to traditional norms. One might argue it begins even earlier when outreach activities attempt to convince children that science and math are fun rather than presenting these subjects as helping, or empowering, people.

Feminist studies that incorporate standpoint theory result in paradigms that draw attention to gendered subjectivities and emphasize the need to revalue and regard femininities as equally or more valuable than masculinities. The increased emphasis on "soft" skills as a differentiating employment factor is an example that is familiar to women engineers. Already there is a basis for greater awareness in the existing engineering outreach and retention activities that aspire to gender reorientation. References to standpoint theory would not be alien concepts for women engineers who have been exposed to these activities, and might work most effectively if grounded in examples of how thinking like a traditional male engineer produced only an adequate rather than a more broadly appropriate engineering solution. Post-structuralism, the current domain of many researchers in gender and Information Society Technology,[1] looks at how gender and technology are co-constructed or mutually shape each other. Put differently, post-structuralist researchers ask "what gendered subjects are being (re)produced in work situations, through (in)formal teaching situations or by becoming a user or designer of technologies" (Zorn et al. 16). This approach, which accommodates more complex formulations of gender identity and practice, aligns better with system-level thinking that is common in engineering projects. Engineers are taught to develop cost-effective solutions, a process which requires the identification of all relevant influences. The female engineers and computer scientists coming from this background might be resistant to the critique of the liberal model and fear that its emphasis on gender subjectivities or standpoint theory paradigms is limiting, so perhaps if they were asked to view post-structuralism as a feedback loop in a controlled system they might be more amenable to seeing that gender is the component missing from the processes.

Third, while the VDC was an effective example of how a gendered lens made a difference, more examples are needed. For example, the editors of a book recently published in Germany, *Gender Designs IT*, reveal how an awareness of gender can bridge the digital divide and improve information technology and its creation process. The authors provide practical, real-world examples that engineers should find useful. The examples came from a symposium that brought together researchers from around the world with the common goal of applying gender research to the information technology sector and supporting women's projects with adequate technology. The authors present new starting points for criticism of technology and provide real examples of methods to influence the development of information society technology. While the book focuses on information and communications technology, its fundamental concepts invite consideration in other fields such as engineering, as reviewers have noted (Montano 68).

Lastly, women engineers must collaborate with each other, with male counterparts, and with others outside the field to increase professional awareness of gender. Feminist theories and methodologies deserve a larger place in the critique of real-world examples. By broadening and deepening their perspectives on technology and its potential implications, women engineers are in a much better position to ask the right questions, and to do so early in the process, so that women's priorities gain visibility during the technology decision and development process. To wait until products or services are available for judgment is too late, especially if those products or services become limiting or punitive forces, as forewarned in 1984 by eminent scientist and social activist Ursula Franklin.

> The exclusion function of [technology], and the explicit foreclosure of future options, should be emphasized much more than they have been in the past, whenever we discuss the nature of contemporary technology. In many cases, it is as important to know what cannot be done anymore because a certain technology is put in place as it is to know what the technology actually achieves (246).

GLORIA MONTANO

CONCLUSION

Now I see one reason why everyone's leaving women out.
Because to bring women in is not just to rectify an inequity ...
it means to change the whole conversation.
　　　　　—Carol Gilligan (qtd in Patterson and Hall 143).

The evidence for the mutually shaping effects of women on technology and technology on women is not hard to find. Unfortunately, the knowledge and understanding remain outside of the conscious minds of most women engineers and computer scientists, due in part to education and training programs and to a professional focus that is mostly directed towards industry or corporate needs. This is especially true in product development groups where the technological artifacts of modern living are created and maintained, but where designers are rarely able to ask why some needs are given higher priority than others.

Recently, there has been an increase in calls by respected authorities in engineering and computer science professions to apply to the realms of information and communications technology the methodologies and approaches routinely used by social scientists. But, will those efforts go far enough to allow populations in general to reassert their authority over technology, or will technology continue to force people into behaving in predetermined ways driven by the limits of the same technology?

Part of the answer lies in encouraging front-line engineers and computer scientists to ask the right questions so that their valuable and rare technical skill and knowledge can be directed to be more inclusive of the world's diverse population. To achieve this as a reflex response to engineering problems, women engineers and computer scientists must recognize and embrace their complete identities, especially gender, so that they can fully see all the dimensions that are important when it comes to technology and its impact on people. In addition, engineers and computer scientists must add to their base of knowledge and skill relevant theories and methods, especially feminist theories and methods, that have already proven effective in the social sciences. Only after all these things happen and only after they are deployed empathetically can the positive future envisioned by Anita Borg be realized.

[1]Information and Society Technology is one of seven sectors of the European Union's Fifth Framework Programme for Research and Technological Development for 1998-2002.

268

WORKS CITED

Anita Borg Institute for Women and Technology. 2006. Web. 18 Dec. 2007.

Anita Borg Institute for Women and Technology. "History." Anita Borg. 2006. Web. 18 Dec. 2007.

Anita Borg Institute for Women and Technology. "Our Initiatives: Grace Hopper Celebration." 2006. Web. 18 Dec. 2007.

Anita Borg Institute for Women and Technology. "Our Initiatives: Systers." 2006. Web. 18 Dec. 2007.

Anita Borg Institute for Women and Technology. "Virtual Development Center." Past Project Archive. 2006.Web. June 18, 2008.

American Society for Engineering Education (ASEE). "Special Report: The National Engineering Education Research Colloquies." *Journal of Engineering Education* 95.4 (2006): 257-56. Print.

American Society for Engineering Education (ASEE). "Special Report: The Research Agenda for the New Discipline of Engineering Education." *Journal of Engineering Education* 95.4 (2006): 259-61. Print.

Borg, Anita. "On Grace Hopper: Celebration for Women in Computing 1997." San Jose, CA, 1997. Keynote Address.

Borg, Anita. "Technology, Democracy, and the Future." *The Spiral* (2001): 1. Print.

Borrego, M. and L. K. Newswander. "Characteristics of Successful Cross-Disciplinary Engineering Education Collaboration." *Journal of Engineering Education* 97. 2 (2008). 123-34. Print.

Dryburgh, H. "Work Hard, Play Hard: Women and Professionalism in Engineering: Adapting to the Culture." *Gender & Society* 13.5 (1999): 664-82. Print.

Emerson, C. J. *Virtual Development Center: Changing the World for Women and for Technology.* Paolo Alto, CA: Anita Borg Institute for Women and Technology, 2005. Print.

Franklin, Ursula M. *The Ursula Franklin Reader: Pacifism as a Map.* Toronto: Between the Lines, 2006. Print.

Frehill, L. M., N. M. D. Fabio, S. T. Hill, K. Traeger and J. Buono. "Women in Engineering: A Review of the 2007 Literature." *SWE Magazine* 2008: 54, 34-70. Print.

Gilligan, Carol. *Unlocking the Clubhouse: Women in Computing.* Cambridge, MA: MIT Press, 2002.

Hewlett, S. A., C. B. Luce, L. J. Servon, L. Sherbin, P. Shiller *et al. The Athena Factor: Reversing the Brain Drain in Science, Engineering, and Technology.* Boston: Center for Work-Life Policy, 2008. Print.

Kline, Nancy. *Time to Think: Listening to Ignite the Human Mind.* London: Cassell Illustrated, 1998. Print.

Li, Q., D. B. McCoach, H. Swaminathan and J. Tsang. "Development of an Instrument to Measure Perspectives of Engineering Education among College Students." *Journal of Engineering Education* 9.71 (2008): 47-56. Print.

Montano, Gloria. Rev. of *Gender Designs IT. SWE Magazine* (2008): 54, 68. Print.

"Mother of Invention." *San Jose Mercury News.* Feb. 20, 2004. Print.

National Academy of Engineering (NAE). *The Engineer of 2020: Visions of Engineering in the New Century.* Washington, DC: National Academy of Engineering, 2004. Print.

National Academy of Engineering (NAE). *Educating the Engineer of 2020: Adapting Engineering Education to the New Century.* Washington, DC: National Academy of Engineering, 2005. Print.

O'Brien, T. "Investor Apologizes For Now Famous Net Quote." *San Jose Mercury News, Morning Final* 20 Feb. 2005. 1A, 4A. Print.

O'Brien, T. "Mother of Invention." *San Jose Mercury News, West Magazine* 9 May 19991.12. Print.

Patent Storm. U.S. Patent 6889991. Cam engaged, lever propelled wheelchair. 2008.

Patterson, M. J. and W. M. Hall. "She Still Challenges the Way We View Human Development." *Pittsburgh Post-Gazette* 22 Apr. 1998. D1, D3. Print.

Robinson, J. G. and J. S McIlwee, "Men, Women, and the Culture of Engineering." *The Sociological Quarterly* 32.3 (1991): 403-421. Print.

Statistics Canada. Canadian Census 2006. 2008. Web. June 18, 2008.

Tonso, K. L. "Teams that Work: Campus Culture, Engineer Identity, and Social Interactions." *Journal of Engineering Education* 95.1 (2006): 27-37. Print.

U.S. Department of Labor. *Highlights of Women's Earnings in 2002.* 2003. Web. Jun. 16, 2008.

Watson, K., and J. Froyd. "Diversifying the U.S. Engineering Workforce: A New Model." *Journal of Engineering Education* 96.1 (2007): 19-32. Print.

Zorn, Isabel, Susanne Maass, Els Rommes, Carola Schirmer, and Heidi Schelhowe. *Gender Designs IT: Construction and Deconstruction of Information Society Technology.* Wiesbaden: VS Verlag für Sozialwissenschaften / GWV Fachverlage GmbH, Wiesbaden, 2007. Print.

11. Film, Feminism and Public Pedagogy, or How to Get a Feminist Education

DANIELLE DEVEREAUX

COMPLETING MY MASTER of Women's Studies degree was not an easy task. I began the program with plenty of energy, completed the coursework for the program successfully and then got stuck, so stuck that I began to doubt the whole endeavour. I have learned from other graduate students that this situation is not unusual, but it was frustrating. Avoidance became my coping strategy. And so, although originally conceived of as a diversion from my academic work, the Media & Culture Screening & Discussion Series (MCSDS) became my Master of Women's Studies project. This chapter is an account of what happened. It will examine what counts as feminist academic work in Women's Studies today; it will profile my growth as a feminist and as a student of Women's Studies interested in both the theory and the practice of feminism; and it will provide grounds for connecting emotional investments, political awareness, and the possibility of change.

The Master of Women's Studies program at Memorial University of Newfoundland (MUN) is interdisciplinary. As part of the coursework for the program, I chose to take a course offered by the Faculty of Education called "Reading and Teaching Popular Culture." A number of films produced by the Media Education Foundation (MEF)[1] were screened in class.

MEF is a U.S.-based, nonprofit organization that produces and distributes documentary films examining the social, political, and cultural impact of American mass media. Many of MEF's titles—its *Dreamworlds: Desire, Sex & Power in Music Video,* and *Killing Us Softly: Advertising's Image of Women* series—will be familiar to instructors and students of Women's Studies, but the film that really seized my mind and heart is not typically used in Women's Studies classes; it was an environmental film called *Advertising and the End of the World*. The film analyzes how advertising, acting as the voice of the marketplace, connects the consumption of goods to our social desires for things like love and friendship, autonomy and independence. While we know that consuming goods will not fulfill these social desires, the money pumped into advertising helps to create the illusion that it will. This illusion, which keeps our capitalist consumer culture in place, is powerful and seductive, but the way of life it promotes and upholds is destroying the planet.

This message may not seem as radical today as it did in 1999 when the film was produced, but I had never seen anything like it. As a graduate student, I watched *Advertising and the End of the World* the way I had watched *Dead Poets Society* as a teenager—again and again. I was so intrigued by the work of MEF that I applied for their internship program and was thrilled to be accepted. During the summer of 2003, I spent five weeks as an intern at the MEF office in North Hampton, Massachusetts; my main job was to write study guides for a number of MEF films. I loved it. Meeting the people behind the films, and learning how film can be used to facilitate critical thinking about the impact of popular mass media on our daily lives, was an exciting experience, but I did not consider it part of my graduate degree. The internship was a summer adventure; I would get back to academic work in the fall. When the internship ended, I was given a series of MEF films as a thank-you gift. During a stopover in the Halifax airport on my way home, I happened to meet a professor[2] I had worked with as a student and teaching assistant. When I mentioned my newly acquired MEF films, his response was, "Well, you should get those shown on campus." After several meetings to discuss how showings might be arranged, the Media & Culture Screening & Discussion Series was born.

The purpose of the series was to facilitate the on-campus viewing and discussion of alternative media, with a particular focus on the social role of mass media and issues of ideology, power, and the politics of representation. The series did not become my Master of Women's Studies project until it was already well underway, but once it did, people would sometimes ask: "Oh, so you're looking at women in the media are you?" While some of the videos screened did deal specifically and exclusively with media images of women, the underlying theme of the series was not women in the media, and the audience was not women-only. What, then, did the Media & Culture Screening & Discussion Series have to do with earning a Master of Women's Studies degree? What counts as appropriate work in Women's Studies in the current climate of feminist research?

THE MEDIA & CULTURE SCREENING & DISCUSSION SERIES: A BRIEF DESCRIPTION

The Media & Culture Screening & Discussion Series took place on the campus of MUN on Thursday afternoons from 12-2 pm during the fall and winter terms of two academic years. It was open to the public and free of charge. While there was no template for the series, a typical screening session looked like this: the door to SN2018 is open, and a poster just outside the door signals that this is the room where the Media & Culture Screening & Discussion Series takes place and what film is being shown. Similar posters have been pinned up around campus during the preceding seven days. I note that the screening series is part of my graduate work and hand out (optional) feedback forms.[3] I introduce the video of the day and explain how the series works: we will watch a video, then discuss it and the issues it raises. I welcome and introduce the discussion facilitator, noting the person's particular interests and expertise as relevant to the film. The film is screened. Then the facilitator stands or sits at the front of the room, speaks briefly (usually from five to ten minutes) to some aspect of the film, and opens the floor for comments and questions. Often participants begin by addressing the facilitator directly, but as the discussion progresses, it usually takes on a group dynamic with participants talking back and forth to each other and the facilitator. Many participants stay for the full discussion period; others leave directly after the screening or stay for part of the discussion.

The videos screened in the series covered a wide range of topics, encouraging discussion of ideology, power, and representation. Representations of gender provided key material (*Playing Unfair: The Media Image of the Female Athlete*; *Wrestling with Manhood: Boys, Bullying & Battering*), but the series also looked at central themes: sexuality (*Spin the Bottle: Sex, Lies & Alcohol*); racism (*Game Over: Gender, Race & Violence in Video Games*); imperialism (*Beyond Good & Evil: Children, Media & Violent Times*; *Independent Media in a Time of War*); the environment (*Advertising & the End of the World*); and class and capitalism (*The Overspent American*). Often the themes intersected; for example, *Mickey Mouse Monopoly: Disney, Childhood & Corporate Power* looked at capitalism, consumerism and childhood, imperialism, and representations of gender and race. The range of topics covered throughout the series was broad, but the guiding theme was critical analysis of cultural systems of power and oppression; and the series used the medium of film to discuss how, in a media-centric society, mass media impact the way we live in the world. To some, it may not be immediately clear that this is a particularly feminist project. The series was not called the Feminist Media & Culture Screening & Discussion Series, but it could have been.

THE *FEMINIST* MEDIA & CULTURE SCREENING & DISCUSSION SERIES?

When the series began, I did not consider turning it into a project that could be used to fulfill the MWS requirements, but as I found myself struggling with whether or not to even continue in the Master of Women's Studies program, one of my supervisors[4] finally said, "Danielle, you're already doing this really interesting project; why not make it your master's project?" But how would I explain the academic-ness of the project, its women's studies-ness? As I began to think about how I might do this, I came to realize that the project connected with much of the feminist theory I had been reading in my Women's Studies classes; that the series itself incorporated many of the lessons of inclusion Women's Studies stresses; that in short the MCSDS was both academic and feminist.

At first glance the series might seem to be an unusual fit for Women's Studies because—well, where are the women? While some of the films screened as part of the series dealt specifically and exclusively with media images of women (e.g. *Playing Unfair: The Media Image of the Female Athlete*), films were not limited to those dealing only with gender or women; the underlying theme of the series was not women in the media, and the audience was not women-only. Nor did I want the theme or audience to be so limited: such constraints would betray the intersecting and compounding nature of social and cultural difference, power and oppression.[5]

In *Feminist Theory: From Margin to Center*, bell hooks argues that feminism must challenge not only a patriarchal society, but also "a political system of imperialist, white supremacist, capitalist patriarchy" (xiv). hooks writes:

> Feminism is a struggle to end sexist oppression. Therefore, it is necessarily a struggle to eradicate the ideology of domination that permeates Western culture on various levels, as well as a commitment to reorganizing society so that the self-development of people can take precedence over imperialism, economic expansion, and material desires…. A commitment to feminism so defined would demand that each individual

participant acquire a critical political consciousness based on ideas and beliefs. (26)

In Kramare and Triechler's *A Feminist Dictionary*, citations defining "feminism" fill five columns, and include the following from "The Combahee River Collective Statement":

> We are actively committed to struggling against racial, sexual, heterosexual, and class oppression and see as our particular task the development of integrated analysis and practice based upon the fact that the major systems of oppression are interlocking. The synthesis of these oppressions creates the conditions of our lives. (159)[6]

Like bell hooks and the Combahee River Collective, many black feminists have challenged feminism to see its aim as ending not only gender oppression, but all systems of oppression so as to radically change society. They argue that this mass movement for change would work to benefit the lives of *all* women and girls, men and boys, and those who do not fit so neatly into a sex or gender binary. Such a movement would acknowledge that within dominant ideologies of imperialist, white supremacist, capitalist, heterosexist structures of domination, very few people live lives free of oppression. It would acknowledge that these systems of domination undermine meaningful identification between people. Further, as eco-feminists point out, feminists who seek to unhinge the interlocking systems of oppression must also bring the environment into an empathic system of relations. An ideology of domination that places women on the underside of a dualistic men/ women divide also places nature on the underside of a humanity/ nature divide. This hierarchical, dichotomous relationship facilitates the overuse and abuse of nature and is leading to the destruction of the planet. An egalitarian society is not possible on a dying planet. *Advertising and the End of the World*, the film that led me to this project, asks us to rethink our relationship with consumerism and insists that, in a world dependent on dwindling resources, questions about who gets access to these resources—from fuel to food, clean air and water—will be intimately linked to who wields the power. While *Advertising and the End of the World* may not typically be screened in Women's Studies classes, its message must be of concern to feminism.

This holistic approach to feminism is sometimes criticized for shifting the focus away from women. However, calling attention to interlocking systems of oppression does not marginalize sexism; it places sexism within a broader context. To insist that feminism must take on racism, heterosexism, classism, imperialism, and sexism, to insist that feminists must also identify with nature and be environmentalists, is to insist that the struggle to end oppression does not follow an either/or approach requiring activists to choose their "ism." Rather it is to acknowledge that "the synthesis of these oppressions create[s] the conditions of our lives" (Kramarae and Triechler 159), the lives of us all. Feminist moves to challenge and eradicate a cultural system of imperialist, white supremacist, capitalist patriarchy in which humans dominate nature have the potential, as a mass-based feminism should, to create a space where all people feel that feminism is relevant to their lives.

FEMINIST WORK/ACADEMIC WORK: WOMEN'S STUDIES AND [MY] UNIVERSITY EDUCATION

In his work on the politics of education, Paulo Freire argues that education is never neutral. It is a political tool often used to reinforce the status quo of social power structures, to uphold an ideology of domination in which those with power are taught to cling to it, and those without power are taught to desire and aspire to it; values, identities and desires outside this ideology of domination are devalued. However, education does not have to, nor should it, be used to keep the *status quo* in place. Education has the potential to challenge, disrupt, and radically transform oppressive ideologies. This type of education, which both Freire and hooks call "education as the practice of freedom," has the potential to be a place of joy, a place of "ecstasy, pleasure and danger" (hooks, *Teaching* 3): the pleasure of learning new ideas, imagining new possibilities; the danger, the challenge, but also the excitement, of bringing these new ideas into daily life and of insisting on radical change. Education as the practice of freedom is about more than acquiring knowledge; it is directly related to how we live in the world.

bell hooks notes that within feminism as a movement a false dichotomy has developed between theory and action. This "tug-of-war" has been fostered by "anti-intellectualism" among activists who insist that they are the ones who know what is going on in the real world, and "elitist academics who believe [and/or act as if] their ideas need not have any connection to real life" (*Feminist Theory* 113-14). As Women's Studies has struggled to become part of the academy, it has sometimes been forced to conform to structures of hegemony and oppression in order to prove its academic worth. Only certain types of work—work that proved Women's Studies could play with the academic "big boys"—counted. hooks argues that the scholarship most often included in this game has been done by straight, white, middle-class women. These women, she posits, fit most easily within academic power structures as held in place by colonialism, capitalism, compulsory heterosexuality and white supremacy. hooks observes that within these structures theory is often used as an instrumental tool "to set up unnecessary and competing hierarchies of thought which reinscribe the politics of domination by designating work as either inferior, superior, or more or less worthy of attention" (*Teaching* 64). Conversely, many feminists active in the women's movement have responded to inaccessible, hegemonic feminist theory by "internalizing the false assumption that theory is not a social practice." Accordingly they dismiss theory, and subscribe to an alternative hierarchy "where all concrete action is viewed as more important than any theory written or spoken" (*Teaching* 66). hooks insists that both theory and action are necessary and that they exist on a continuum: feminists must find ways to use both theory and action to create a "liberatory feminist praxis" (*Feminist Theory* 17). To argue that either theory or action is more or less feminist is counterproductive, since where feminism seeks to radically challenge and change systems of domination and oppression there is much at stake.

The MCSDS was an example of engaged feminist theory and practice, as well as education as the practice of freedom, on a number of levels. The series aimed to provide an interdisciplinary space where the many and varied intersections of power and oppression could be examined, analyzed and talked about. Naming, thinking critically about, and discussing these systems of oppression may help, in some small measure, to begin the process of dismantling them, as we envision how our lives might be lived differently, in more egalitarian, feminist ways. One example of how the series shaped my own understanding of feminist theory as part of everyday practice and education as the practice of freedom can be seen in a simple shift in terminology. When the MCSDS began, discussion facilitators were listed on the series schedule and posters as "speakers," a term which reinforced conventional learner/educator hierarchies. There were a number of reasons for my choice of this term. Firstly, "speaker" was the format I was used to seeing in public education/public lecture settings. It did not occur to me to call the person who agreed to stand at the front of the room, to speak and direct the conversation, as anything but the speaker. And, as a student, I found myself in the position of asking people, including professors, to make time to facilitate discussion at this thing I had started and, well, who was I? They certainly did not need to agree to participate to impress me (as might be the case if asked by the head of their department or the dean of their faculty). Nor could I offer a stipend or other recompense to anyone who agreed to participate. So it seemed that I should at least offer the venue up as a speaking engagement, marking the speaker as an expert and imbuing the task with a little prestige. The least I could do was to publicize their names on the posters. Finally, I feared that no one would come to the screening series and if they did come, that they would not talk[7]; if this were to happen, then the speaker would indeed be charged with speaking to the audience.

Partway through the first term of the series, a professor I had asked to act as guest speaker[8] for a screening of the MEF film *Mickey Mouse Monopoly* mentioned she was surprised to see herself billed as "speaker" on posters advertising the screening. She said that she was not really planning to speak to the audience, but lead and participate in the discussion. Her comments and our pursuant discussions around the notion of expert and the role of the people I had been calling speakers, helped me realize that although the speakers did indeed have a great deal of expertise to offer, their role as the one who opened up and then directed discussion was actually more in line with that of equal participant. "Discussion facilitator" more accurately described their task. Further, the people viewing the films also had a great deal of expertise to offer by virtue of their experience as people living in a mass-mediated world. The central themes of the films screened at the MCSDS included gender, sexuality, racism, imperialism, class, capitalism, the environment, and mass media: issues which all people have some experience with. I came to also realize that the term "participants" more accurately described the role of screening series attendees than "audience," as every person in the room had important contributions to make. After the first semester of the screening series, speakers were referred to as discussion facilitators and the audience referred to as participants, which better reflected the series' aspirations to emulate Freire's philosophy of education wherein "education is a live and creative dialogue in which everyone knows something and does not know others, in which all seek together to know more" ("To the Coordinator" 113).

The fact that the screening series was not part of a credit course enabled it to disrupt traditional professor/student classroom hierarchies on a variety of levels. As bell hooks suggests, the practice of grading students' work makes it difficult to fully challenge traditional professor/ student hierarchies in most academic settings, since neither the student who wants a good mark, nor the professor charged with assigning it, can ever completely forget this power dynamic (*Teaching*). Not being an academic course, the screening series charged no "tuition" fee and was open to the public. A person did not have to be registered at the university or employed by it in order to participate. And because all the videos I screened were free—through my affiliation with MEF—I did not have to be concerned about costs. Though charging a fee might have made it possible to order new screening material, it was important to me that the series be available as a cost-free learning and thinking space. Most interactions in capitalist society require that people assume the role of consumer. This is increasingly true in university settings where a corporate model of operation sees students as clients who must be won over by the university marketing team; and where students are wooed into attending university in order to become contributing members of the capitalist economy. By offering a learning space without these assumptions, the series addressed participants as people—citizens, co-learners and co-educators—not clients or consumers. Education as the practice of freedom: education as free.

The non-credit factor also disrupts conventional notions of learning that see education as something that is necessarily institutionally recognized. In her chapter "Educating Women" in *Feminist Theory*, bell hooks calls on feminist educators to educate women, to spread the feminist word, so to speak, in non-academic settings. Educating outside the realm of the institution may be seen as a specifically feminist endeavour. Institutional sanction is not necessary for the legitimization of learning; learning can and does take place without administrative approval. The screening series could surely form the basis of a university-level credit course. However, feminism challenges us to recognize the value of work/knowledge/learning that has not been traditionally valued within institutionalized social systems of power.[9] And yet not pursuing a post-secondary degree is often seen as a mark of failure in North America today, even where this choice means a person will still learn and develop skills—get an education—in non-institutionalized ways (for example by not going to university or college in order to pursue fishing or farming). In this climate, it is particularly important to have spaces where, metaphorically speaking, pedagogy can take place outside the classroom. I say *metaphorically speaking* because it is not the actual physical classroom that is necessarily the problem. The screening series did take place in a classroom and thus was affiliated with the university. However, hierarchal classroom dynamics, like conventional notions of what an education is and who can have access to it, were challenged. This does not mean the university classroom setting was non-problematic. Holding the screening series on campus meant that I could access a screening space, projector and university-related media outlets. However, people disenfranchised from such spaces often do not come to on-campus events, even when these events are free and open to the public.

THE RESPONSE

Responses to the Media & Culture Screening & Discussion Series were overwhelmingly positive, both on solicited feedback forms and in informal conversation. Despite the success of the series, at each screening I worried that no one would show up, and if they did, that no one would talk (this fear diminished with each term but never vanished entirely). But people kept showing up and they kept talking! Though discussion facilitators were offered nothing but a thank-you in exchange for their time and efforts, they kept agreeing to participate and even thanked me for asking them to participate. The success of this optional, middle-of-the-day activity indicates that many people are simply interested in learning, discussing, sharing their experiences, listening to others share their experiences, and engaging in critical analysis and critical thinking. People are interested in and seek out education as the practice of freedom. In response to the question, "What do you think is the use/value of having and/or attending a series like this?" one undergraduate student simply wrote, "Learning, talking together." That s/he underlined the word "together" indicates the important role empathy played in the series. A sense of togetherness helped to create a learning community: one that came to see everyone present as an equal participant in post-screening discussions, and where most people seemed to feel comfortable participating. One undergraduate student, who indicated s/he had been to the series once before, wrote: "This is unique. You don't need to invest yourself the same way (put yourself on the line the same way) as in an actual class. You really can consider the information and deliver your ideas without worrying about how it will be accepted."

The MCSDS aimed to provide an interdisciplinary space where the many and varied intersections of power and oppression could be examined, analyzed, and talked about. The films discussed and challenged ideologies of domination as reinforced through media systems in a media-centric society, and the series took issue with traditional learner/ educator hierarchies as reinforced through conventional education systems. The evolution of the MCSDS and my own growth as a graduate student in Women's Studies may be seen as examples of feminist theory in practice, of a feminist education.

[1] For further information about the Media Education Foundation and their films see www.mediaed.org

[2] Dr. David Thompson, whose encouragement and support played an integral role in getting the Media & Culture Screening & Discussion Series going. I am grateful to him.

[3] Before the screening series became part of my graduate work, blank feedback sheets were periodically distributed for comments and suggestions.

[4] Dr. Elizabeth Yeoman, to whom I am grateful.

[5] I am grateful to Dr. Ursula Kelly for this insight.

[6] The Combahee River Collective was a black feminist group formed in Boston in 1974. The Combahee River Collective Statement was drafted in 1977 for inclusion in Zilla Eisenstein's anthology *Capitalist Patriarchy and the Case for Socialist Feminism* (Smith xxxii).

[7] This fear was probably related to my own shyness when attending public lectures, where there always seemed to be many (mostly male) experts in the audience with many comments and questions to share: comments and questions which tended to make a non-expert like me want to keep my mouth shut.

[8] Dr. Elizabeth Yeoman.

[9] Another reason why, ideally, project-based graduate work should be seen as no less legitimate than thesis-based graduate work in Women's Studies Departments.

WORKS CITED

Combahee River Collective. *The Combahee River Collective statement: Black Feminist Organizing in the Seventies and Eighties.* Foreword by Barbara Smith. Latham, NY: Kitchen Table: Women of Color Press, 1986. Print.

Freire, Paulo. *Education: The Practice of Freedom.* London: Writers and Readers Publishing Cooperative, 1976. Print.

Freire, Paulo. "To the Coordinator of a Cultural Circle." *Convergence* 4.1 (1971): 111-116. Print.

hooks, bell. *Feminist Theory: From Margin to Center*. 2nd ed. Cambridge, MA: South End Press, 2000. Print.

hooks, bell. *Teaching to Transgress: Education as the Practice of Freedom*. New York: Routledge, 1994. Print.

Kramarae, Cheris and Paula A. Trichler. *A Feminist Dictionary*. Boston: Pandora Press, 1985.

Smith, Barbara, ed. *Home Girls: A Black Feminist Anthology*. New York: Kitchen Table: Women of Color Press, 1983. Print.

Contributors

Jill Allison received a Ph.D. in Anthropology from Memorial University of Newfoundland, where she is currently the Global Health Coordinator in the Faculty of Medicine. Her work in medical anthropology merges her experiences as a nurse with an academic interest in medical institutions, technology, global health and health and social justice. Her research interests include medicalization of reproductive health, health of underserved and marginalized populations, relations of power and structural inequalities in health care, and gender and health.

Faith Balisch is an Associate Professor in the Department of English Language and Literature at Memorial University. Her primary research area is Canadian humour and satire with particular interests in the nineteenth-century and in Canadian women's humour. Her publications include papers on eighteenth-century Canadian humour, the nineteenth-century romance as written by women in the Maritimes, and the humour of Robertson Davies and Lynn Johnston, among others. She is currently working on a history of women's humour in Canada and an anthology of Canadian women's writings about war beginning with the American Revolution.

Valerie Burton is a Professor of History at Memorial University and is currently the Academic Director of the University's "First Year Success" Program. Her most recent publication is a *Signs* symposium, "Fish/ Wives." As co-editor of *Changing Places* she continues the interest in collaborative projects using feminist methodologies that was important to her when, as the Memorial University's Women's Studies Program Graduate Coordinator and Speakers' Series Chair, she first met several of the collection's authors.

Danielle Devereaux graduated with a Master of Women's Studies degree from Memorial University of Newfoundland and Labrador in 2005. Since then she has worked as a sessional instructor in Women's Studies, an organic farmer, and a freelance writer and editor. Her poetry has appeared in *Arc, The Fiddlehead, Riddle Fence, QuArc,* and *The Best Canadian Poetry in English 2011* (Tightrope Books). An alumna of the Banff Writing Studio, her poetry manuscript-in-progress was shortlisted for the 2009 Fresh Fish Award for Emerging Writers. *Cardiogram,* a limited edition chapbook of her poems, has been published by Baseline Press. Danielle currently works in research communications at Memorial University.

Sonya Corbin Dwyer is Professor of Psychology at Grenfell Campus, Memorial University of Newfoundland in Corner Brook, where she teaches contemporary issues in personality, the psychology of education, psychotherapy, and the psychology of women. Her current research includes cross-cultural post-secondary teaching and transnational adoption. She recently returned from China where she taught graduate students at Jilin University for a semester. Sonya became a mother after she received tenure and promotion to associate professor.

Pauline Greenhill has been Professor of Women's and Gender Studies at the University of Winnipeg since 1996. Her recent books include *Transgressive Tales: Queering the Grimms* (Kay Turner, co-editor, Wayne State University Press, 2012); *Make The Night Hideous: Four English-Canadian Charivaris* (University of Toronto Press, 2010); *Fairy Tale Films: Visions of Ambiguity* (Sidney Eve Matrix, co-editor, Utah State University Press, 2010). She has published in scholarly journals including *Signs; parallax; Theoretical Criminology; Marvels & Tales;* and *Resources for Feminist Research.*

Jean Guthrie retired in 2007 from Memorial University of Newfoundland, where she taught rhetoric and composition in the Department of English and contributed to the translation of Alciato's emblems for the Memorial University Alciato Web Site. She served as Coordinator, First Year English; Associate Director, General Studies; Associate Dean, Faculty of Arts; Coordinator, Graduate Program in Teaching; Coordinator, Women's Studies. She was awarded the President's Award for Distinguished Teaching (Memorial 2002) and the Anne-Marie MacKinnon Award for Educational Leadership (Association of Atlantic Universities 2004).

Willeen Keough is the Chair of Gender, Sexuality, and Women's Studies and an Associate Professor of History at Simon Fraser University. Recent publications include "Contested Terrains: Ethnic and Gendered Spaces in the Harbour Grace Affray" in the *Canadian Historical Review*, "(Re-)telling Newfoundland Sealing Masculinity: Narrative and Counter-narrative" in the *Journal for the Canadian Historical Society*, and "Unpacking the Discursive Irish Woman Immigrant in Eighteenth- and Nineteenth-Century Newfoundland" in the *Irish Studies Review*. Her co-authored textbook (with Lara Campbell), *Gender History: Canadian Perspectives,* has just been published with Oxford University Press. She is also working on a SSHRC-funded book-length project tentatively titled "Seal Wars: Conflicting Masculinities at the Labrador Front."

Kathleen Lahey is Professor and Queen's National Scholar in the Faculty of Law and Co-director of Feminist Legal Studies at Queen's University in Ontario. She specializes in matters of women and taxation, equality law, and the gender analysis of poverty. Kathleen has served on the Ontario Fair Tax Commission, the Law Reform Commission of Canada Advisory Panel on Adult Relationships, and the Ontario Advisory Council on Women's Issues, as well as participating in equality cases brought under the Canadian Charter of Rights and Freedoms. She is the author of numerous papers and studies on women and fiscal policy, including *Women and Fiscal Equality* (2010), and was the founding editor of the *Canadian Journal of Women and the Law*.

Gloria Montano holds a bachelor of science in electrical engineering from the University of Texas at El Paso and a master of education from Memorial University of Newfoundland. She has held administrative and academic staff positions at Memorial University, directed a national service-learning program in the U.S., and has over twenty years of engineering and management experience at high tech companies in the Silicon Valley. Additionally, Gloria has a long history of working with organizations dedicated to diversifying participation in engineering and science, most notably Women in Science and Engineering Newfoundland and Labrador and the Society of Women Engineers.

Christine Overall is a Professor of Philosophy and holds a University Research Chair at Queen's University, Kingston. She has held visiting positions at the University of Waterloo (Ontario), Mount Saint Vincent University (Nova Scotia), and, most recently, Kwansei Gakuin University

(Japan). Her research and teaching are in feminist philosophy, applied ethics, philosophy of religion, and philosophy of education. She is the editor or co-editor of four books and the author of six. Her most recent book, *Why Have Children? The Ethical Debate*, was published by MIT Press in 2012.

Ruth Perry, an authority on eighteenth-century British literature and culture, was the founding Director of the Women's Studies program at MIT, where she is currently the Ann Fetter Friedlaender Professor of Humanities. Past President of the American Society for Eighteenth-Century Studies and co-founder of the Boston Graduate Consortium of Women's Studies, her most recent book is *Novel Relations; The Transformation of Kinship in English Literature and Culture 1748-1818*. Her current project is a biography of Anna Gordon, an eighteenth-century Scotswoman whose repertoire of ballads is the earliest unique source of these magnificent narrative songs.

Marie Wadden is a radio producer with the Canadian Broadcasting Corporation, and the author of two books. *Nitassinan, the Innu Struggle to Reclaim their Homeland* was published in 1991 and won the Edna Staebler Award for Creative Non-Fiction. *Where the Pavement Ends, the Aboriginal Recovery Movement, and the Urgent Need for Reconciliation* was published in 2008, and nominated for the Winterset Award, and the Shaughnessy Cohen award for political writing. She lives in St. John's.